IMAGES
of America

NORTH POINT MILWAUKEE LIGHTHOUSE

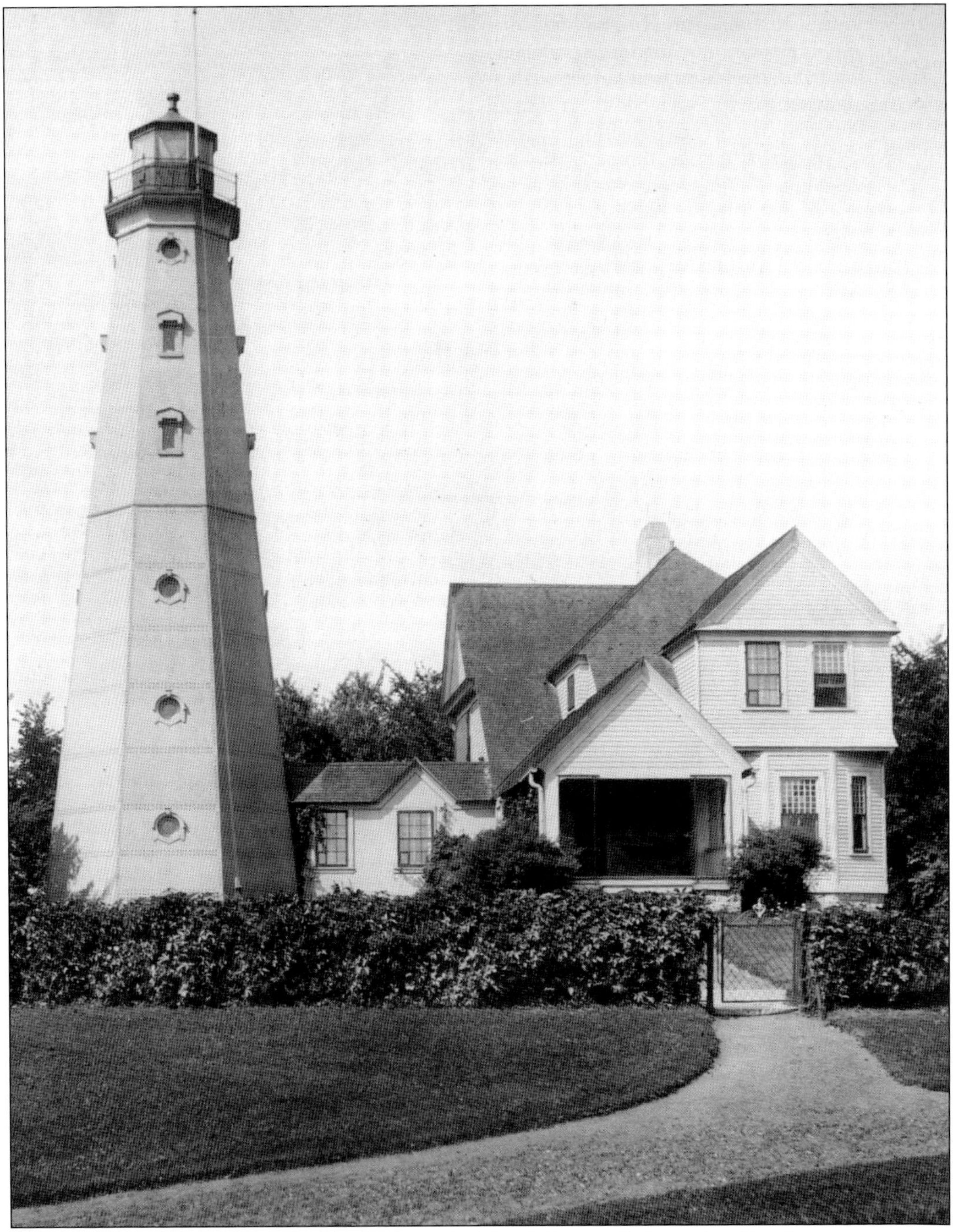

A lighthouse has stood atop the bluff named the North Point of Milwaukee Bay for over a century and a half. Constructed in 1912, the last of three distinctly different beacons is pictured here. (Courtesy of the US Coast Guard.)

On the Cover: Pictured is the North Point Lighthouse as it appeared around 1898. (Courtesy of Milwaukee Public Library.)

IMAGES
of America

NORTH POINT MILWAUKEE LIGHTHOUSE

Ken and Barb Wardius
and the NPLH Friends

ARCADIA
PUBLISHING

ISBN 978-0-7385-8264-1

Published by Arcadia Publishing
Charleston, South Carolina

Printed in the United States of America

Library of Congress Control Number: 2011929853

For all general information, please contact Arcadia Publishing:
Telephone 843-853-2070
Fax 843-853-0044
E-mail sales@arcadiapublishing.com
For customer service and orders:
Toll-Free 1-888-313-2665

Visit us on the Internet at www.arcadiapublishing.com

To John Enright, a researcher's researcher; the epitome of the spirit and dedication of North Point's lighthouse keepers.

Contents

Acknowledgments

This latest lighthouse story has taken the most work of any of our writings. We dug extra hard for some of this history and photographs—quality topics take time. We had an extraordinary amount of help. The efforts of the North Point Lighthouse Friends, especially John Enright, May Klisch, John Scripp, David Allen Jones, Mark Kuehn, and David O'Brien among others, have been without equal. Their collective help and cooperation is the chief reason this book exists. Additionally, the very significant research of Terry Pepper, executive director of the Great Lakes Lighthouse Keepers Association, was invaluable.

At the risk of omitting someone, other contributors include: Al Muchka and Susan Otto of the Milwaukee Public Museum; the staffs of the Milwaukee Public Library and Milwaukee County Historical Society, especially Steve Daily; Ed Werner; Lake Park Friends; Tom and Phyllis Tag of Great Lakes Lighthouse Research; Jane Fadel Murphy; Linda Nenn, Rick Smith, and the Port Washington Historical Society; lighthouse researcher Candace Clifford; Eric Greenfeldt and the Washington Island Archives; Tim Harrison, of *Lighthouse Digest*; Bob and Sandra Shanklin (the Lighthouse People); Dale Hanson; Pam Cook; Julie Bastin; Dick Moldenhauer of Burkhart Construction; Dorothy Peissig; Kathleen Redmond; James and Bill Donahue and Patty Donahue Brooks; Ellen Puerzer; Kimm Stabelfeldt; Wayne Sapulski; our editor, Jeff Ruetsche, for his calm guidance and patience; our family, in particular Sarah Lacey Wardius; and the Zikmund and Schaefer families for their continued support and encouragement.

The photographs in this book appear courtesy of a variety of sources, many of which will be credited by the following codes:

AINL—Apostle Islands National Lakeshore
FOWP—Friends of the Wind Point Lighthouse
MCHS—Milwaukee County Historical Society
MPL—Milwaukee Public Library
MPM—Milwaukee Public Museum
NARA—US National Archives and Records Administration
NASA—National Aeronautics and Space Administration
NOAA—National Oceanic and Atmospheric Administration
NPLHF—North Point Lighthouse Friends
PWHS—Port Washington Historical Society
USCG—US Coast Guard
WIA—Washington Island Archives

We paid special attention and gave extra effort to ensure the accuracy of this book. At times, there were some conflicts surrounding information and dates. Please accept our apologies for any errors or omissions.

INTRODUCTION

Mariners have relied on lighthouses from ancient to contemporary times. Beginning with the first lighthouse in the Alexandria harbor in ancient Egypt over 2,000 years ago, people may have depended on something as simple as a coal fire on a tree stump for safe passage. All around the globe, countless beacons warned of dangerous waters and guided humans, ships, and cargoes into a myriad of ports. Today, these signals continue to represent numerous themes, including history, attention to duty, commitment, and bravery.

From the earliest days of the United States, lighthouses have been an integral and important part of the nation's heritage. The first lighthouse on what would eventually become American soil was at the Boston Harbor in colonial Massachusetts, built in 1716. When the country was in its infancy, the federal government was charged with establishing dozens of lighthouses because the founders knew the nation's economic advancement and business interests were linked to maritime commerce. In time, as European settlers expanded to the West, hundreds of lights dotted the country's shores, from the original structures on the East Coast, then to the Southern and Great Lakes regions, and eventually to the Gulf and West Coasts. America would ultimately be a lighthouse leader in the world.

As the country grew, the movement of commodities depended extensively on water routes. The Great Lakes provided a path from the times of Native Americans and European immigrants to today. New cities, ports, and expanded harbors were born, and scores of lighthouses logically followed. The Great Lakes were a vital link for the transportation and distribution of raw materials, resources, and fundamental foodstuffs.

Of the five Great Lakes, only Lake Michigan is entirely within the borders of the United States. Its shores encompass hundreds of miles. For several centuries, humans have traveled Lake Michigan, beginning with canoes, wooden ships, and ultimately modern metal freighters that still traverse her waters today. Lighthouses have dotted many of the big lake harbors for over a century and a half. The states of Michigan and Wisconsin especially prospered because of Lake Michigan's abundant resources and commerce.

Wisconsin is partially encompassed by several important waterways, including the Great Lakes Michigan and Superior, as well as the grand Wisconsin and Mississippi Rivers. Its maritime past is closely tied to dozens of lighthouses that can be found in almost every locale coupled to these lifeblood bodies of water. Historically, over 48 lighthouses lit Wisconsin's waterways.

Southeastern Wisconsin and its major lakeshore cities of Kenosha, Racine, and Milwaukee were some of the busiest ports in the Badger State. Bustling maritime commerce began hundreds of years ago with the many Native American tribes in the area. It continued with the European pioneers and their migration westward across the United States. These nautical connections allowed this area to prosper economically. Today, modern commercial vessels come and go less regularly, and the emphasis has shifted to sport and recreational craft for a pleasure and tourist economy.

Milwaukee has been an important Wisconsin port since the mid-1800s. Like many typical Great Lakes harbors, the city initially handled basic materials of the time, including lumber, coal, various grains, and other raw food staples, in addition to basic machinery. This business dictated the eventual building of several lighthouses, including the North Point Milwaukee Lighthouse.

The North Point Milwaukee Lighthouse has changed at times in its long and interesting history. The first light, built in 1855, sat precariously closer and closer to an eroding bluff. In 1888, a new lighthouse was constructed a bit further inland at North Point. In 1912, the height of the lighthouse was increased. A new steel base was added to accommodate growing trees in Lake Park and city lights that obscured North Point's beam.

Being lifelong Milwaukeeans, we have been drawn to Lake Michigan and the city's embrace of this water treasure for many years. Lake Park has been a destination we have sought for walking and leisure. We walked by the North Point Milwaukee Lighthouse as children; little did we know that some day the history of the lighthouse would intrigue us enough to want to intimately delve into its storied past.

North Point Milwaukee Lighthouse is our attempt to capture the wonderful history of this venerable beacon and familiar Lake Park sentinel. Our hope is that we have done the grand lighthouse and its keepers justice. Please feel free to contact us regarding this book.

Barb and Ken Wardius
2240 West Marne Avenue
Glendale, WI 53209
(414) 228-8947
E-mail: bkw@crestwoodcreek.com
Internet: www.crestwoodcreek.com

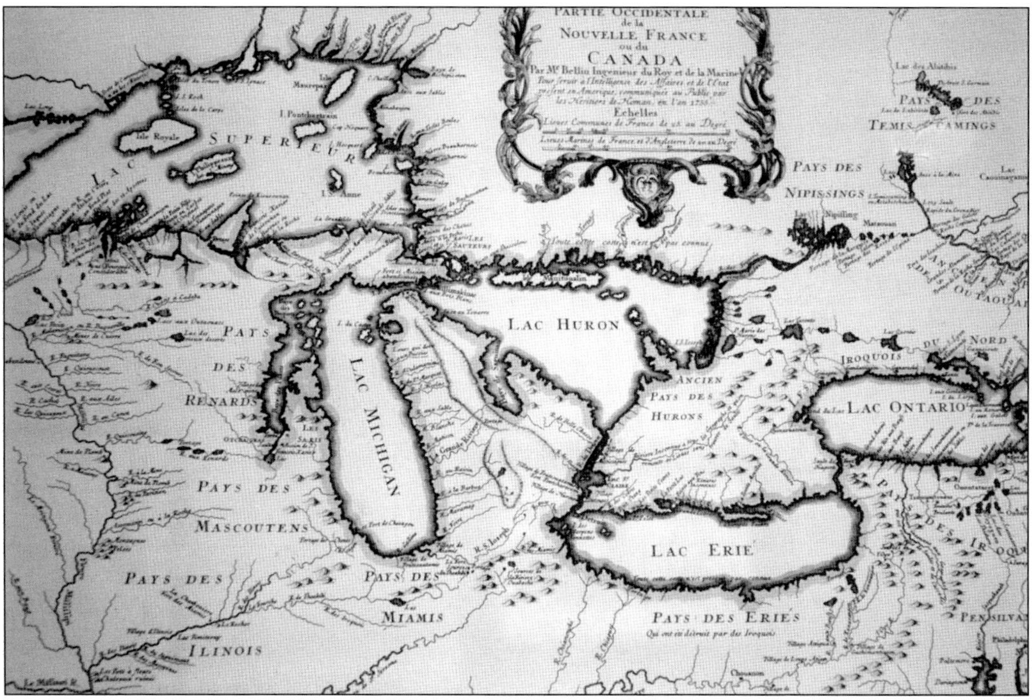

This 1755 French map shows a fairly simplified but accurate graphic of the Great Lakes region, including what later would become Wisconsin. For hundreds of years, native peoples, as well as European explorers, merchants, and settlers, used these water passages as highways for commerce. The region had abundant natural resources and waterways to facilitate the movement of essential goods. (Courtesy of AINL.)

One

Maritime Milwaukee
The Brew City's Nautical History

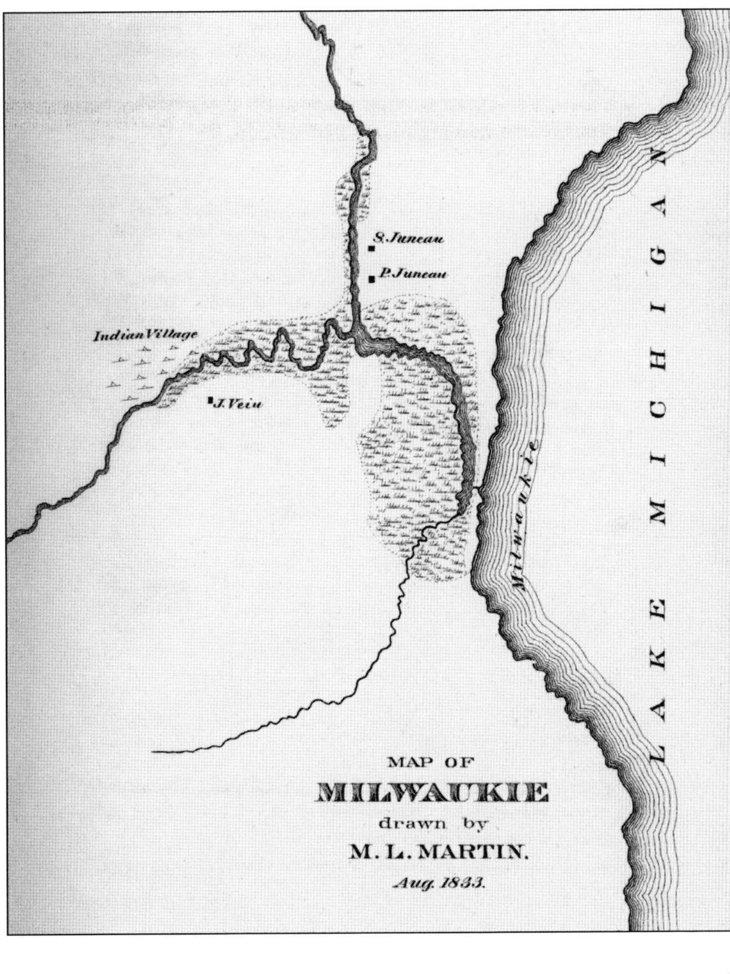

One of the earliest maps of Milwaukee is this August 1833 drawing by Morgan Lewis Martin. Just the most basic features of the area are depicted here, including Lake Michigan, the marshland, the area's three unnamed rivers, a few homes of some of Milwaukee's earliest white settlers, and an Indian village. Note the mapmaker's spelling of the city's name as "Milwaukie." Native Americans called the location Mahn-ah-wauk, or "gathering place by water." Fur trading and ample natural resources drew frontiersmen. The area offered considerable commercial potential. (Courtesy of MPM.)

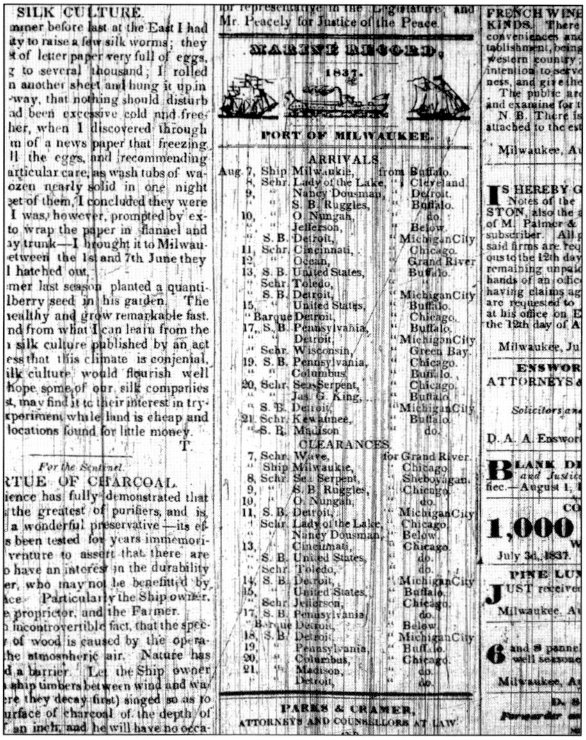

MARINE RECORD.

1837.

PORT OF MILWAUKEE.

ARRIVALS.

Aug. 7, Ship Milwaukie, from Buffalo.
8, Schr. Lady of the Lake, " Cleveland.
9, " Nancy Dousman, " Detroit.
" S. B. Ruggles, " Buffalo.
10, " O Nungah, " do.
" " Jefferson, " Below.
" S. B. Detroit, " MichiganCity
11, Schr. Cincinnati, " Chicago.
12, " Ocean, " Grand River
13, S. B. United States, " Buffalo.
" Schr. Toledo,
" S. B. Detroit, " MichiganCity
15, " United States, " Buffalo.
" Barque Detroit, " Chicago.
17, S. B. Pennsylvania, " Buffalo.
" " Detroit, " MichiganCity
" Schr. Wisconsin, " Green Bay.
19, S. B. Pennsylvania, " Chicago.
" " Columbus, " Buffalo.
20, Schr. Sea Serpent, " Chicago.
" " Jas. G. King, " Buffalo.
" S. B. Detroit, " MichiganCity
21, Schr. Kewaunee, " Buffalo.
" S. B. Madison " do.

CLEARANCES.

7, Schr. Wave, for Grand River.
" Ship Milwaukie, " Chicago.
8, Schr. Sea Serpent, " Sheboygan.
9, " S. B. Ruggles, " Chicago.
10, " O. Nungah, " do.
11, S. B. Detroit, " MichiganCity
" Schr. Lady of the Lake, " Chicago.
" " Nancy Dousman, " Below.
13, " Cincinnati, " Chicago.
" S. B. United States, " do.
" Schr. Toledo, " do.
14, S. B. Detroit, " MichiganCity
15, " United States, " Buffalo.
" Schr. Jefferson, " Chicago.
17, S. B. Pennsylvania, " do.
" Barque Detroit, " Below.
18, S. B. Detroit, " MichiganCity
19, " Pennsylvania, " Buffalo.
20, " Columbus, " Chicago.
21, " Madison, " do.
" " Detroit, " do.

PARKS & CRAMER,
ATTORNEYS AND COUNSELLORS AT LAW.

Milwaukee was only an infant city when the *Milwaukee Sentinel*, a local newspaper, published the marine record on August 22, 1837. It was a listing of vessels that had arrived and departed from the port. Ships listed include schooners, barques, and barges. They came from and left for many other Great Lakes ports, including Chicago, Detroit, Michigan City, and Buffalo. (Authors' collection.)

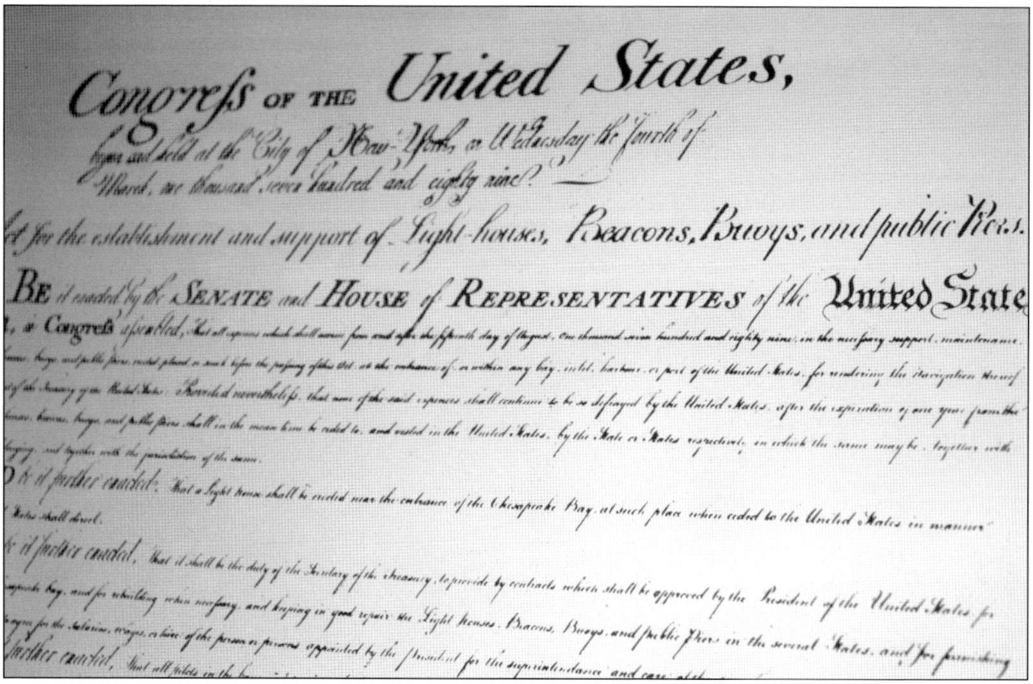

Congress of the United States,

begun and held at the City of New-York, on Wednesday the fourth of March, one thousand seven hundred and eighty nine.

Act for the establishment and support of Light-houses, Beacons, Buoys, and public Piers.

Be it enacted by the Senate and House of Representatives of the United State[s] in Congress assembled, ...

Some of the earliest essential business of the US government, including the president and Congress, dealt with maritime issues such as the establishment and maintenance of lighthouses, beacons, buoys, and public piers. Economic growth depended on safer ways of transporting commodities via water, the most economical method employed during those days. (Authors' collection.)

The first steam-powered ship arrived in what would become Milwaukee in 1835. The city would soon develop into a Great Lakes port of major importance. Schooners and other vessel types crisscrossed Milwaukee Bay, and the local rivers teemed with ships. Loaded with lumber, basic foodstuffs, and a variety of natural resources and materials needed for a growing industrial center, lighthouses were needed to increase safety due to this bustling boat traffic. (Courtesy of MCHS.)

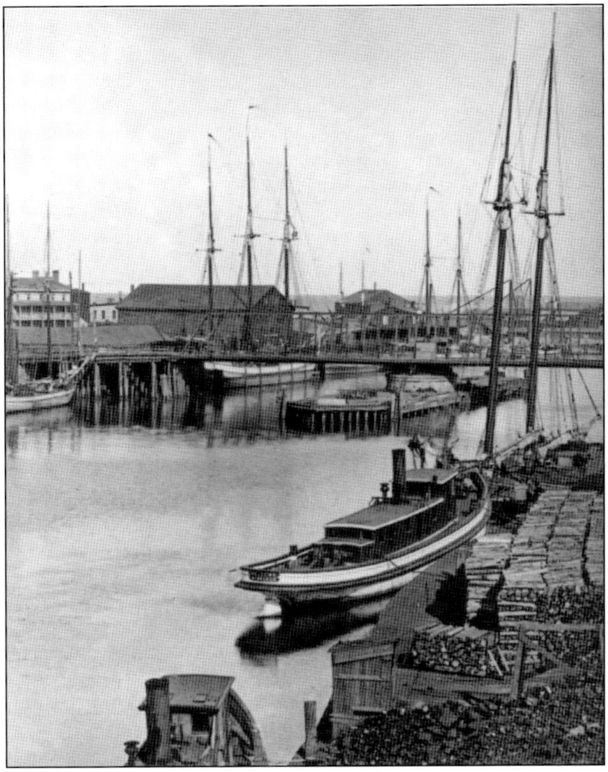

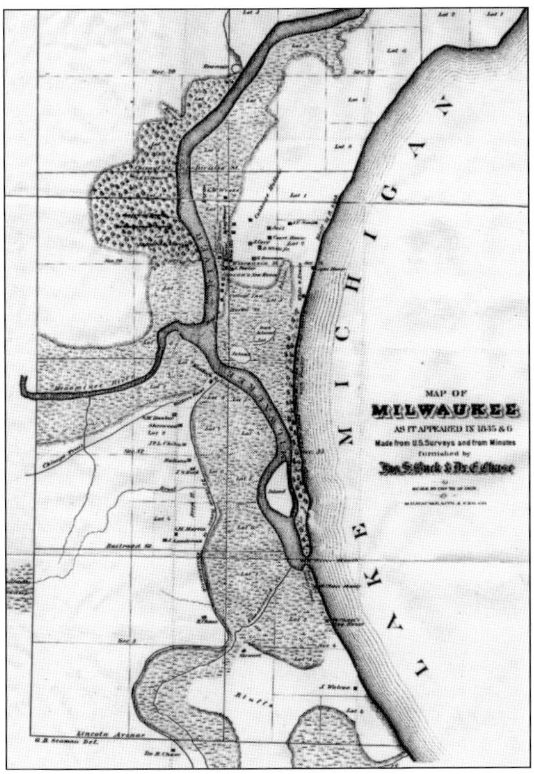

This 1835 Milwaukee map illustrates what the area looked like before any large-scale harbor development and improvement took place. Marshy areas surrounded the Milwaukee and Menominee Rivers and Kinnekenneck Creek (later spelled Menomonee and Kinnickinnic). The combined rivers flow into Lake Michigan, south of an island that was later named Jones Island. The eastern end of Wisconsin Street notes a lighthouse, the inaugural light at Milwaukee. It is seen to the left of the *H* in "Michigan." (Courtesy of MCHS.)

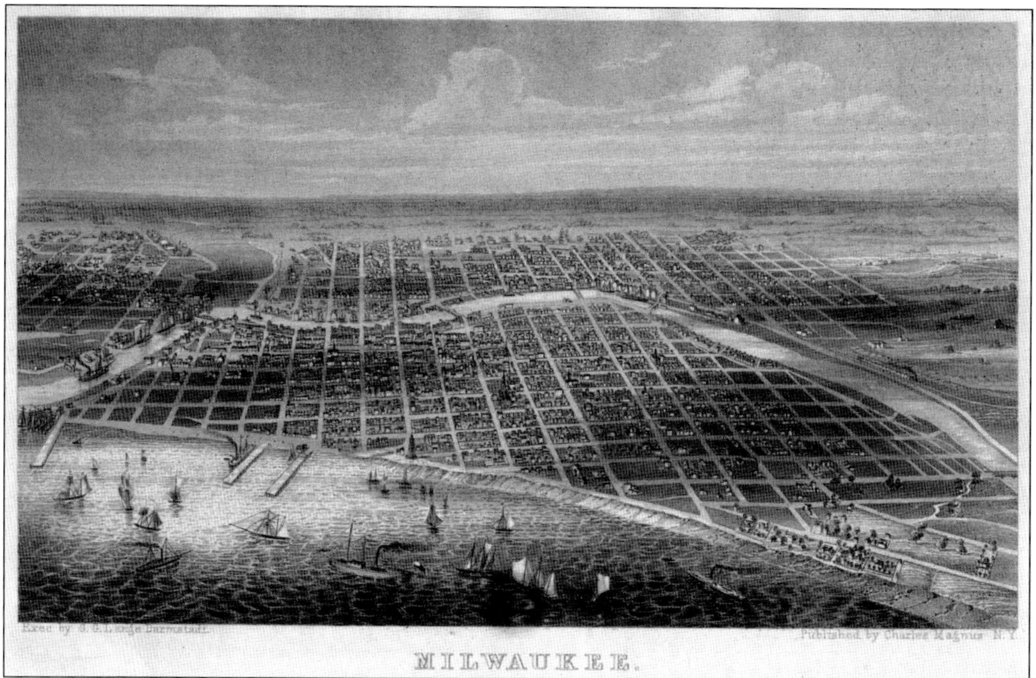

Like many fledgling cities on the Great Lakes, Milwaukee was teeming with immigrants. Founders Byron Kilbourn, Solomon Juneau, and George Walker, along with other Germans, Poles, Italians, and Irish, brought the area to life. Milwaukee became an important center for the shipment of grains, especially wheat, as well as a major manufacturing locale. Breweries, butcher shops, and bakeries were some of the other mainstays of the local economy. Here, Milwaukee's first lighthouse is visible on the shoreline, immediately to the right of some piers. (Courtesy of Mark Kuehn.)

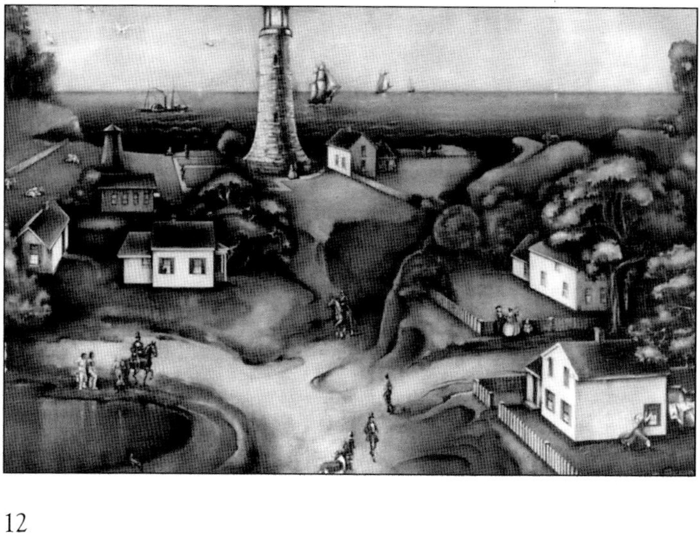

The first lighthouse in the Milwaukee Bay area was a small brick building and 30-foot tower positioned somewhat north of where Milwaukee's rivers drain into Lake Michigan. It was completed in 1838 and located on Wisconsin Street (now East Wisconsin Avenue). While not the most favorable position for a beacon, the light did alert sailors that the port of Milwaukee was close by. (Courtesy of MCHS.)

Milwaukee's first lighthouse stood atop a rather low bluff. Government officials realized too late that it was not strategically placed. They decided to replace it with a beacon three miles north of Milwaukee Bay on a much higher bluff called North Point that jutted into Lake Michigan. Milwaukee's 1838 lighthouse was dismantled in 1855. This is an artist's version of what the area might have looked like. (Courtesy of Pioneer History of Milwaukee.)

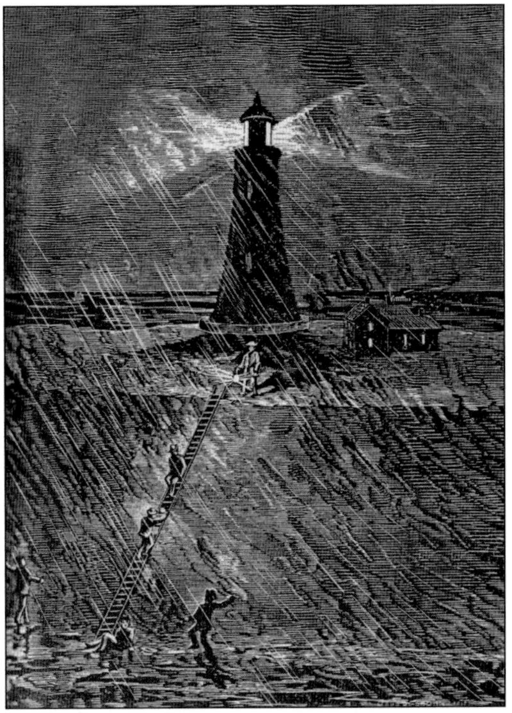

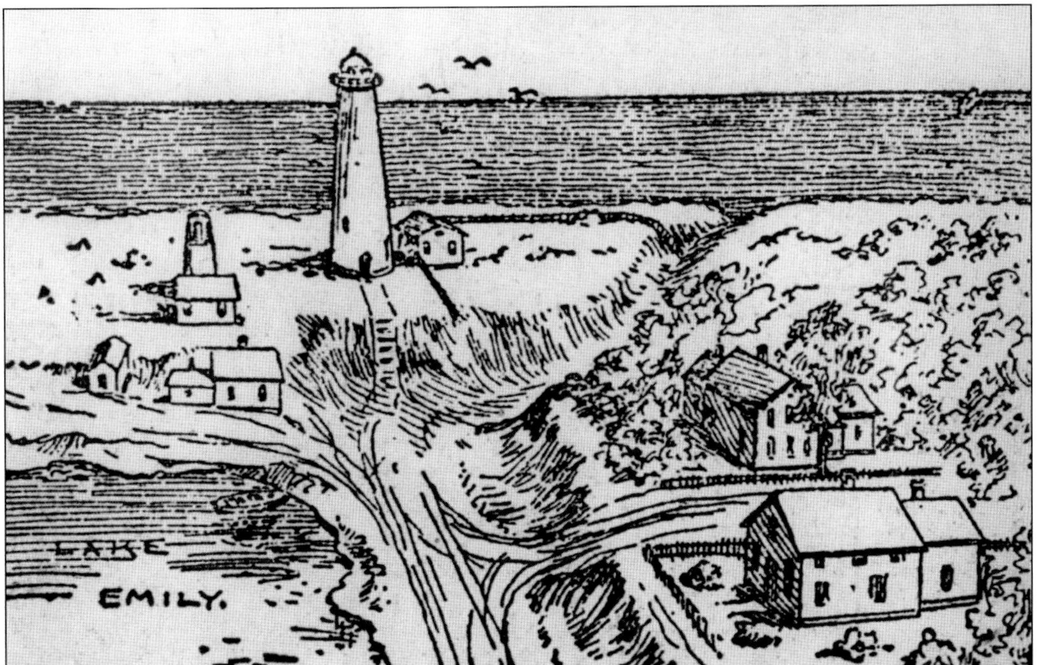

This 1840s view of downtown Milwaukee features a large body of water, Lake Emily. It is immediately west of Milwaukee's first lighthouse, which was built in 1838. Located along the street now known as Wisconsin Avenue, the lake was eventually filled in. The large office buildings currently at this location stand on wood pilings that are soaked due to the subsurface water that continues to exist there. (Courtesy of MCHS.)

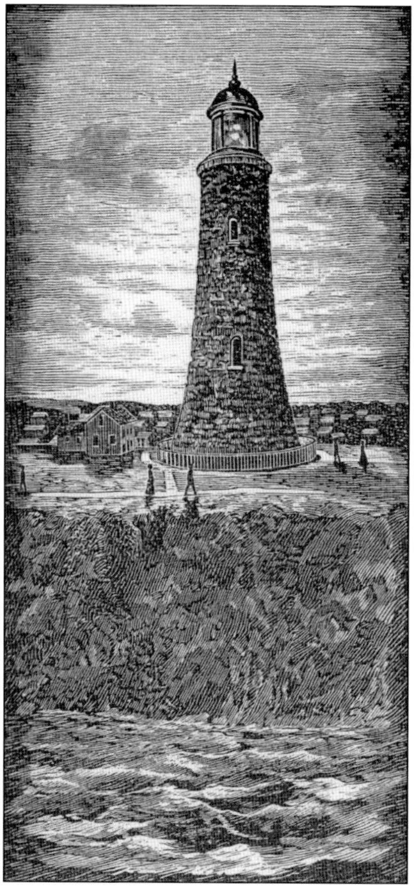

The first known lighthouse keeper here, from 1845 to 1847, was Eli Bates Jr. Bates was an interesting character. Born in 1806, his family was quite poor. In addition to his lighthouse job, he supplemented his $300 annual salary by reportedly running a local tavern and gambling establishment. Having lost a leg to disease as a teenager, he walked with an artificial cork limb. (Courtesy of Pioneer History of Milwaukee.)

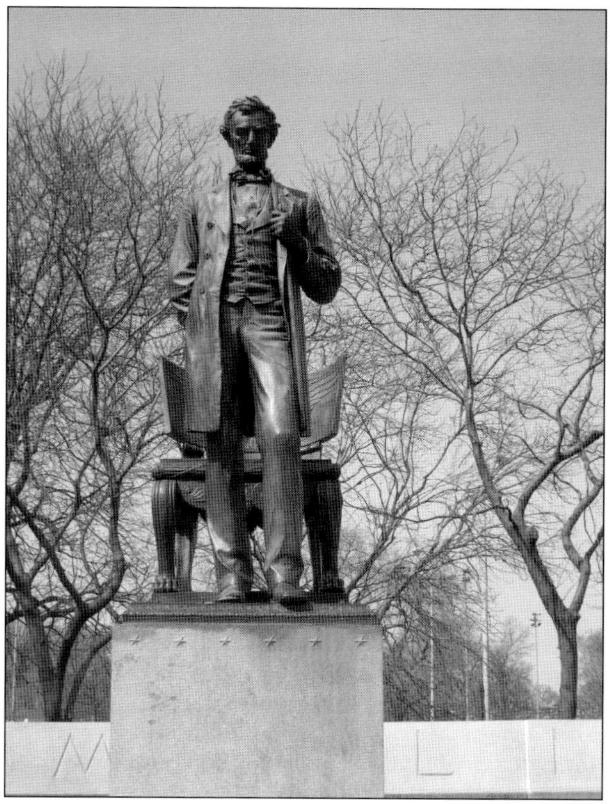

After his few years at Milwaukee's lighthouse, Eli Bates moved to Chicago in 1840. His occupations included teaching, farming, and being the superintendent of a lumberyard. Although Bates came from very modest roots and did not make his fortune from lighthouse tending, he died in 1881 with a large estate. A believer in charity, one of his bequests was a large donation for a statue of Abraham Lincoln in Lincoln Park in Chicago. (Courtesy of Zagalejo.)

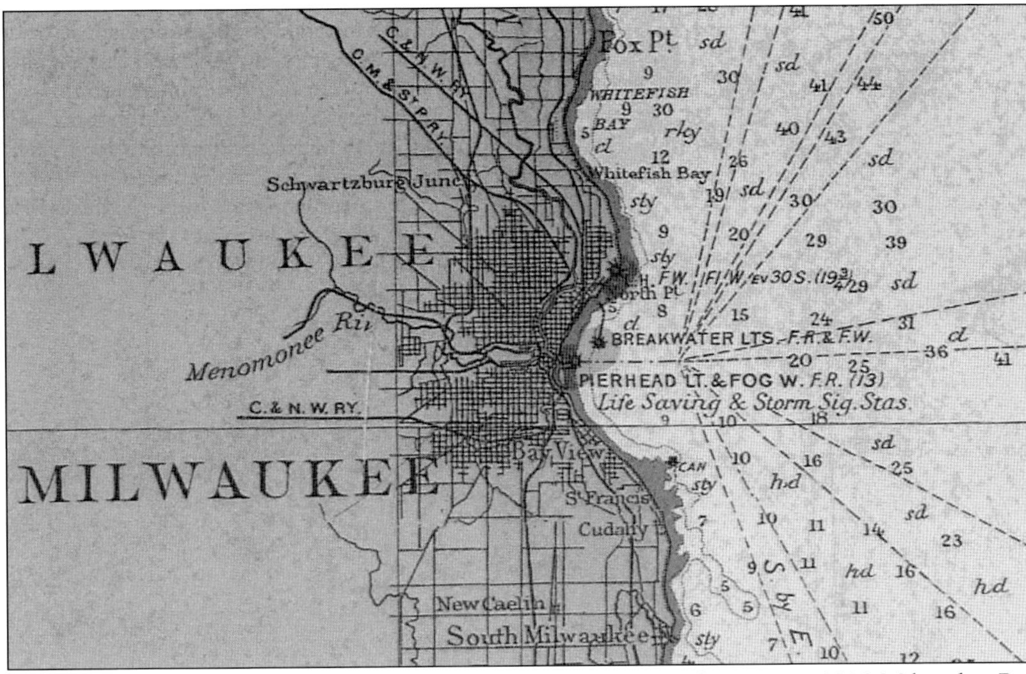

Milwaukee became a Great Lakes port in 1835 and was incorporated as a city in 1846. Milwaukee Bay and harbor developed into a bustling port, as illustrated by this nautical map. The immediate harbor area contained several structures related to maritime safety, including pierhead and breakwater lights, a fog signal, and lifesaving and storm signal stations. The North Point Lighthouse, with its distinct white flashing beacon, stood three miles north of town. (Courtesy of NOAA.)

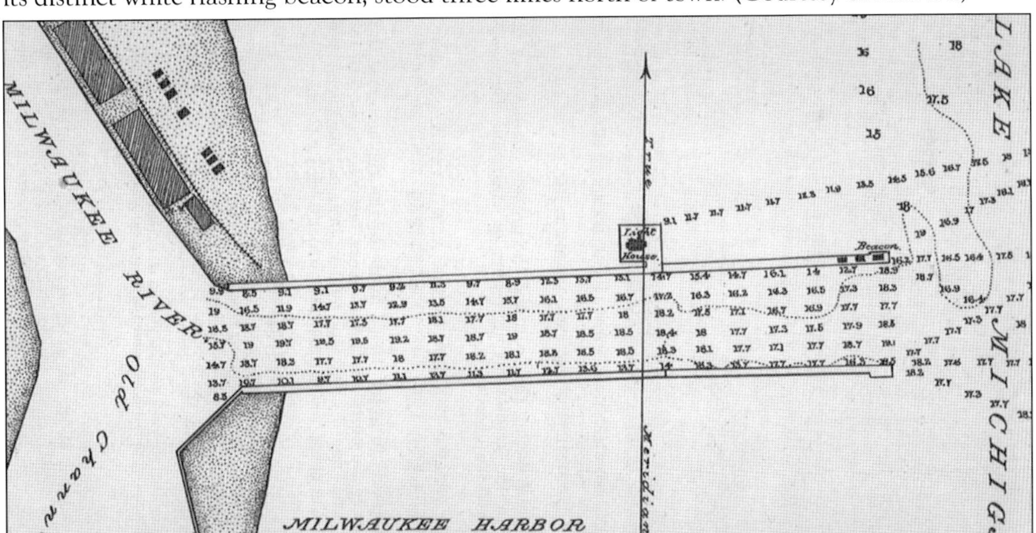

Milwaukee's rivers naturally emptied into Lake Michigan on the southern end of the harbor area. Although discussed for several decades, the straight cut, or man-made channel, about a half mile north of the original outlet, was not completed until 1857. An 1884 harbor map shows depths in the new waterway, as well as the pier beacon and keeper's residence. (Courtesy of NPLHF.)

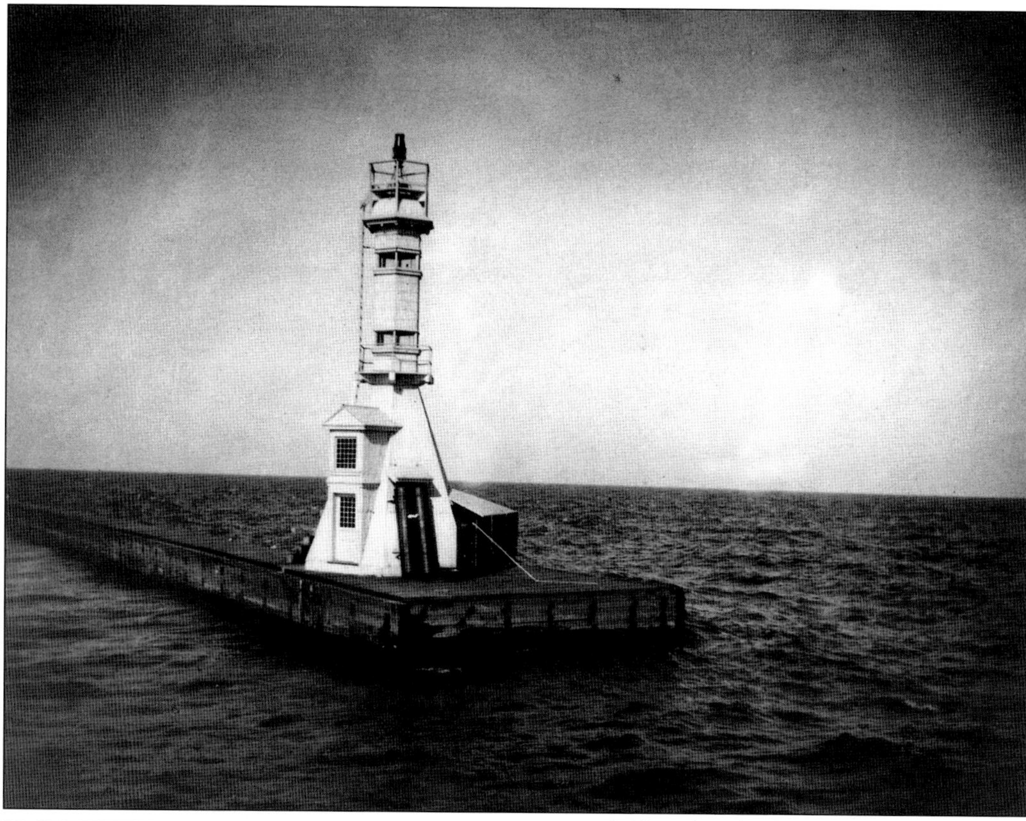

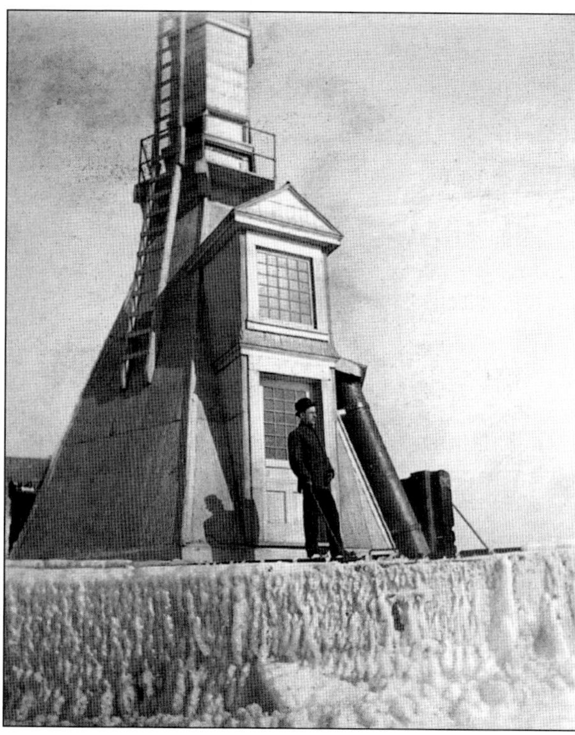

Milwaukee had a number of long, crude wooden piers early in its history. One unique style of pier light was this peculiar pagoda lighthouse. Structures such as this would have sported smaller fifth- or sixth-order Fresnel lenses, which were strong enough to guide ships as they came closer to their intended port. Early breakwaters and piers at Sheboygan and Racine also featured this interesting beacon. (Courtesy of Tim Harrison.)

A closer examination of this image of the pagoda-style lighthouse yields some rather interesting observations. The gentleman out front appears at first glance to be a lighthouse keeper, but his clothing is not a uniform. He is standing on ice-skates with what looks like a hockey stick in his hand. The icy conditions may have been good for hockey, but the location was certainly not safe. (Courtesy of Tim Harrison.)

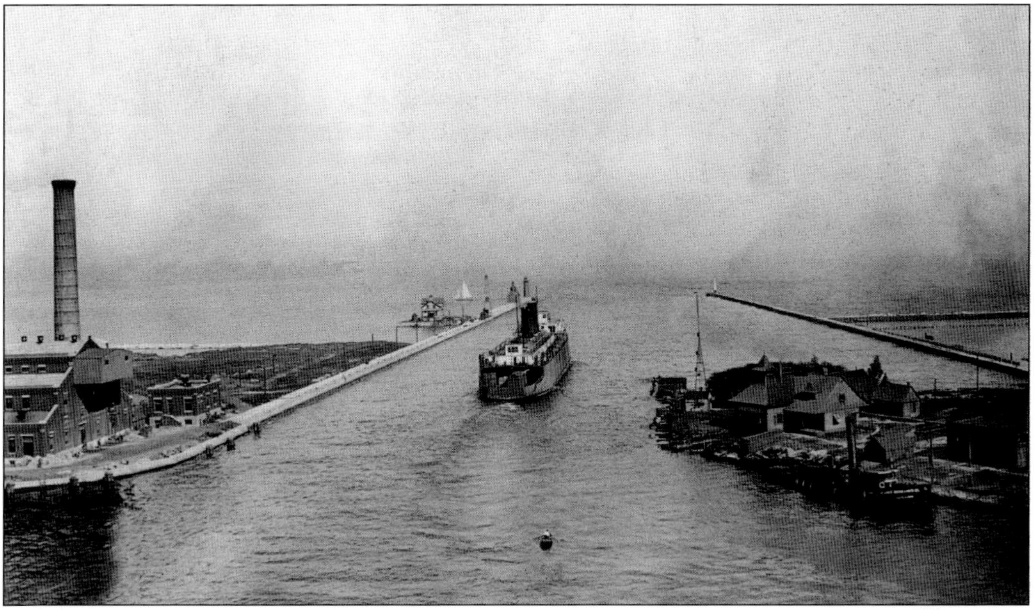

This early 1900s view captures maritime Milwaukee quite well. A large ship plies eastward, away from the harbor, through the man-made waterway known as the straight cut. Both channel sides are lined with concrete piers and beacons on their corresponding ends. In addition to the lighthouses, the city's incinerator is on the left, and the US Life Saving Station and associated tower are on the right. (Courtesy of MCHS.)

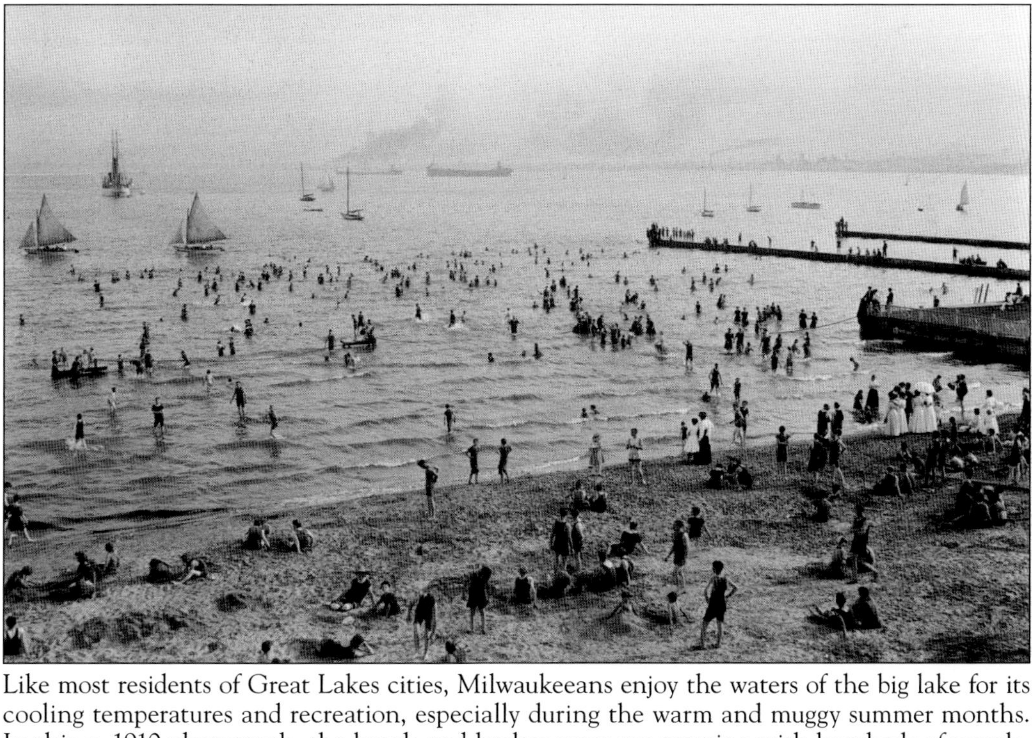

Like most residents of Great Lakes cities, Milwaukeeans enjoy the waters of the big lake for its cooling temperatures and recreation, especially during the warm and muggy summer months. In this c. 1910 photograph, the beach and harbor areas are teeming with hundreds of people, sailboats, and large cargo-hauling vessels. (Courtesy of MPM.)

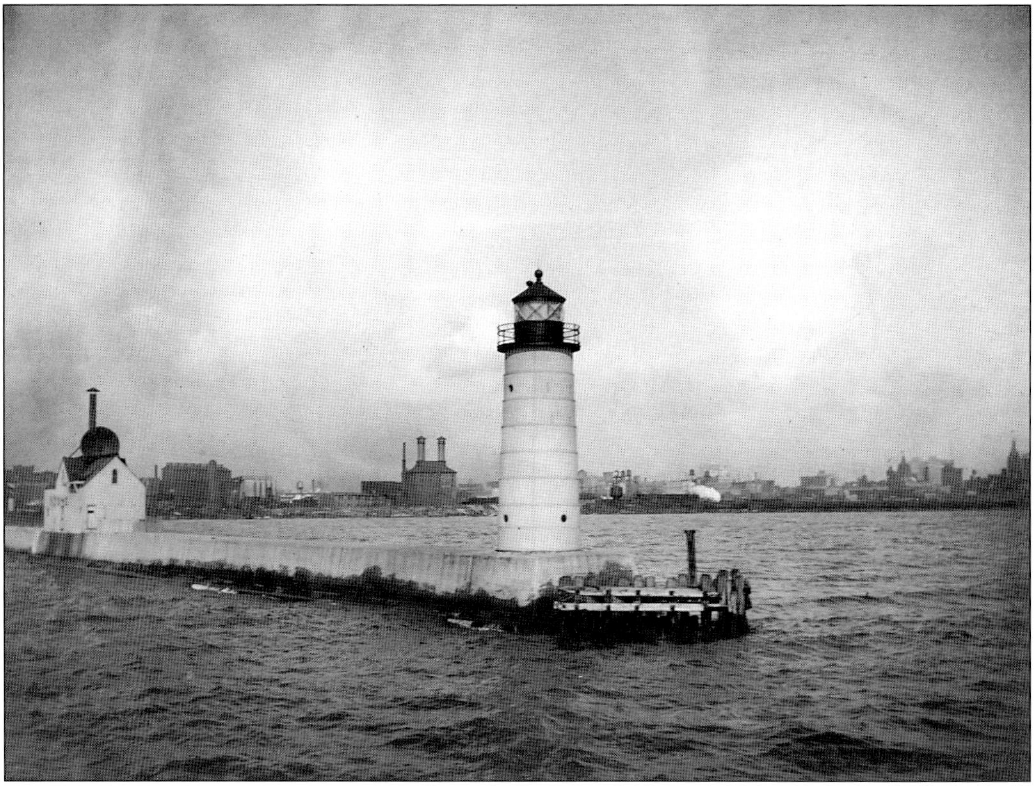

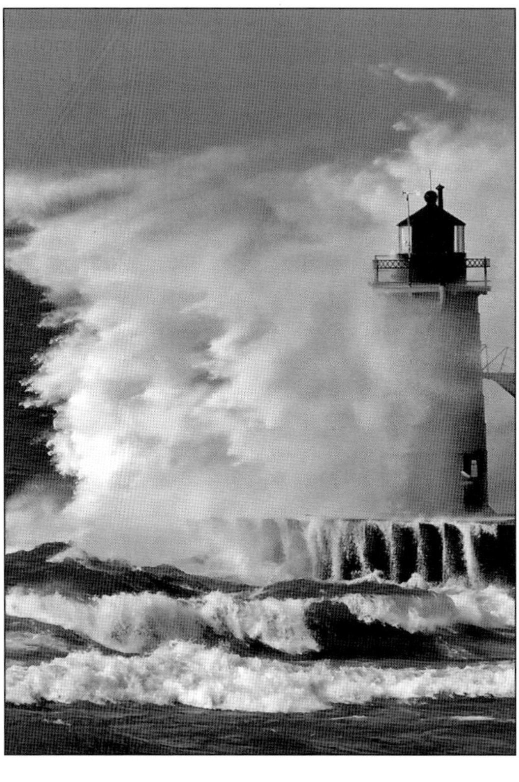

Milwaukee, like many Great Lakes ports, had various other pier lights in its history. The first pier light was a wooden framed structure dating to the mid-1800s. This 1914 photograph depicts a standard conical metal lighthouse, found in several Lake Michigan cities, along with a large fog signal building. Different designs existed, and the location of pier and breakwater lights could change as harbor improvements occurred over the years. This steel lighthouse has moved more than once in its lifetime. (Courtesy of USCG.)

Lighthouses are at times exposed to the full wrath of a stormy Lake Michigan. Out in the open, harbor pier and breakwater lights were especially vulnerable and might be pummeled for days. Light keepers were still expected to venture out in dangerous weather. Some Great Lakes lights had elevated catwalks that would assist lighthouse personnel in fulfilling their appointed rounds and duties. North Point's elevated position minimized direct damage from the lake. (Courtesy of Gary Martin.)

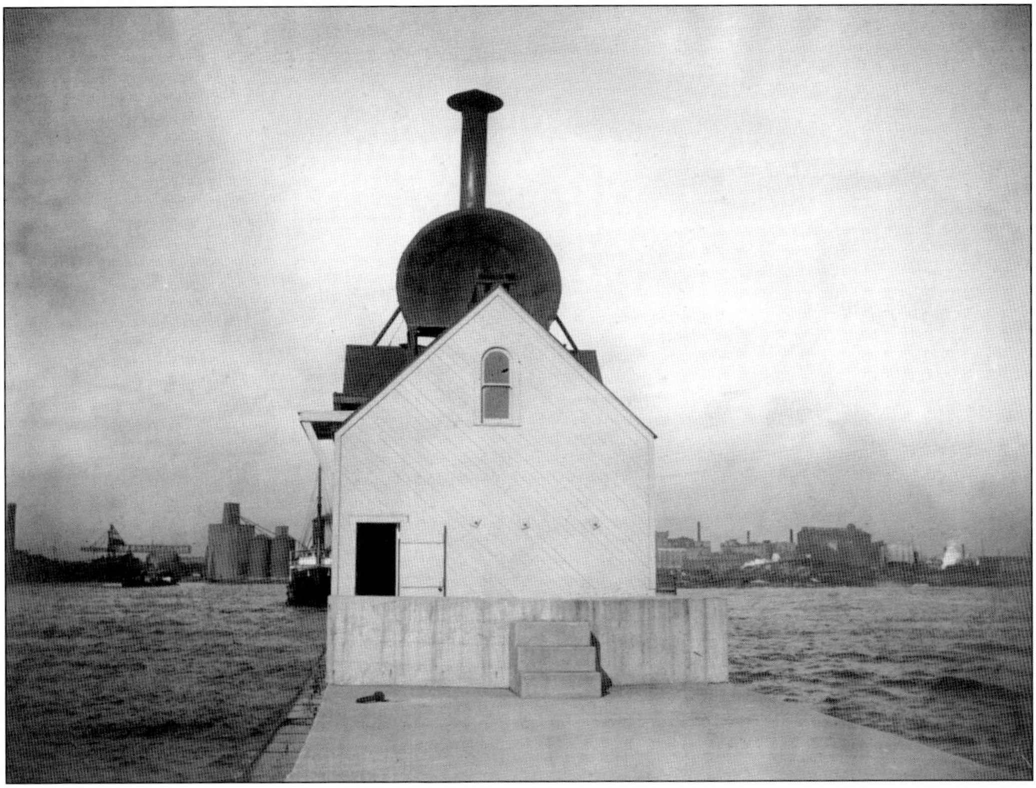

With the 1914 city skyline and malt, seed, and other manufacturers as a backdrop, the harbor entrance at Milwaukee was also guarded by this mammoth fog signal on its main pier, a short distance inland from the pier light beacon. The keeper's quarters also share the pier. Fog signal buildings such as this were common on the Great Lakes. Ships often heard the distinctive moans of the foghorn, or the clang of a fog bell, even if the lighthouse's beam was obscured by foggy conditions. (Courtesy of USCG.)

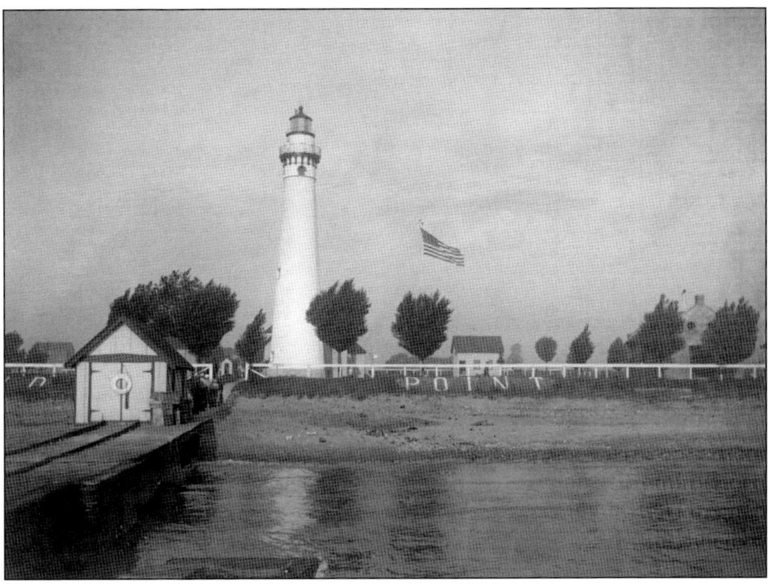

Many foghorns on the Great Lakes were so powerful that they could be heard in nearby cities. Logbooks from the 1880s from the Wind Point Lighthouse, 22 miles to the south in Racine, noted that the light from the North Point Milwaukee Lighthouse was visible and that the Milwaukee pierhead fog signal could be heard. (Courtesy of USCG.)

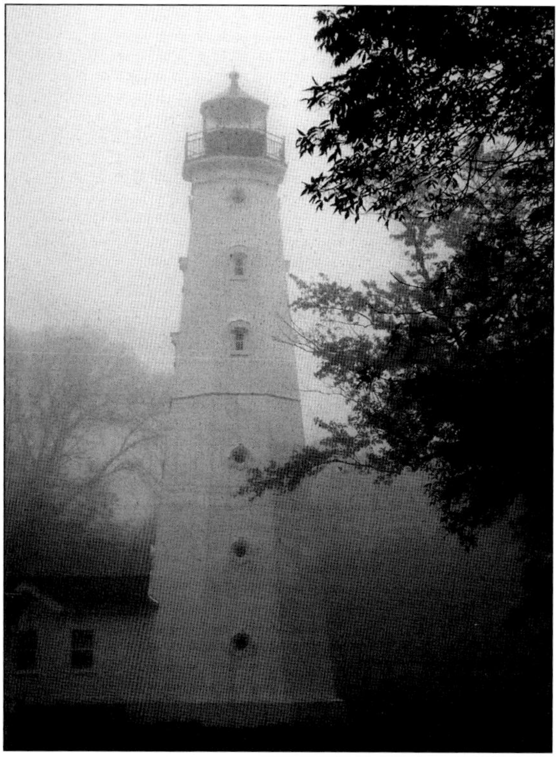

In extremely foggy conditions, lighthouse beams would be rendered impotent. While many Great Lakes light stations also employed foghorns, the North Point Lighthouse never did. The position of the lighthouse, north of the city, may have played a role in not needing a fog building at North Point. Mariners navigating in the vicinity of Milwaukee's harbor would have heard the pier or breakwater fog signals. Here, the North Point Lighthouse is shrouded in thick fog. (Courtesy of Jeff Grzeca.)

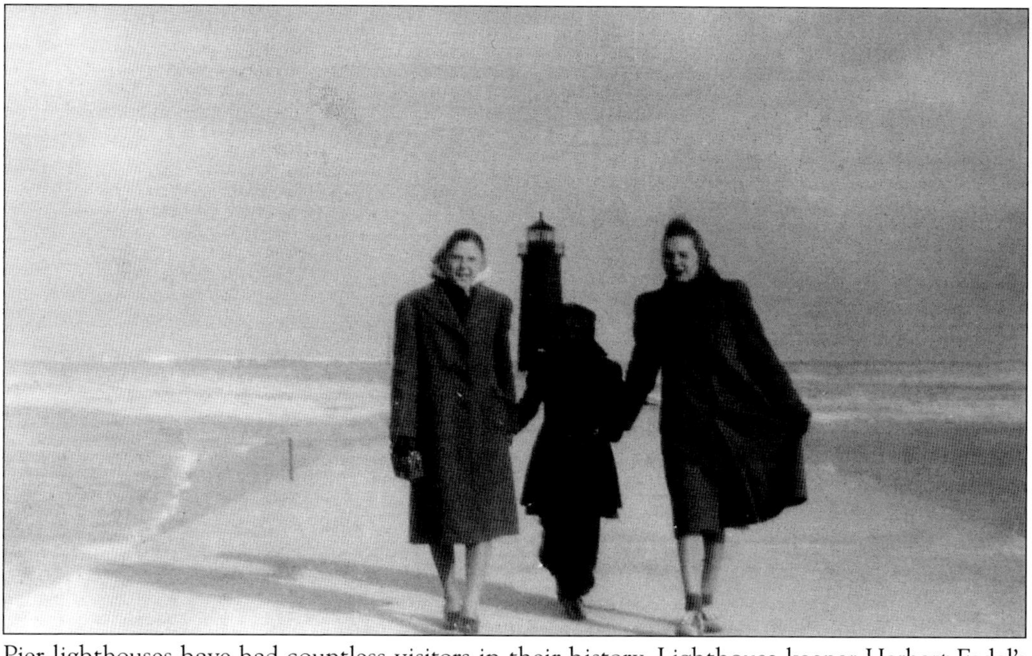

Pier lighthouses have had countless visitors in their history. Lighthouse keeper Herbert Fadel's daughters Lois (left) and Jane (right) and friend Maxine Wilke walk inland with the Milwaukee pier light in the background around 1940. The North Point Lighthouse has attracted the public since its earliest days. People enjoy walking through Lake Park or taking a leisurely stroll out on the piers to take in a closer view of a beacon. (Courtesy of Jane Fadel Murphy.)

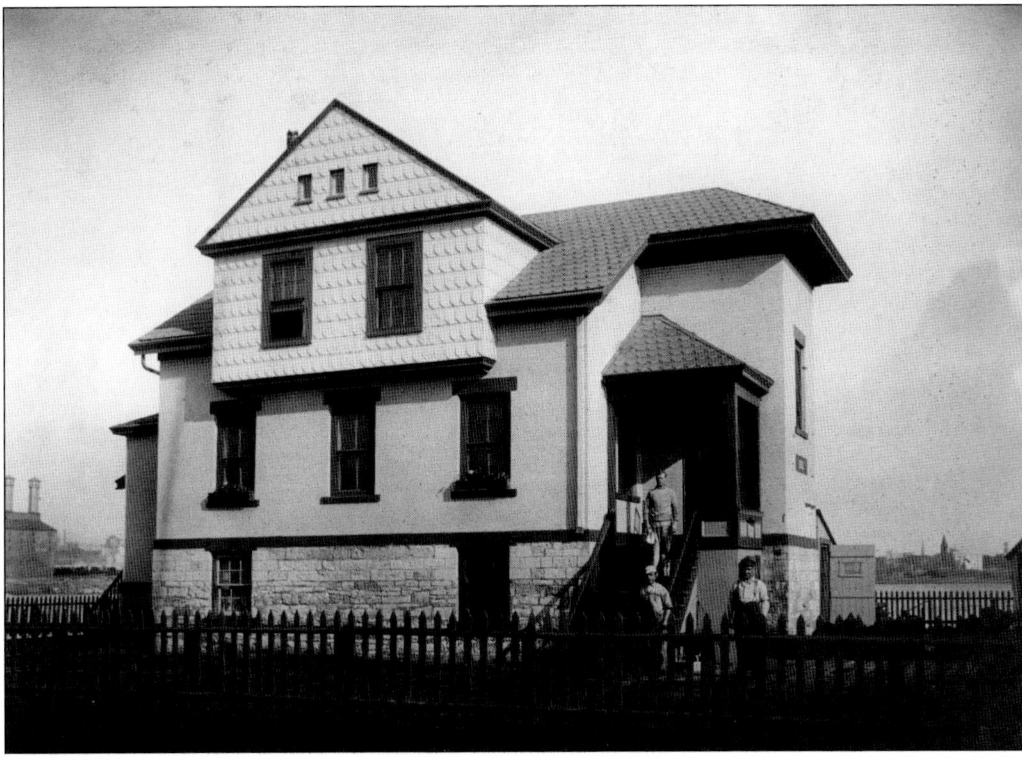

This photograph, taken on September 11, 1914, beautifully shows the quarters for the light keepers who were assigned to the pier and breakwater lighthouses in Milwaukee. This two-story dwelling sat on a concrete and wooden wharf area that was connected to the main north pier in the harbor. Keepers would routinely trek from the lakeside residence out to the fog signal and pierhead beacon to tend to lighthouse chores. (Courtesy of USCG.)

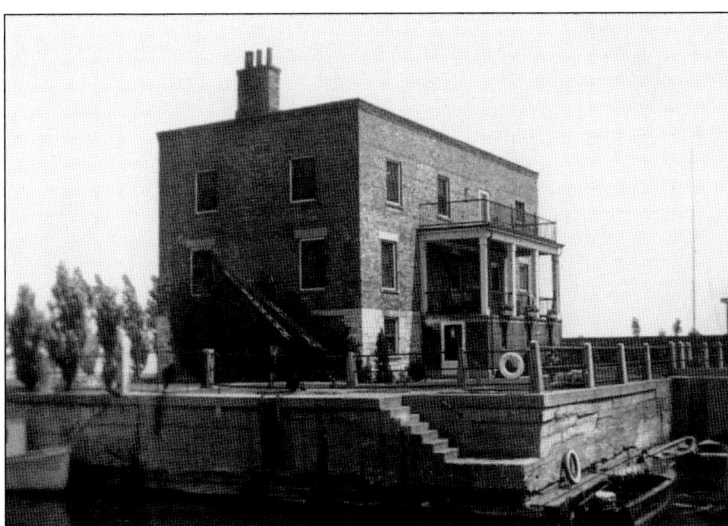

The building that housed Milwaukee's harbor lighthouse crews was later changed and remodeled. This image shows the wharf area with its multiple boats and ring buoys. The lakeshore area immediately north of here was eventually filled in and an airstrip, Maitland Field, was constructed. The small airport ultimately made way for more lakefront progress. (Courtesy of Jane Fadel Murphy.)

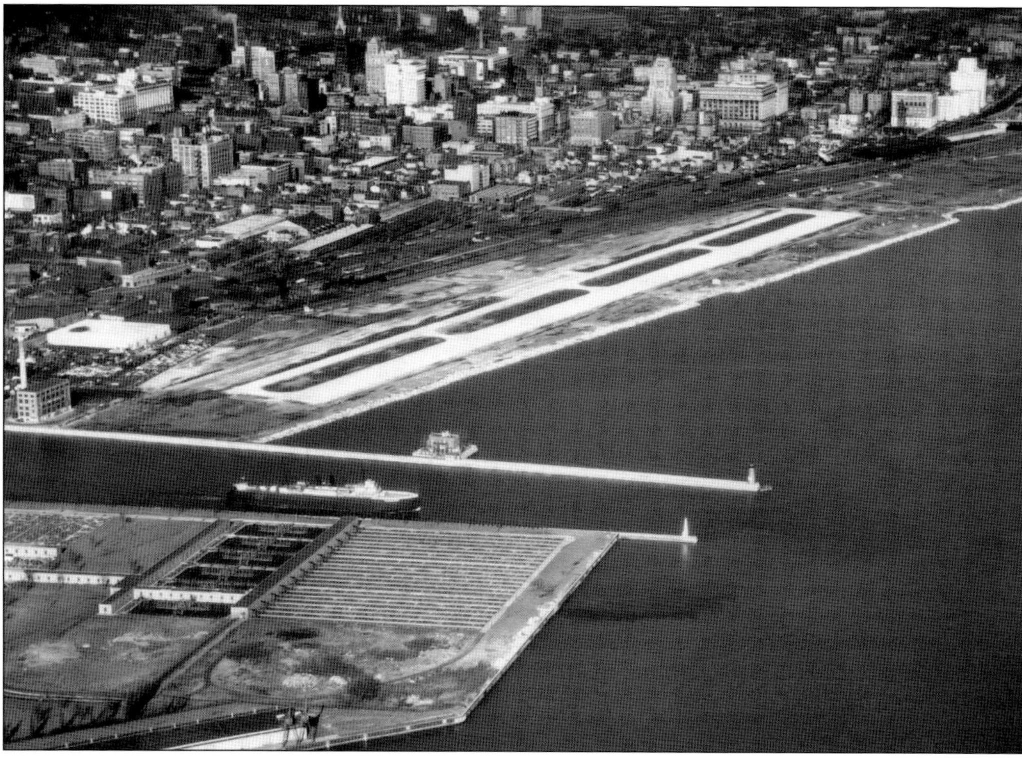

This c. 1935 bird's-eye view of the Milwaukee harbor shows a ship leaving port and two pier lighthouses, as well as the light keeper's quarters along the concrete piers. Immediately beyond those structures is a small airfield. Opened in 1927, Maitland Field was named after Lester Maitland, a pioneering Milwaukee pilot and World War I veteran. It was later filled in for additional development along Lake Michigan. (Courtesy of MPL.)

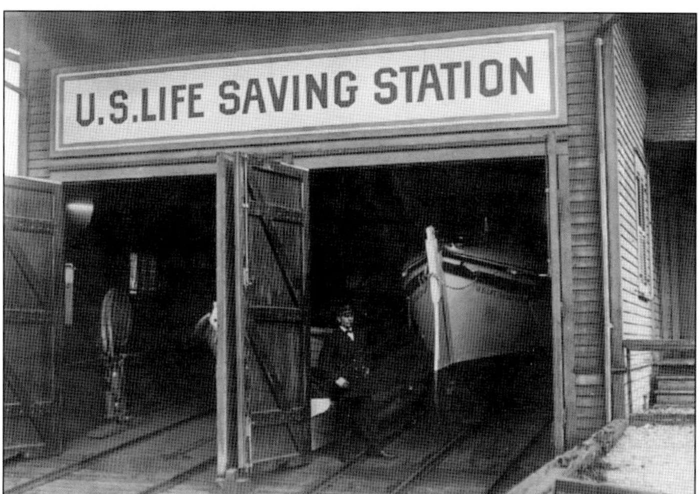

Another facility in the Milwaukee harbor devoted to maritime safety was this US Life Saving Station, located on the northern end of Jones Island. Here, the highest person in charge, known as the keeper, stands near the doorways, which opened to launch the rescue vessels down a rail system. Stations also had seven or eight crew members called surfmen, who were given numerical rank designations. (Courtesy of MCHS.)

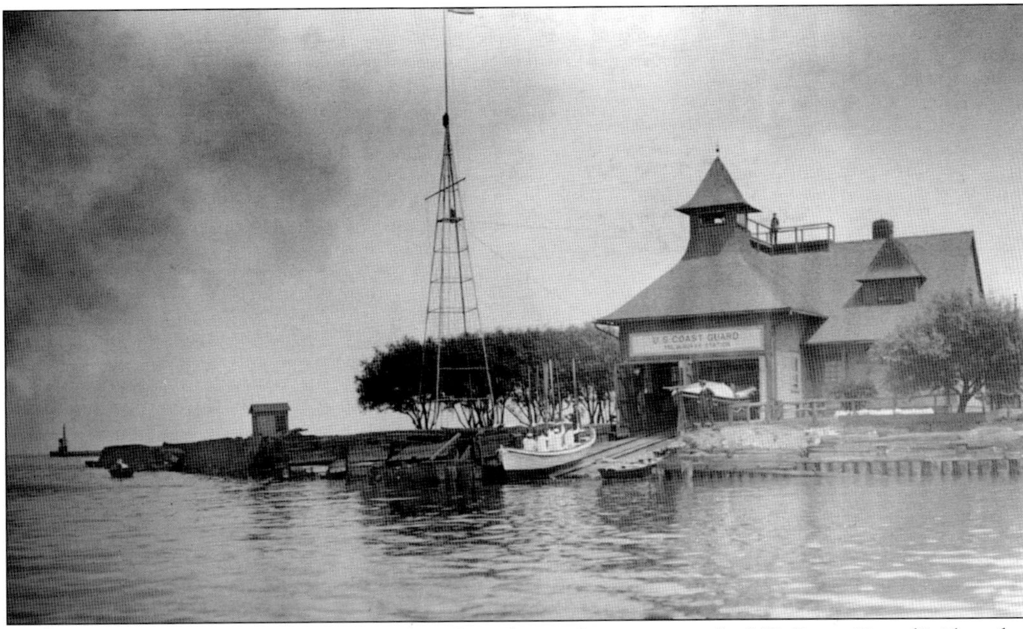

Later, the US Life Saving Station in Milwaukee changed its name to the US Coast Guard Milwaukee Station and performed the same important activities. Those stationed here were responsible for lending help to vessels and personnel in need on the waters in the Greater Milwaukee area. In this early-1900s photograph, note the crew in a white boat being launched into the water and also the lookout man atop the building. (Courtesy of MCHS.)

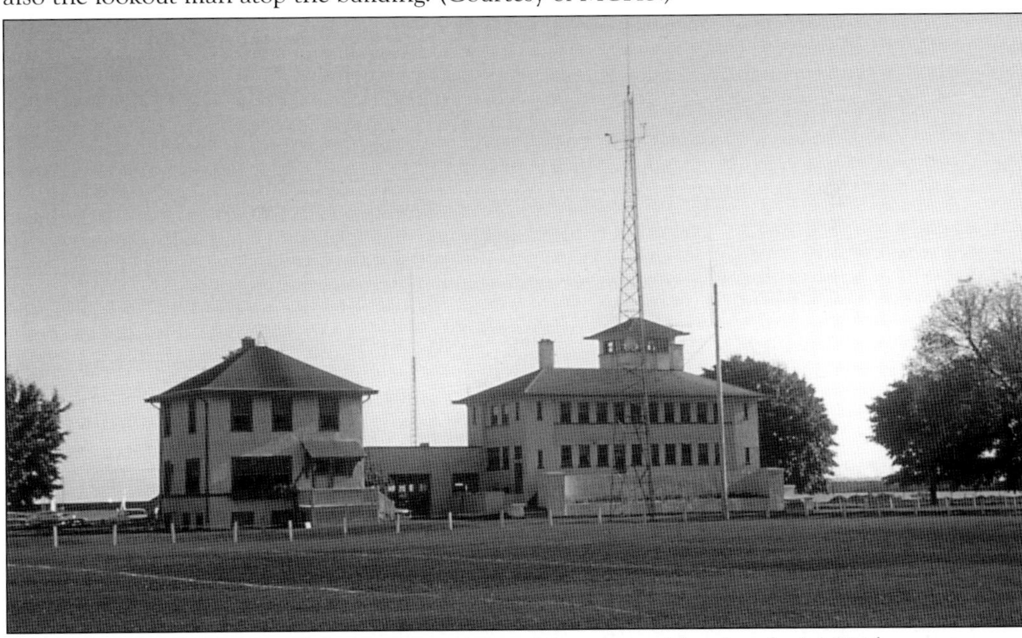

In 1915, the US Coast Guard Station was relocated from Jones Island to the McKinley marina area because of poor water quality in Milwaukee's inner harbor. It was in service until 1970. Various other uses were proposed for the structure, but none materialized. After many efforts to preserve its picturesque prairie-style architecture and historic significance, the building was eventually demolished in 2008. (Courtesy of MCHS.)

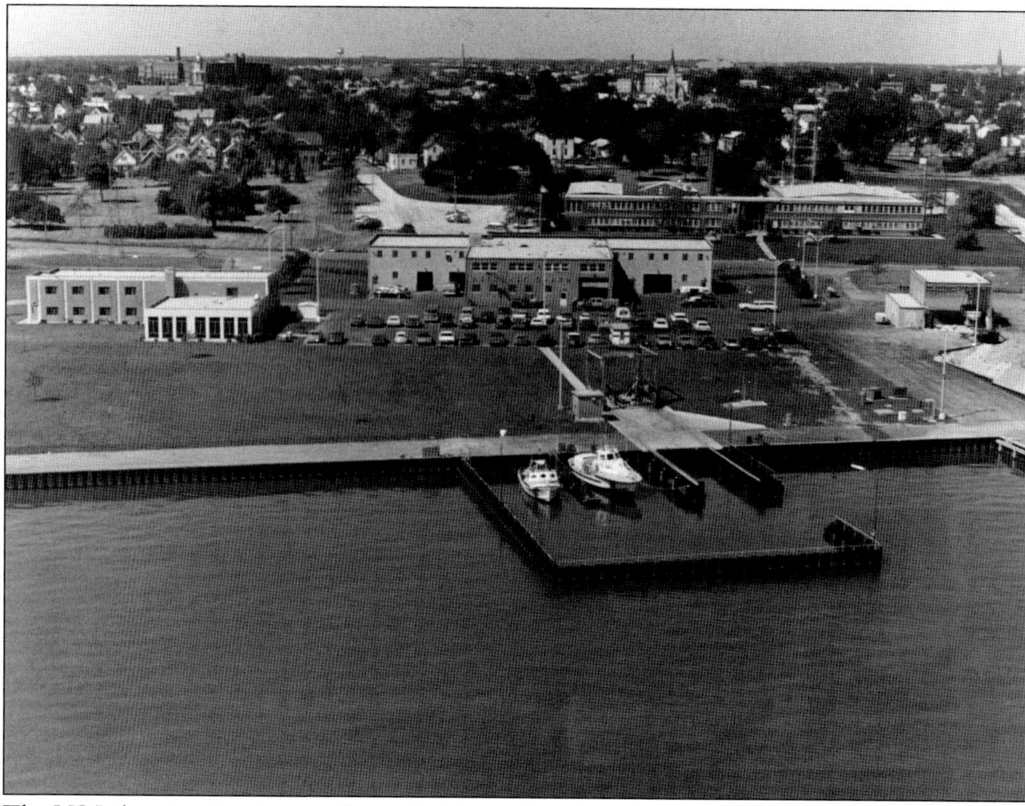

The US Lifesaving Service, and later the Coast Guard, have had facilities in Milwaukee for over 130 years to assist ships and crews in distress. The location of these facilities changed over the years, as the city's harbor and nautical safety needs evolved. This aerial photograph features the current US Coast Guard Station, on the southern end of Milwaukee's harbor along South Lincoln Memorial Drive, which opened in 1970. (Courtesy of USCG.)

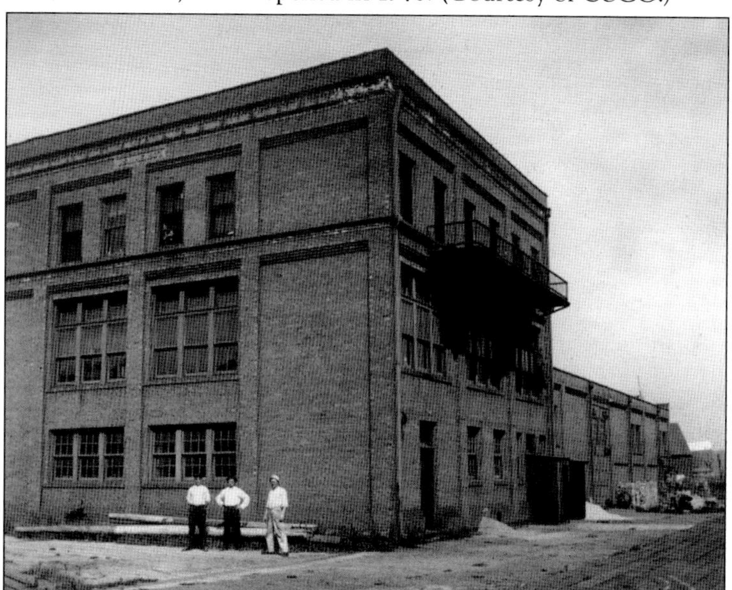

Milwaukee was home to a US Lighthouse Establishment Depot, constructed in 1907 and later enlarged. The facility repaired and refurbished equipment and kept supplies and materials that related to lighthouses. Nestled on the Kinnickinnic River, just south of the city's downtown, the warehouse not only provided for Milwaukee's lighthouse needs, but also many other Wisconsin beacons. (Courtesy of Tom Tag.)

This rare photograph, taken in 1938, shows the all-important lamp shop in an interior area at the Milwaukee Lighthouse Depot. The Fresnel lens pictured here sits atop a pedestal and is about the same size as North Point's, a fourth-order lens. The apparatus shown also features a gear-driven mechanism used to rotate the lens. (Courtesy of Jim Woodward and Tom Tag.)

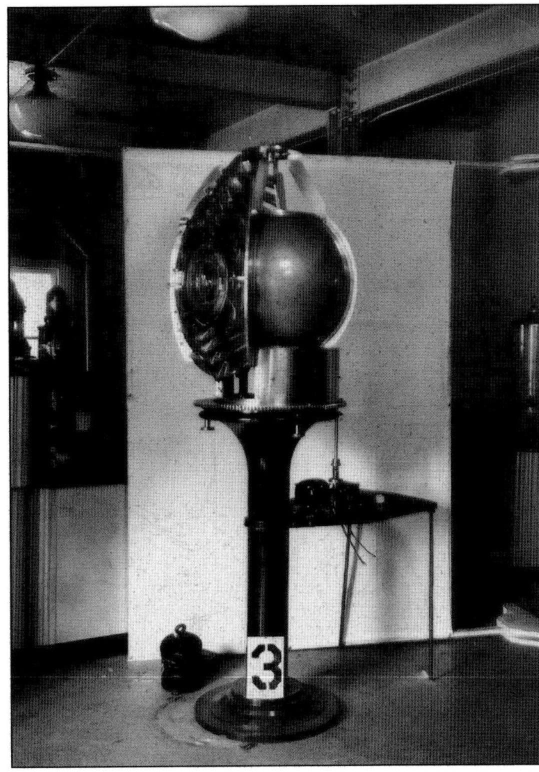

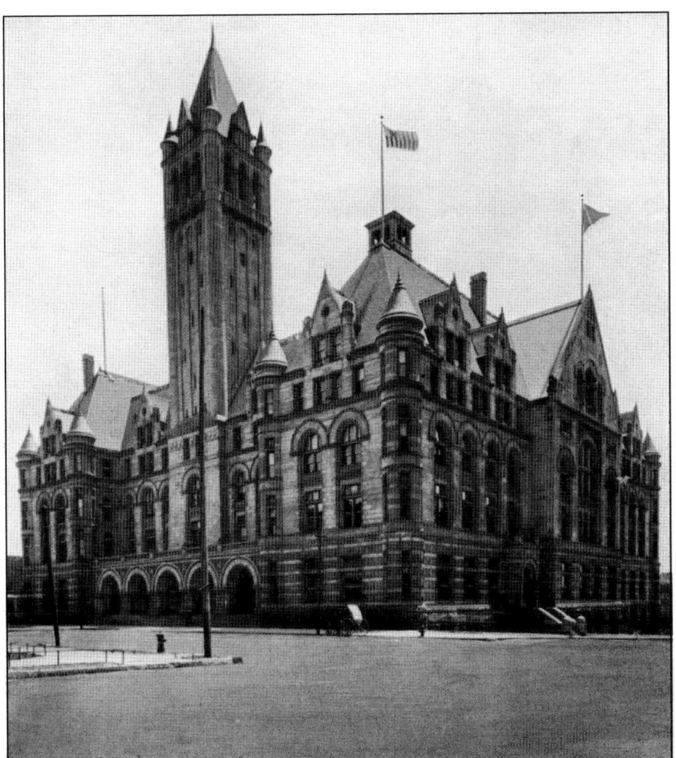

The Federal Building in downtown Milwaukee was the home of the US Lighthouse Service offices for many years. Constructed in 1899, numerous decisions involving the dealings and activities at North Point came from inspectors and lighthouse authorities that were employed here and in Chicago. Milwaukee lighthouse operations were also connected to the 1907 lighthouse depot on the nearby Kinnickinnic River. (Courtesy of MPM.)

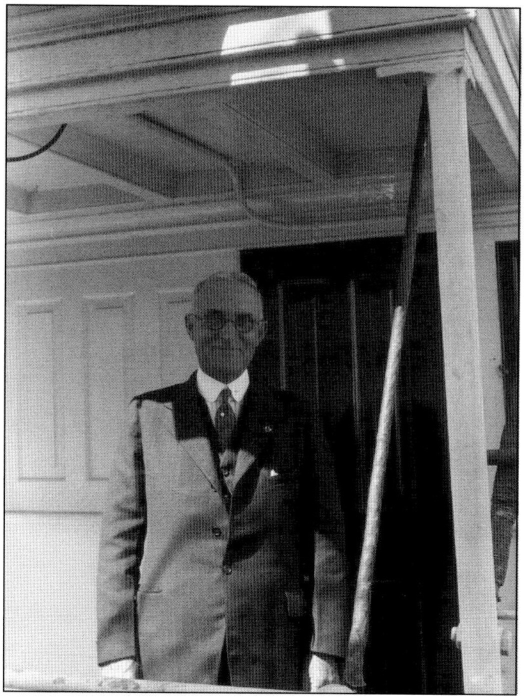

Capt. Charles H. Hubbard had an office in the Federal Building in Milwaukee. The superintendent in charge of the 12th Lighthouse District from 1918 to 1935, Hubbard made many decisions involving North Point. At one time, he was the youngest skipper on the Great Lakes and captained the tenders *Dahlia* and *Sumac*. Captain Hubbard once visited assistant keeper Charles Linsmeier at North Point when Linsmeier became sick after sandblasting the tower's interior. (Courtesy of MPM.)

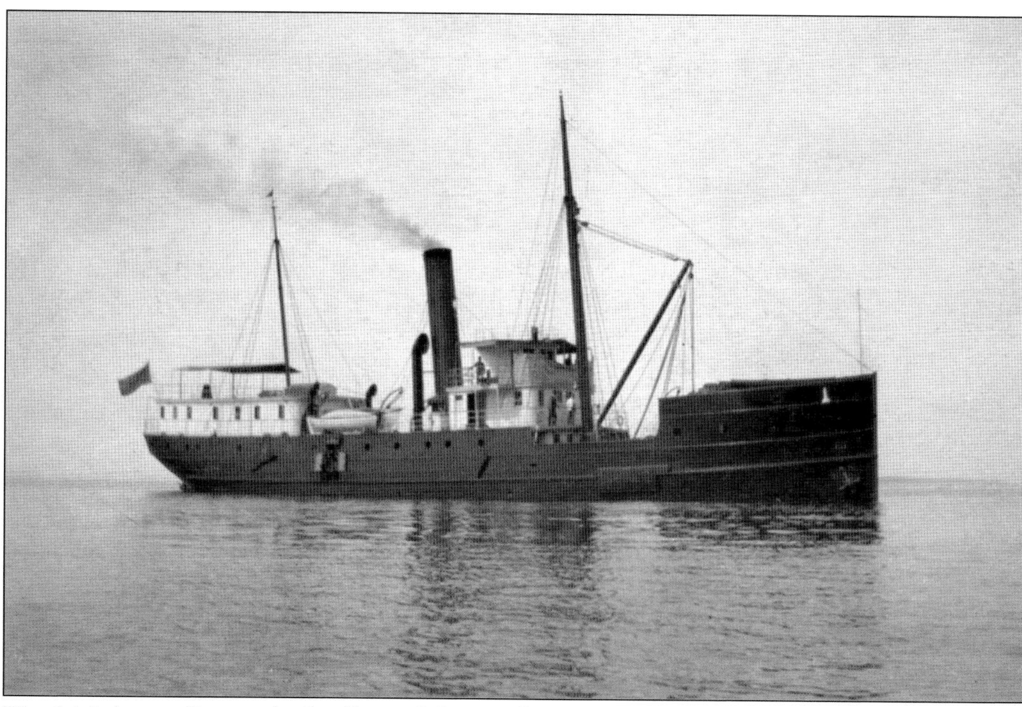

The Lighthouse Service had a fleet of ships called tenders that crisscrossed the Great Lakes, delivering supplies, equipment, and machinery to lighthouses. The North Point station did not have enough water depth or a usable pier to accommodate a tender, so the Milwaukee Lighthouse Depot in the Kinnickinnic River basin received North Point's supplies. Materials bound for the lighthouse had to travel via roadways from the depot. (Courtesy of Connie Sena.)

Two

Lighthouse Basics
Lenses, Lanterns, and Technology

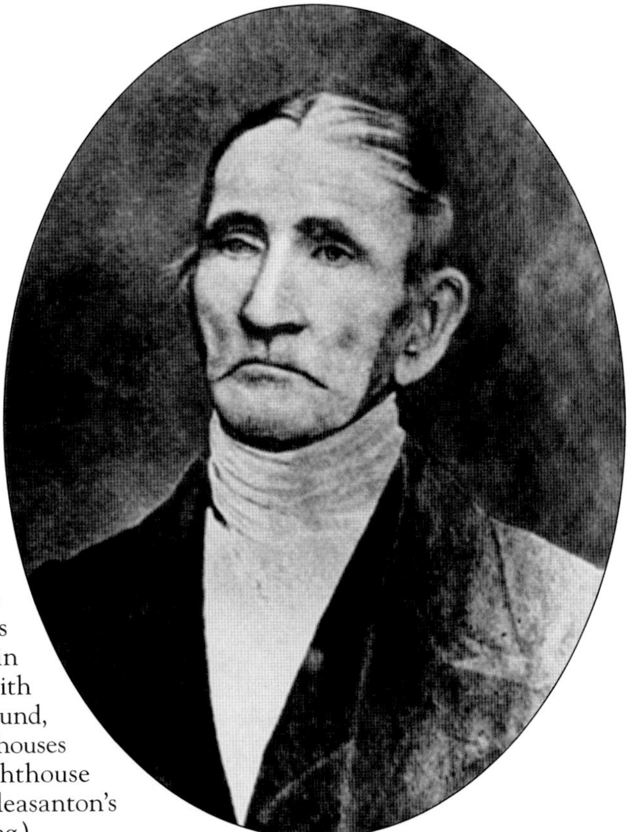

Early mariners clamored for brighter and more dependable lighthouses. The US government was sluggish, though, in implementing new technology. Stephen Pleasanton, the fifth auditor of the US Treasury, was responsible for aids to navigation in the United States. A bureaucrat with no engineering or nautical background, many of his decisions involving lighthouses were based strictly on money. Lighthouse advancements were impeded by Pleasanton's administration. (Courtesy of Tom Tag.)

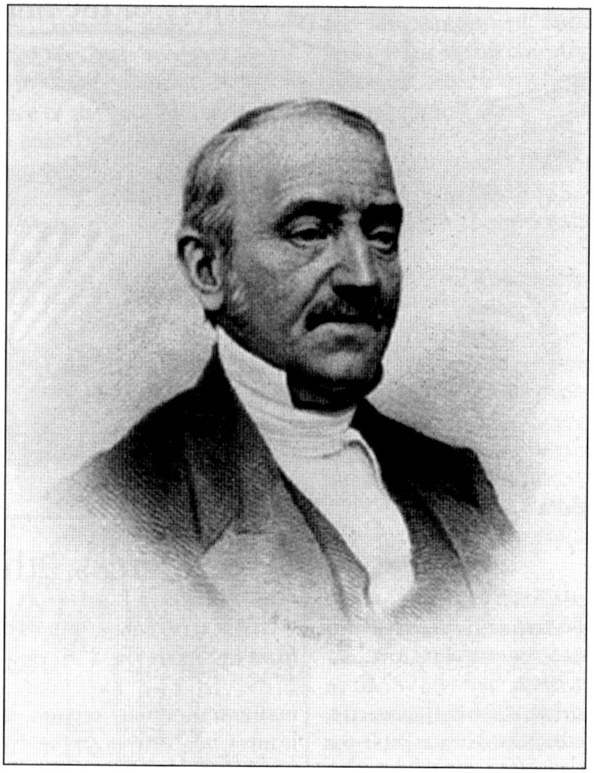

Winslow Lewis is considered one of the early pioneers of lighthouse technology. Born in 1770, his background in seafaring and engineering motivated him to invent a lighthouse lamp. Patented in 1810, Lewis's light was a combination of lamps with reflectors and lenses that magnified the light beam. Early American lighthouses used this design, but it proved inferior to other devices. Milwaukee's first lighthouse, as well as North Point's original tower, employed Lewis lamps. (Courtesy of Tom Tag.)

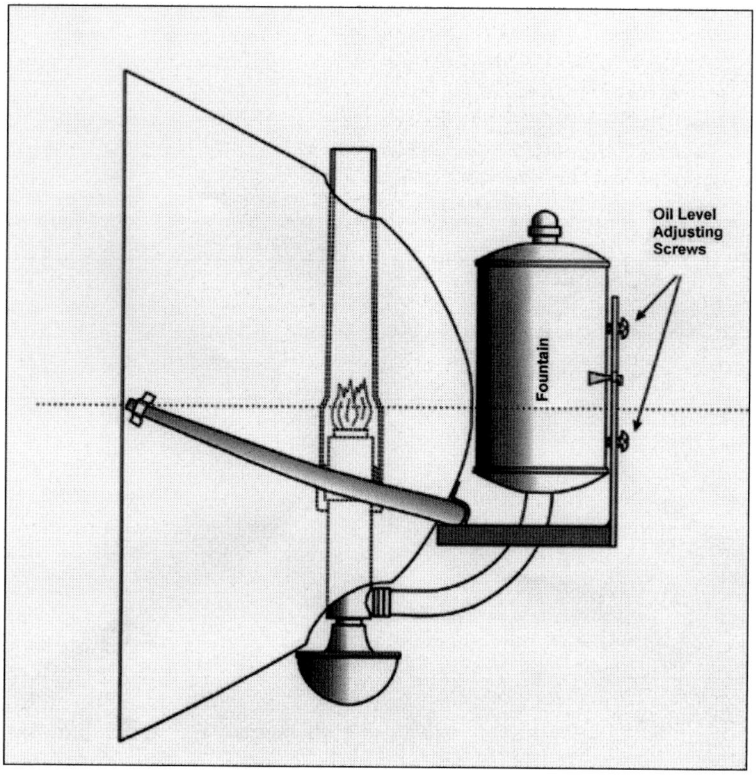

Milwaukee's inaugural 1838 lighthouse was equipped with an array of 11 Winslow Lewis lamps, each with a large individual copper-and-silver-plated reflector. Oil was stored in a reservoir, combined with air, and was burned using a hollow wick system. Surrounded by glass chimneys, the Lewis lamp set-up was used very early in Great Lakes lighthouses. Although flawed in many respects, the Lewis system replaced cruder previous lighting technology. (Courtesy of Tom Tag.)

Augustin Jean Fresnel (pronounced *fruh-nell'*), a French physicist who specialized in optics, was born in 1788. His studies of light and glass prisms were instrumental in the technological advances in lighthouse lenses. Not appreciated until after his death, Fresnel lenses were tremendously brighter and could be seen many more miles out on the water by mariners than previous lighthouse beams. (Courtesy of FOWP.)

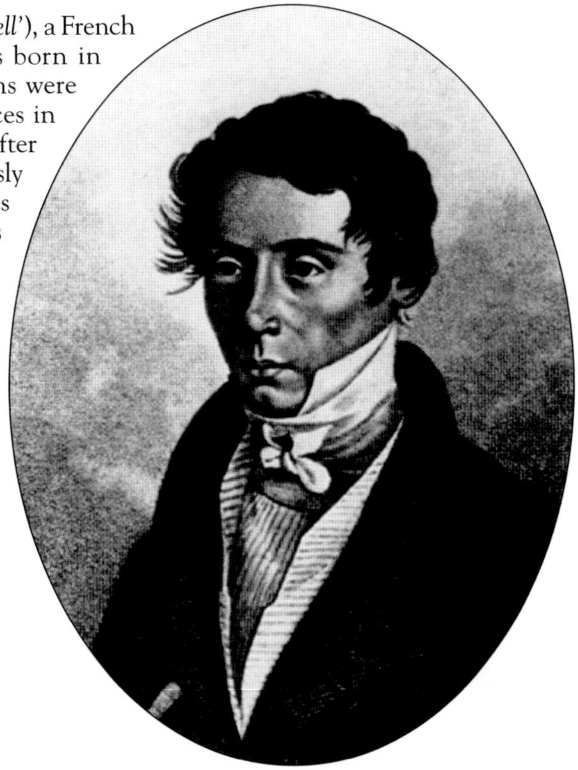

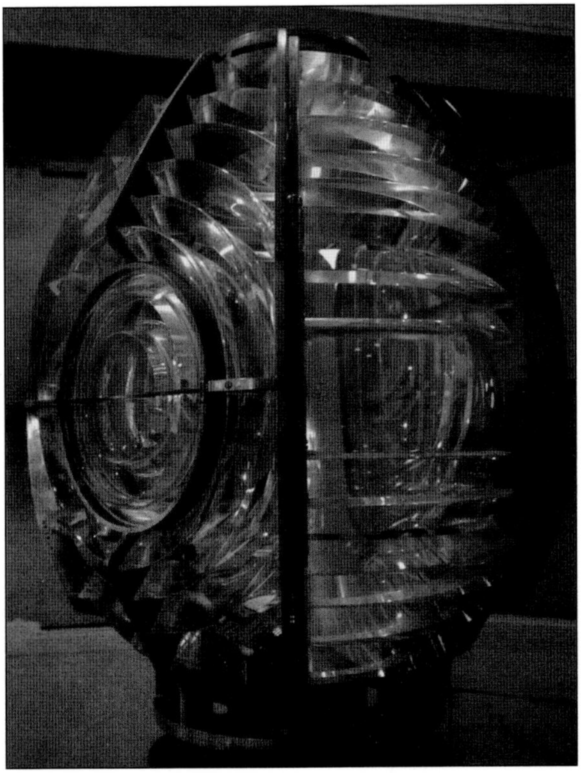

Fresnel lenses come in six different sizes called orders. The largest is a first order, which was used along coastlines throughout the world. The smallest, a sixth order, was used to alert ship captains and to identify town and city entrances. The larger the lens, the more powerful it was. North Point's lens was a fourth order, a medium size, that weighed about a quarter of a ton. (Authors' collection.)

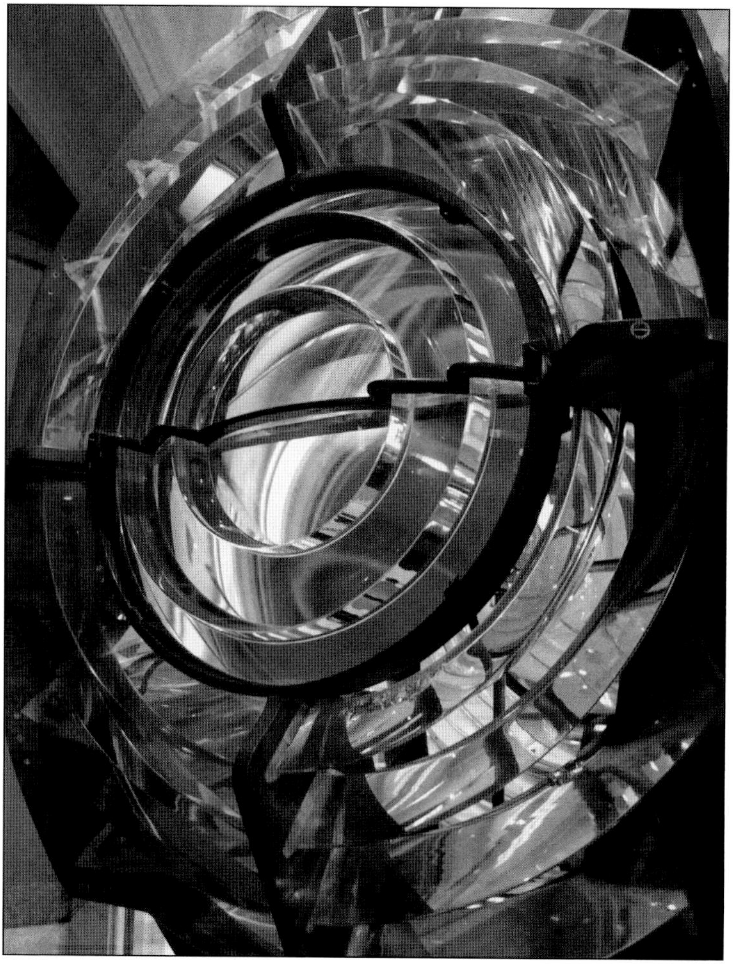

A Fresnel lens is a combination of dozens of glass prisms encased in a brass framework that gives the apparatus a barrel shape. A striking piece of technology, these lenses still have many applications today. Light keepers not only polished the priceless lens elements, but they also made the brass framework sparkle. (Authors' collection.)

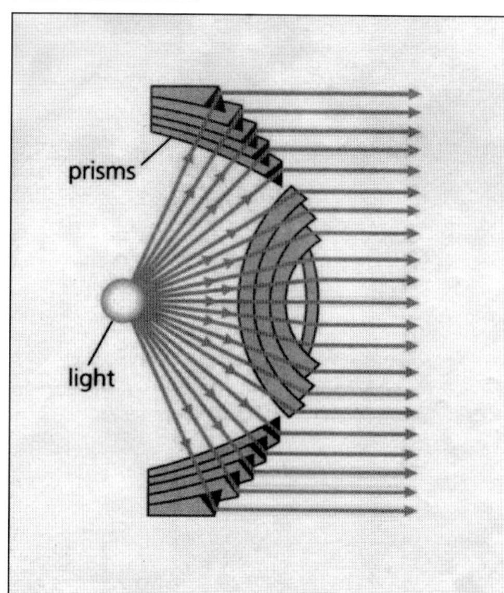

While Fresnel lenses are intricate instruments, their theory and application are very straightforward. The many hand-polished glass pieces bend and magnify the light, which comes from a source positioned in the inner middle of the lens. The resulting light beams, projected outward, are extremely intense. A very high percentage of the initial light source is utilized, and the result is a powerful beam. (Authors' collection.)

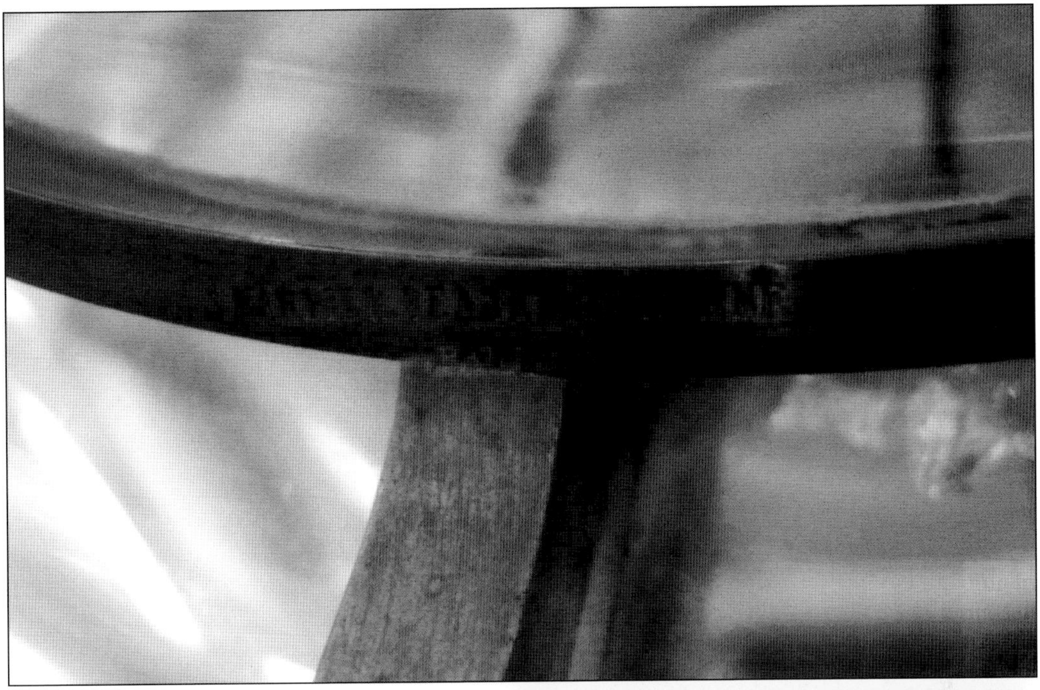

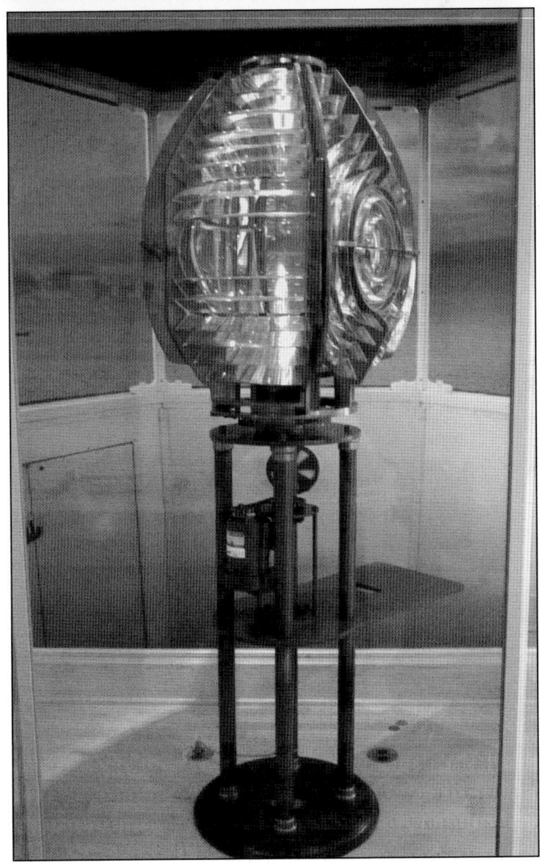

Several French companies based in Paris were the primary manufacturers of Fresnel lenses. One of North Point's lenses was produced by Barbier, Benard & Turenne. The maker's name is normally stamped or engraved somewhere on the brass frame of the lens. The units were disassembled in France for the trip to America and put back together at the designated lighthouse. (Courtesy of John Enright.)

One of the most interesting facts uncovered regarding the North Point Lighthouse involves its Fresnel lenses. North Point had four different lenses in its history, all of which were of the fourth order, a medium-sized lens. Larger lenses would have been used in taller towers, typically in what are termed "coastal beacons." Smaller Fresnel lenses are found in harbor, breakwater, and pier lights. At least two different French companies created North Point's priceless glass optics. (Authors' collection.)

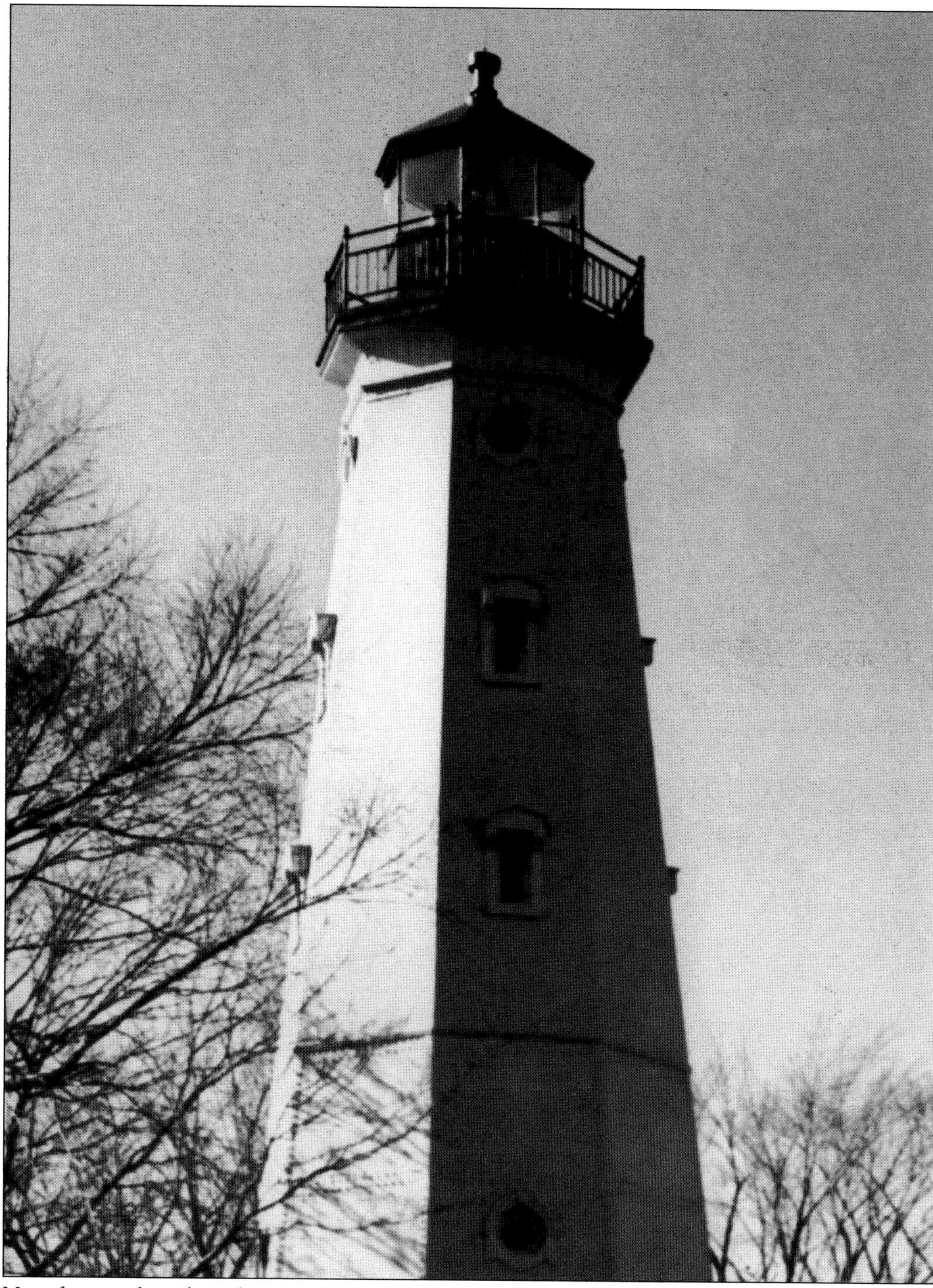

Very few good-quality photographs exist of a North Point Fresnel lens actually situated in the lighthouse's lantern, which is the space immediately at the top of the lighthouse. This 1945 image clearly shows the beacon atop the tower. Since North Point's lens was positioned at such a lofty vantage point above Lake Michigan, the fourth order beam was seen at great distances, even farther than some more powerful Great Lakes lights. (Courtesy of USCG.)

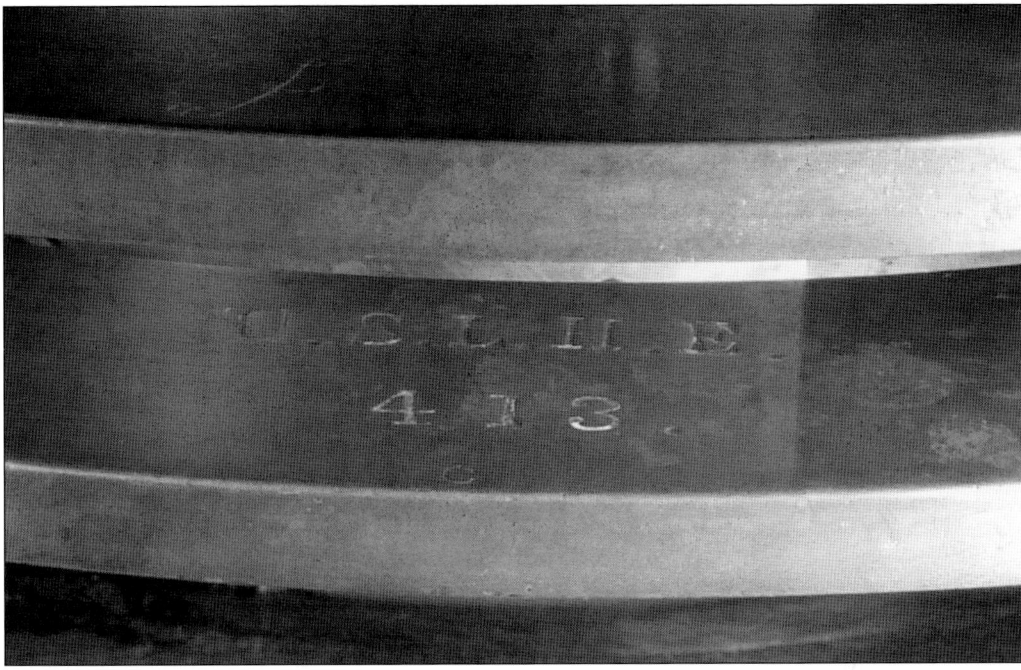

The US Lighthouse Establishment, later named the US Lighthouse Service, was the government entity responsible for all lighthouse construction, operations, maintenance, and maritime safety issues. Many pieces of equipment bore an identifier; usually an embossed stamping could be found on lenses, fuel containers, and other pieces of lighthouse property. North Point's final Fresnel lens sports the designation USLHE 413. (Authors' collection.)

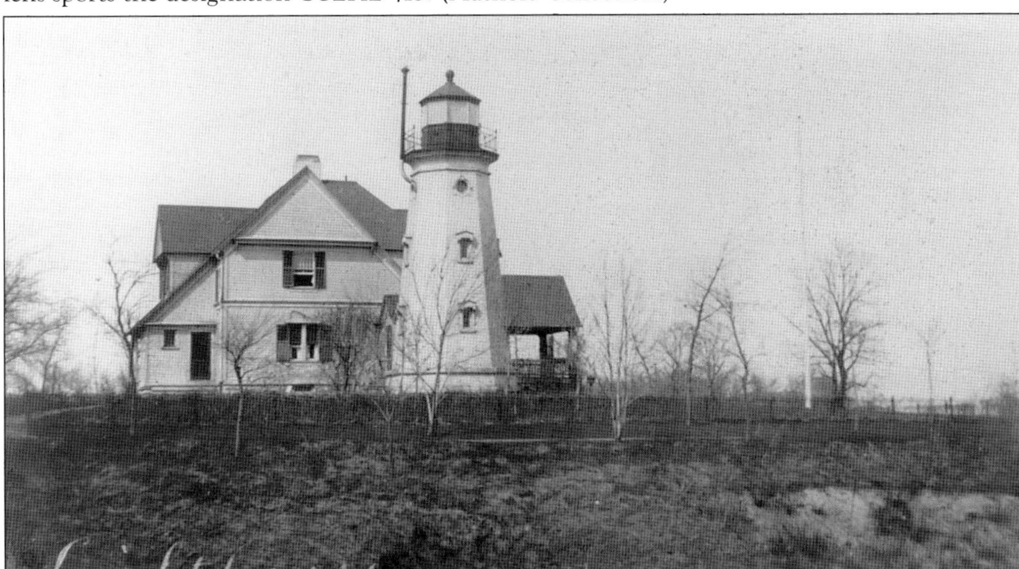

The lantern of most lighthouse towers featured curtains. During daylight hours, these coverings, hung with brass hooks, were closed across the glass panes. Prolonged exposure to intense sunlight could potentially degrade the Fresnel lens. It also shielded the room from becoming overheated and possibly igniting fuel vapors that might be present. In this image, North Point's shades are fully closed. (Courtesy of MPL.)

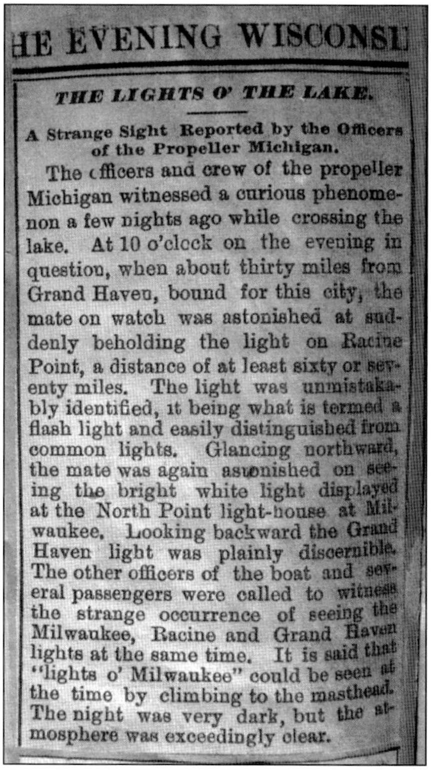

HE EVENING WISCONSI

THE LIGHTS O' THE LAKE.

A Strange Sight Reported by the Officers of the Propeller Michigan.

The officers and crew of the propeller Michigan witnessed a curious phenomenon a few nights ago while crossing the lake. At 10 o'clock on the evening in question, when about thirty miles from Grand Haven, bound for this city, the mate on watch was astonished at suddenly beholding the light on Racine Point, a distance of at least sixty or seventy miles. The light was unmistakably identified, it being what is termed a flash light and easily distinguished from common lights. Glancing northward, the mate was again astonished on seeing the bright white light displayed at the North Point light-house at Milwaukee. Looking backward the Grand Haven light was plainly discernible. The other officers of the boat and several passengers were called to witness the strange occurrence of seeing the Milwaukee, Racine and Grand Haven lights at the same time. It is said that "lights o' Milwaukee" could be seen at the time by climbing to the masthead. The night was very dark, but the atmosphere was exceedingly clear.

The normal physics and properties of light sometimes appear to behave in mysterious ways. Under certain atmospheric conditions, lighthouse beams can be seen many more miles away, beyond the horizon, than can be explained. Occasionally, North Point's light was visible near the eastern shores of Lake Michigan some 80 miles away. This archival newspaper account documents the phenomenon, seemingly impossible with the earth's curvature, known as "looming." (Courtesy of the Stebbins family.)

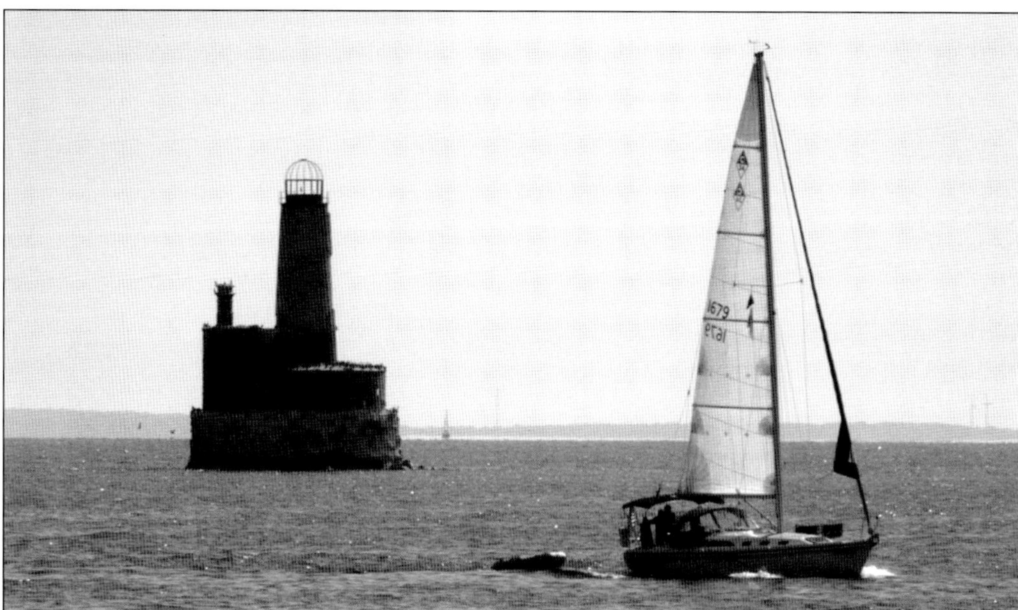

Milwaukee's North Point Lighthouse had some connections to and shared some equipment with another Great Lakes beacon, the Waugoshance Lighthouse, which was located west of the Straights of Mackinac in Lake Michigan. One of North Point's Fresnel lenses was originally shown at Waugoshance. A lens pedestal from it was moved to North Point when the Michigan lighthouse was decommissioned in 1912. (Authors' collection.)

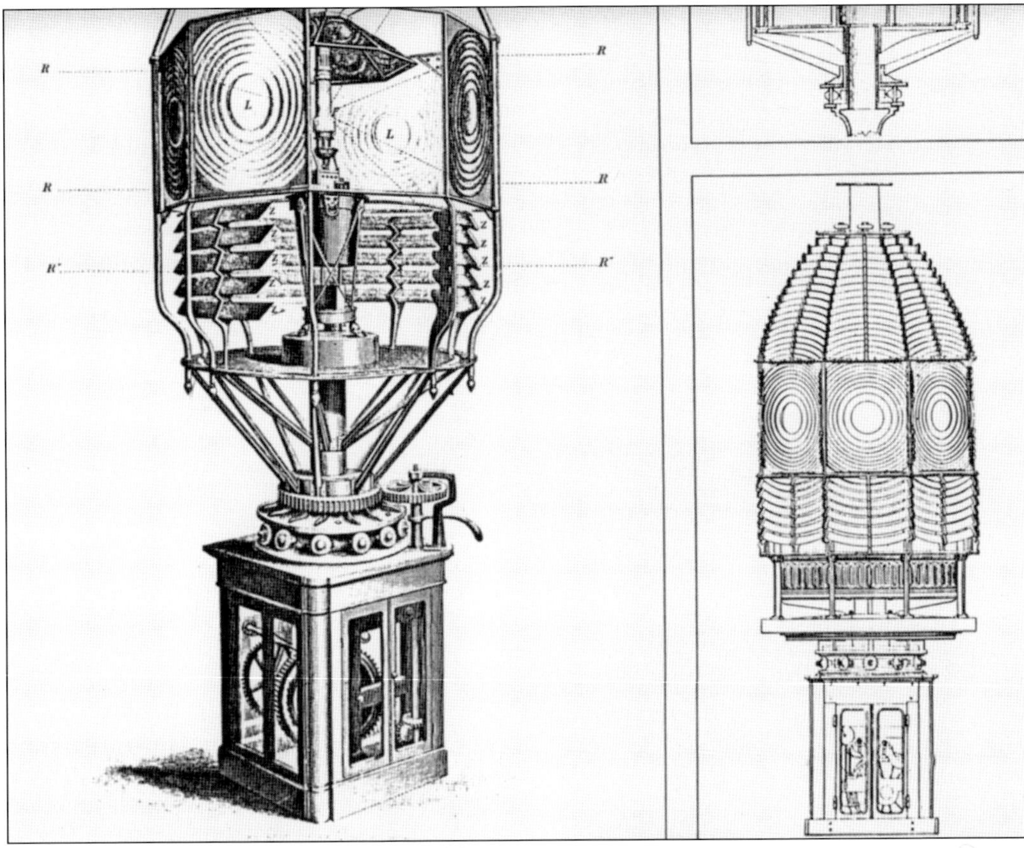

The Fresnel lens at North Point revolved by means of a clockwork mechanism. At one time, a galvanized cord, which was one-eighth of an inch in diameter with heavy weights, hung in a 60-foot metal drop tube in a center column in the tower that extended to the cellar. In a groove system, metal ball bearings allowed the massive lens to turn freely. In 1915, it took 60 seconds for North Point's lens to complete one revolution. At times, this apparatus could be uncooperative. (Courtesy of Mike and Liana Cooper.)

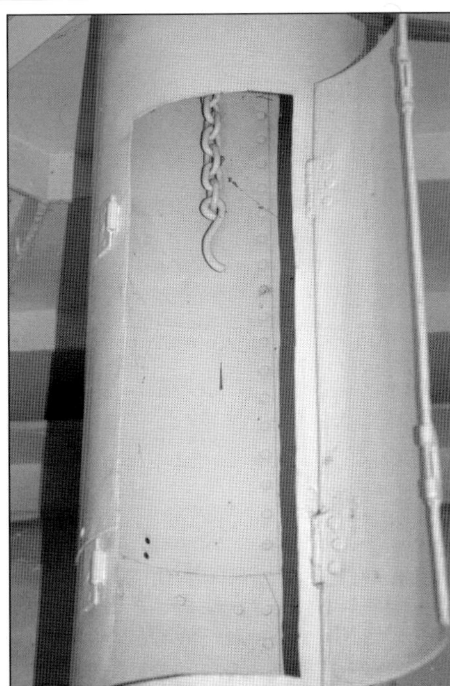

The clockwork system at North Point that rotated the lens was aided by the use of weights. A central metal cylinder called a drop chute ran the entire length of the tower and was the casing that held the weights and attached metal cable. This mechanism insured that the lens turned in its prescribed time frame. In 1915, North Point's lens flashed a clear white light every 30 seconds. (Authors' collection.)

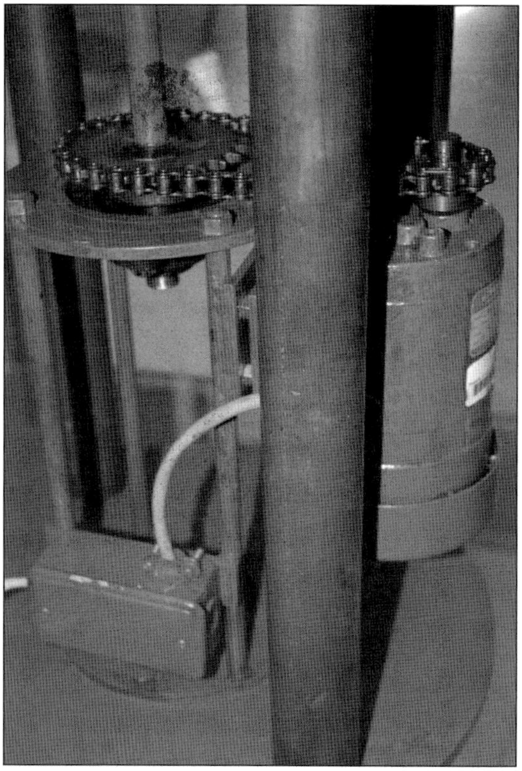

North Point's original revolving apparatus and clockwork mechanism was a fairly elaborate piece of machinery and a workhorse. After the lighthouse was automated, the Coast Guard replaced that equipment and installed a much simpler device that was dependable for years. The latest system employs a small motor and chain drive that turns the Fresnel lens in its display case at the nautical museum at North Point. (Authors' collection.)

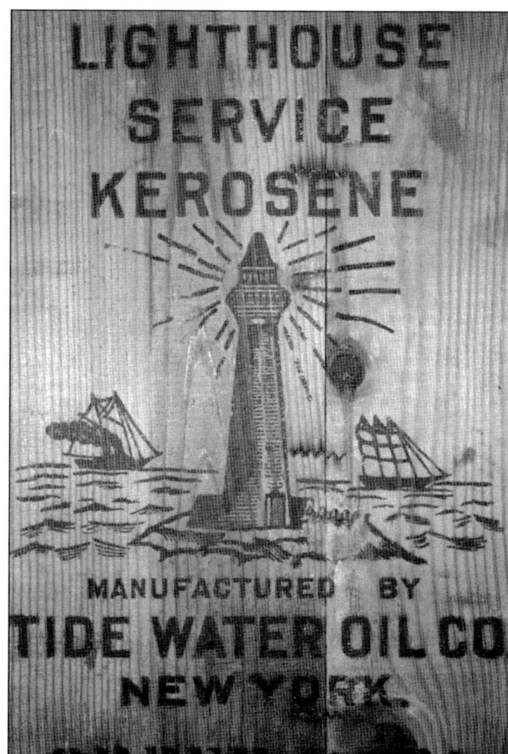

Liquid fuels burned at lighthouses changed over the years as technology advanced. Historically, whale oil, lard oil, and later kerosene (also known as mineral oil), provided the light in the world's lighthouse lanterns. The North Point Lighthouse benefited from being in an urban setting, with early illuminants quickly giving way to more modern coal gas and eventually electricity in 1929. (Authors' collection.)

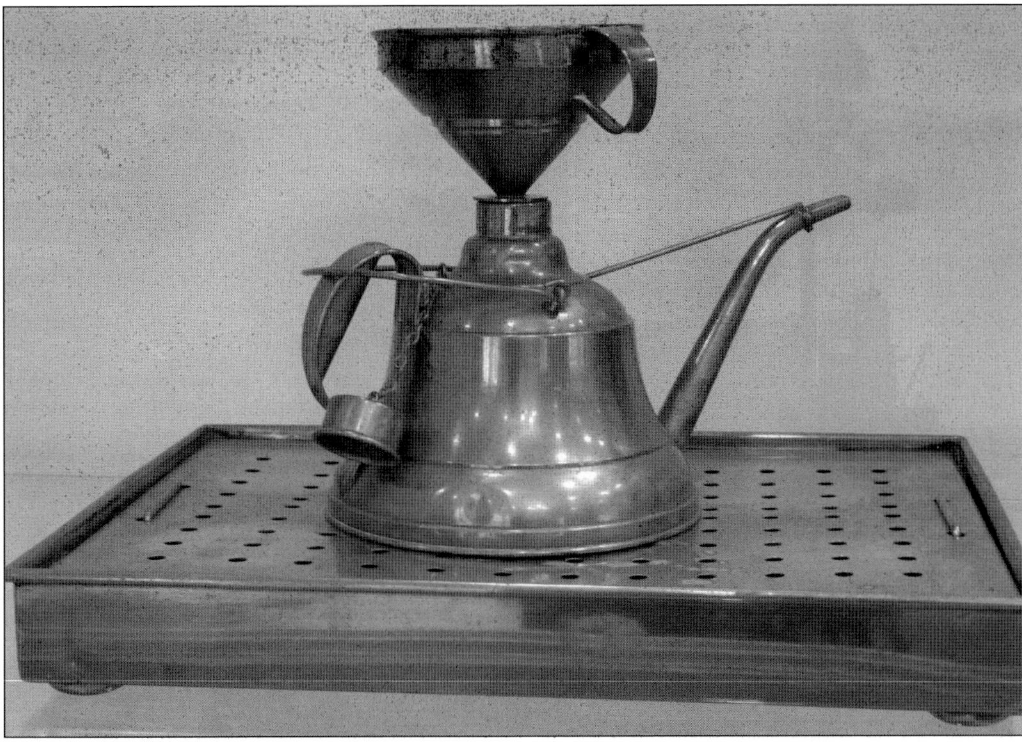

Liquid fuels, such as mineral oil (kerosene), used in the early history of the lighthouse at North Point, were stored in manageable-sized containers. Lamps in the lantern could be filled with the can and funnel apparatus shown here. Any spilled oil was collected in the grid pan below and reused. Light keepers were careful not to waste valuable fuel. (Authors' collection.)

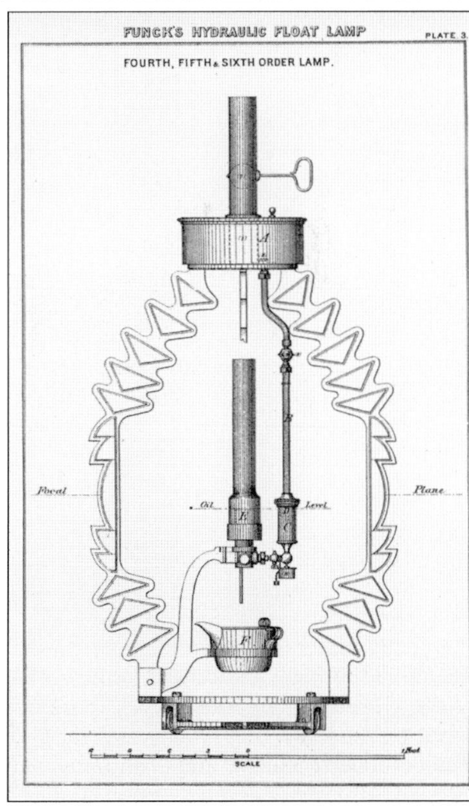

Not much is known about the lighting apparatus employed at North Point's original 1855 lighthouse. The most likely device used in that era would have been this hydraulic fountain lamp. Centered within the glass, fourth-order Fresnel lens, gravity-fed oil and air were combusted. Joseph Funck, a lamp-shop foreman, later improved on the design of lighthouse lamps by improving the airflow and flame within the burner. (Courtesy of Tom Tag.)

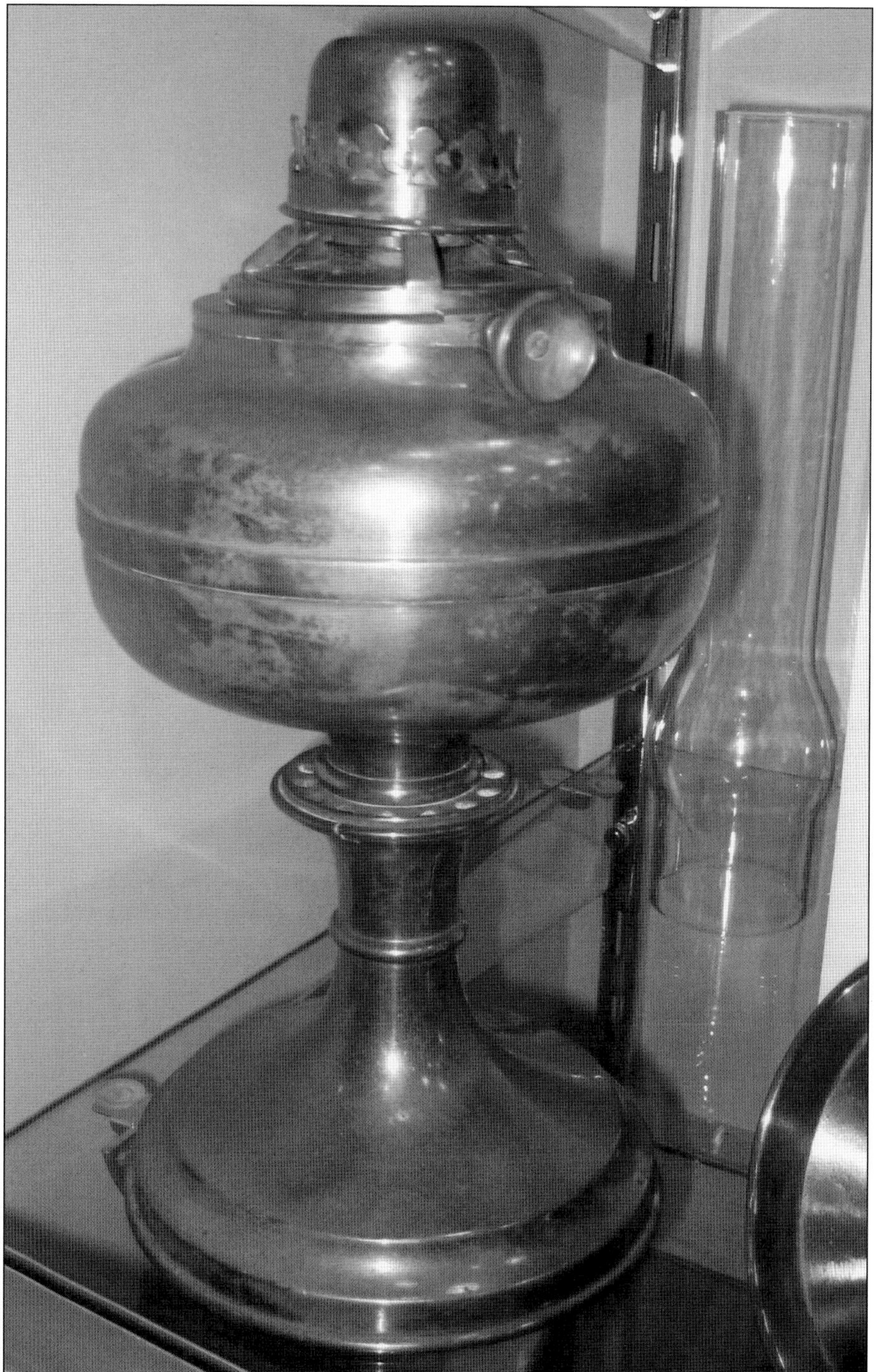

An 1897 *Milwaukee Journal* article quotes keeper Georgia Stebbins as describing the North Point lamps: "The lamps are brass, about 18 inches high and have what is commonly known as Argand burners. The flame of the lamp is about one and a half inches square. The lamps are filled with mineral oil especially prepared for the government lighthouses." North Point's nautical museum features this Argand lamp. (Courtesy of Tom Tag.)

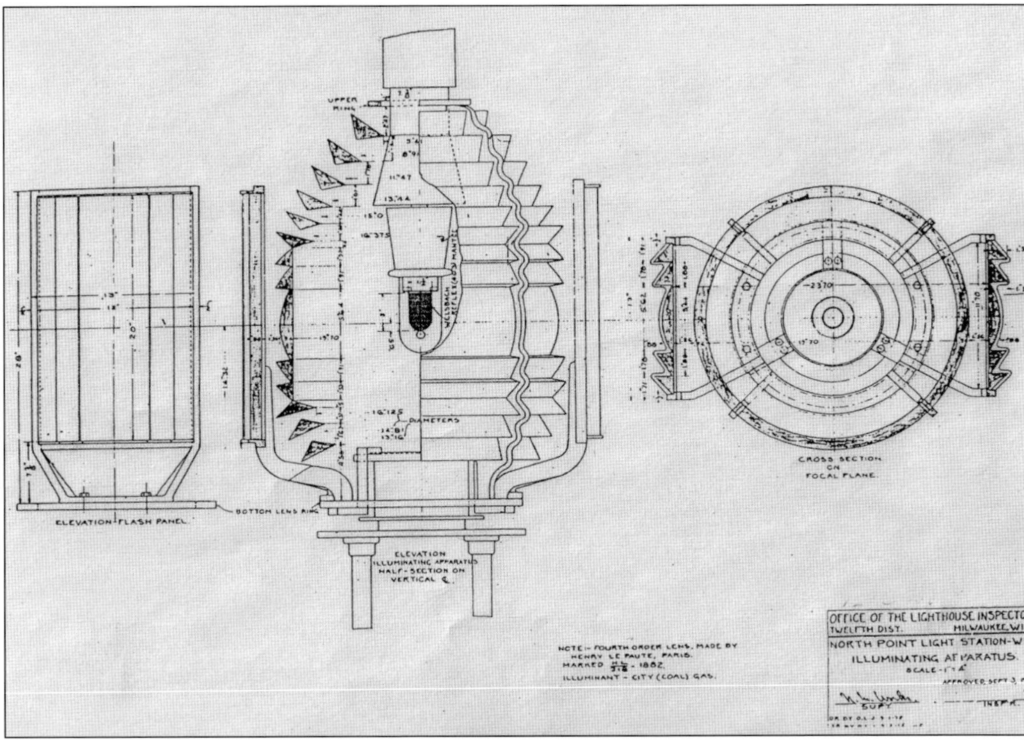

The heart of a lighthouse is the beacon. This 1913 drawing, from the office of the 12th District Lighthouse inspector in Milwaukee, shows the intricate details of North Point's fourth-order Fresnel lens, technically called the illuminating apparatus. The drawing outlines various views of the many glass prisms, the brass frame, the interior lamp mechanism, and an accompanying flash panel. (Courtesy of NPLHF.)

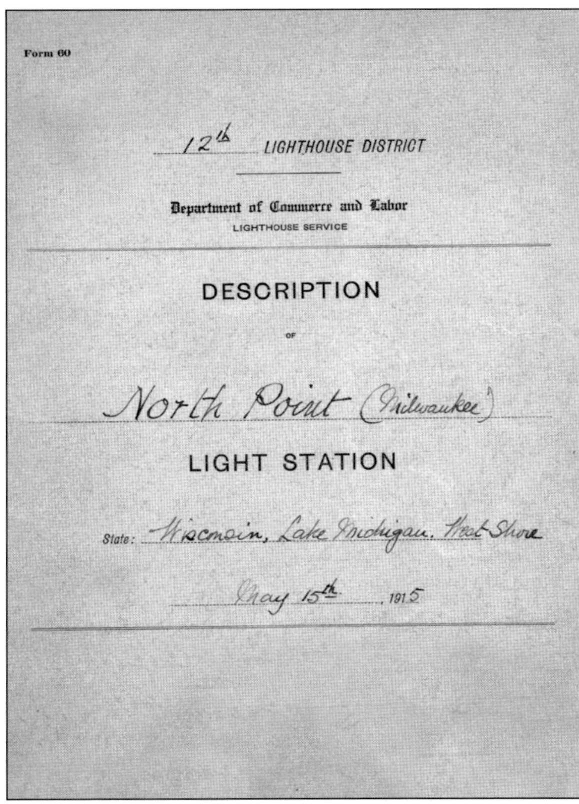

Form 60

12th LIGHTHOUSE DISTRICT

Department of Commerce and Labor

LIGHTHOUSE SERVICE

DESCRIPTION

OF

North Point (Milwaukee)

LIGHT STATION

State: Wisconsin, Lake Michigan, West Shore

May 15th, 1915

Official government lighthouse documents, such as this May 1915 Form 60 Description of the North Point Milwaukee Light Station, can give great insight into the structures and technology utilized at a lighthouse. This manuscript details the general premises, buildings, lantern, lens type, revolving apparatus, and lamp style, among other particulars, at North Point in 1915. (Courtesy of NPLHF.)

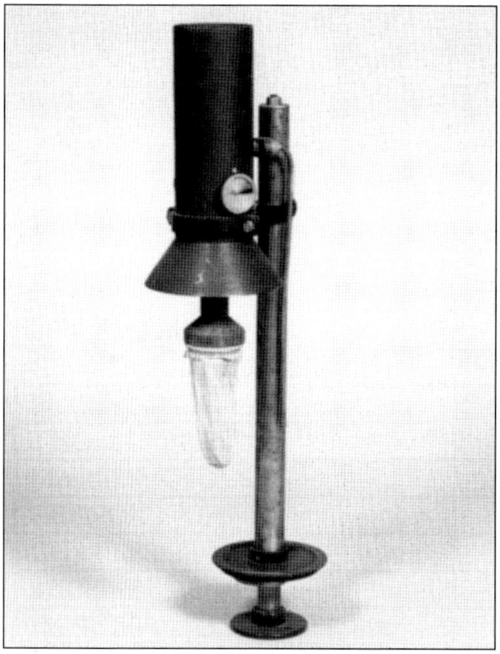

The official 1915 description document of North Point shows that the lamp in the lantern was a Welsbach reflex mantle type. Similar to today's Coleman lantern, fuel was vaporized under pressure and mixed with air, producing a dependable and brilliant light. City coal gas eventually replaced oil fuels at North Point and may have been used with the Welsbach set-up. (Courtesy of Tom Tag.)

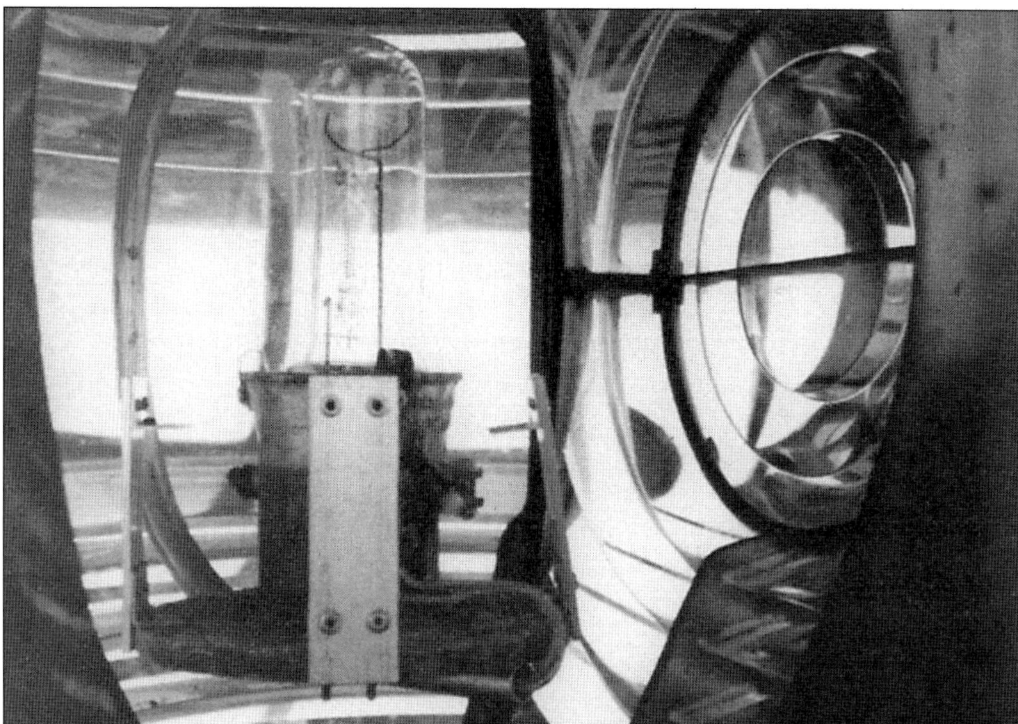

As technology advanced, lighthouses adapted to improvements in machinery. The light at North Point initially used oil as a fuel. Around 1913, North Point's nearness to an urban locale led to the use of coal gas. The *Milwaukee Journal* touted North Point as America's first gaslit lighthouse. Beginning in 1929, electricity powered the lens. This rare photograph shows the large bulb inside the lens at North Point around 1980. (Courtesy of Jim Woodward and NPLHF.)

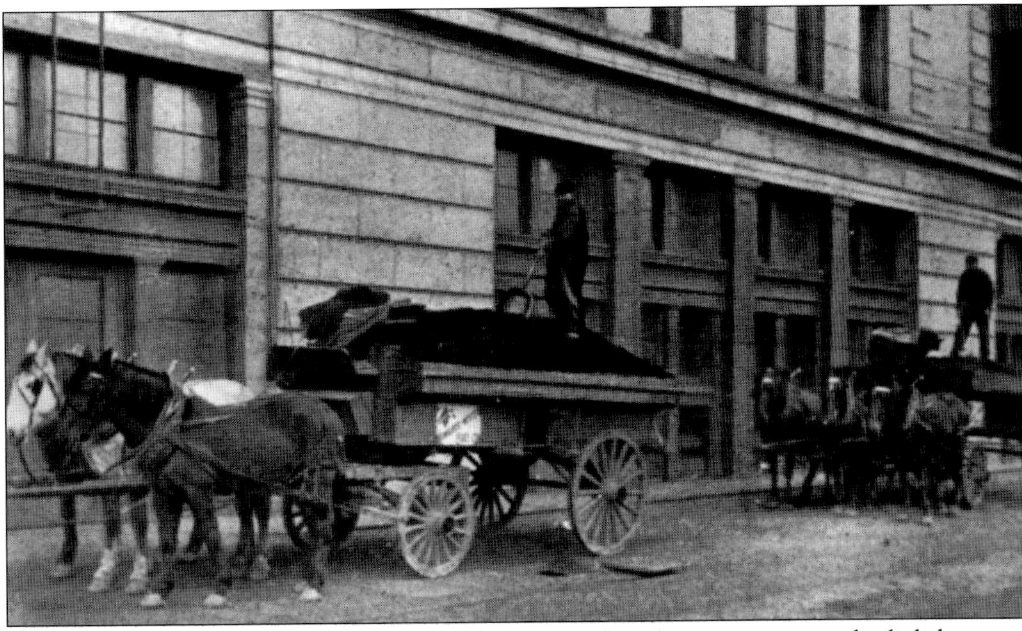

For many years, coal was used as a fuel for heating and cooking purposes at the lighthouse. A stove in the tower also kept certain areas warm. Coal was delivered to North Point in its earliest days via horse-drawn wagons. Being within a city, North Point later had a supply of gas, which eventually replaced coal in a furnace in the keeper's basement. (Courtesy of MPL.)

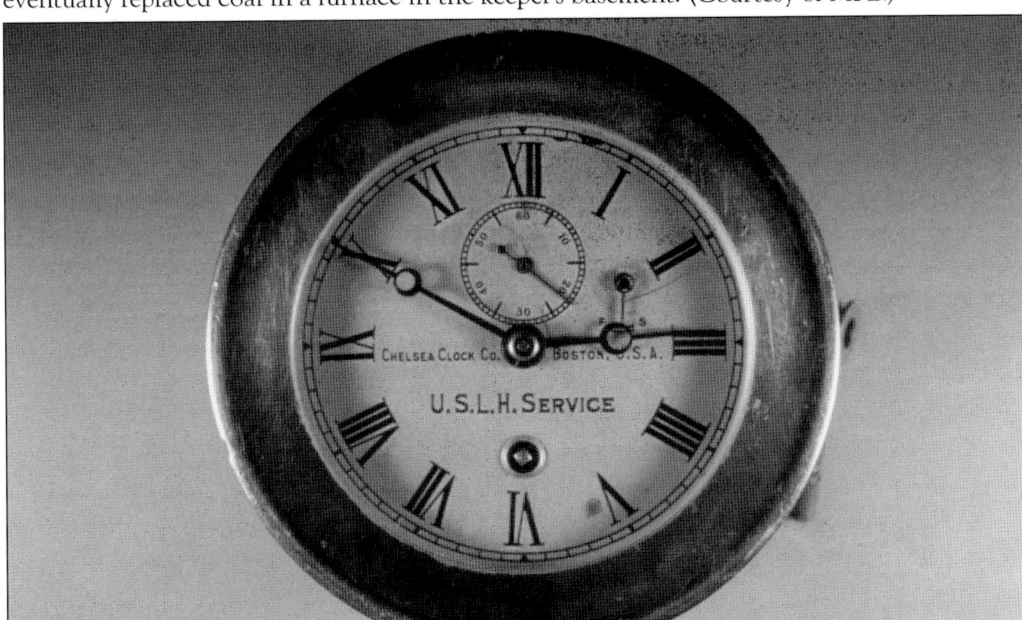

The US Lighthouse Service provided lighthouse keepers with some basic instruments, equipment, and utensils. One very important piece of gear was an official government-issued clock. North Point's beacon needed to be lit and extinguished at very specific times of day, and the lens's rotating and flash timing required it to be precise. The clock ensured accurate operations. (Courtesy of James Claflin.)

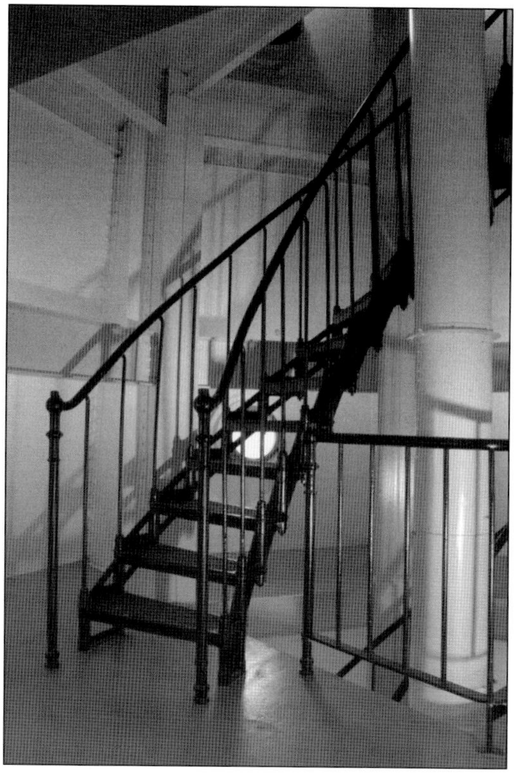

A spiral metal staircase wound its way from the bottom of the tower to the upper lens area at North Point. Most lighthouses had twisting steps to allow the keeper to travel easily from the base of the tower to the top. North Point's final tower, a combination of a new base and the second lighthouse at this location, has two separate sets of stairways combined. (Authors' collection.)

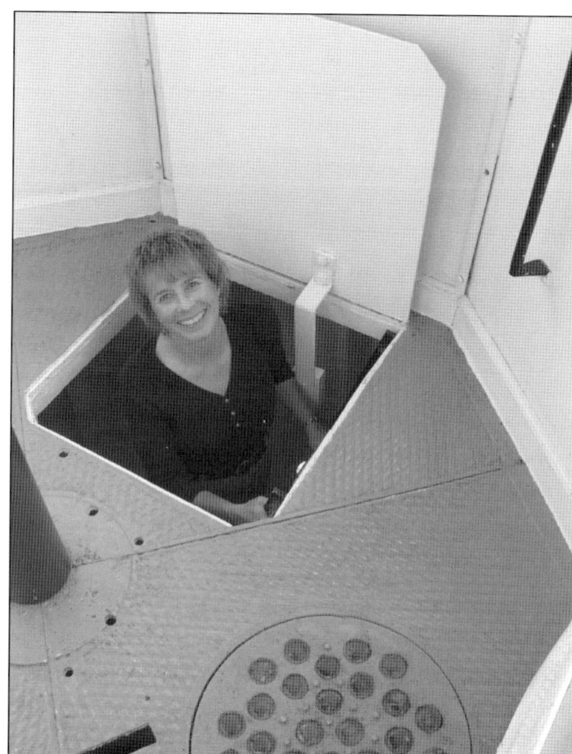

Lighthouses normally have at least one hatch in the tower; tall towers can have multiple hatches. North Point's tower has one at the base of the lantern. The main purpose of the hatch is to regulate the amount of air flowing through the tower. Years ago, airflow could affect the performance of liquid-fueled lamps. Early in its history, North Point had issues with poor light efficiency. Perhaps this was improved by adjusting the hatch. (Authors' collection.)

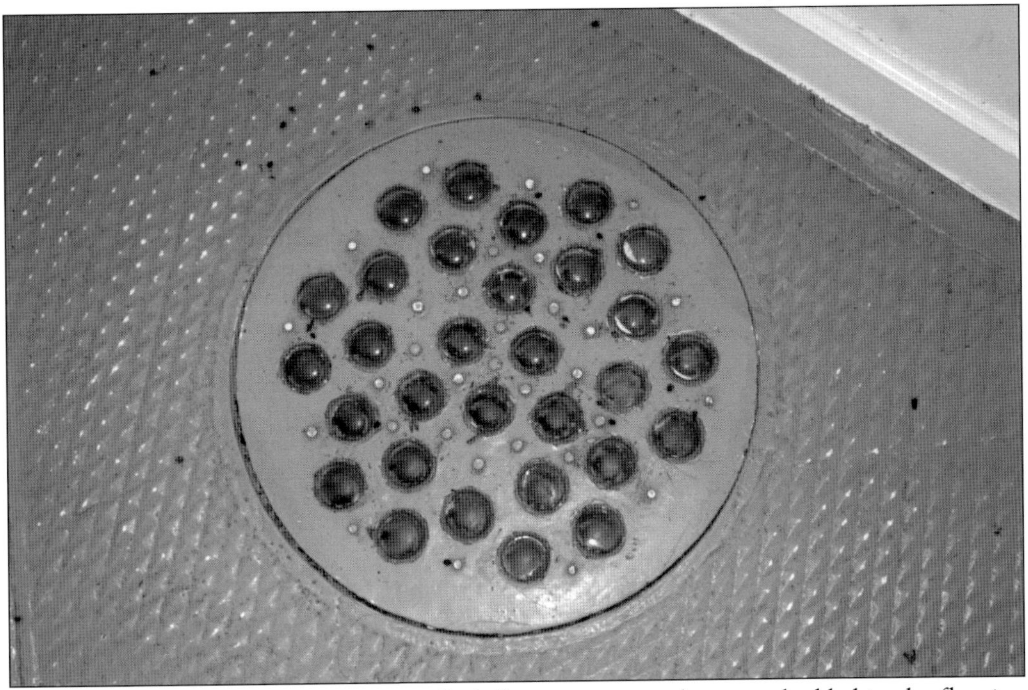

Three of these circular glass features, called illuminating panels, are embedded in the flooring of North Point's lantern. Resembling clear marbles, these handy devices allowed the light keeper to know for certain if the lamp was still lit without opening and entering the lantern itself. Personnel at lighthouses were always looking for ways and methods to make their jobs easier and more efficient. (Authors' collection.)

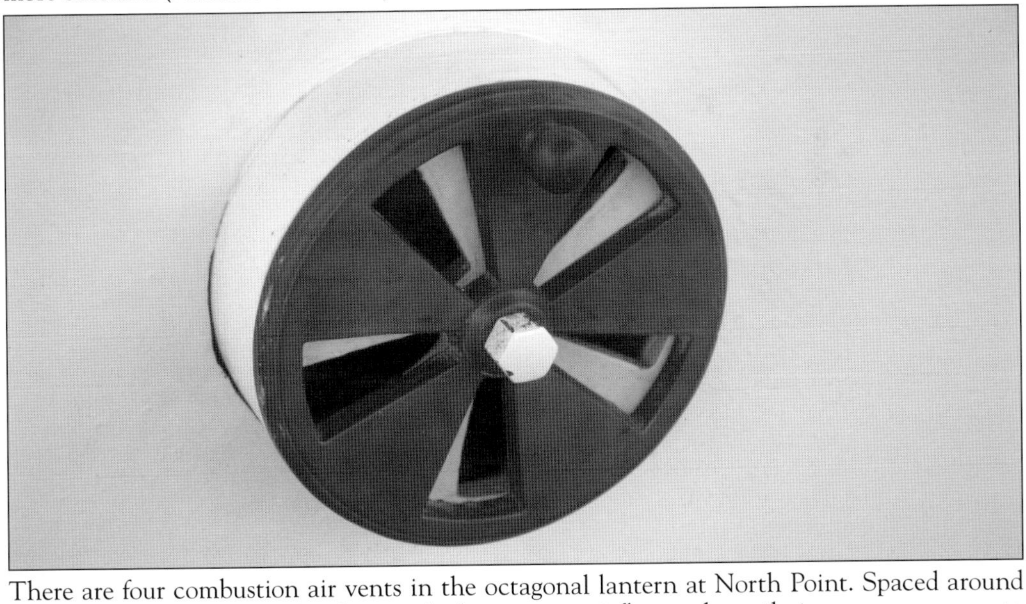

There are four combustion air vents in the octagonal lantern at North Point. Spaced around the perimeter of the room that houses the lens, proper airflow and ventilation were necessary to allow the liquid fuels to burn evenly and efficiently in the tower. Too little or too much air would affect the light. Based on experience, keepers knew how far to open or close the vents depending on weather and wind conditions. (Authors' collection.)

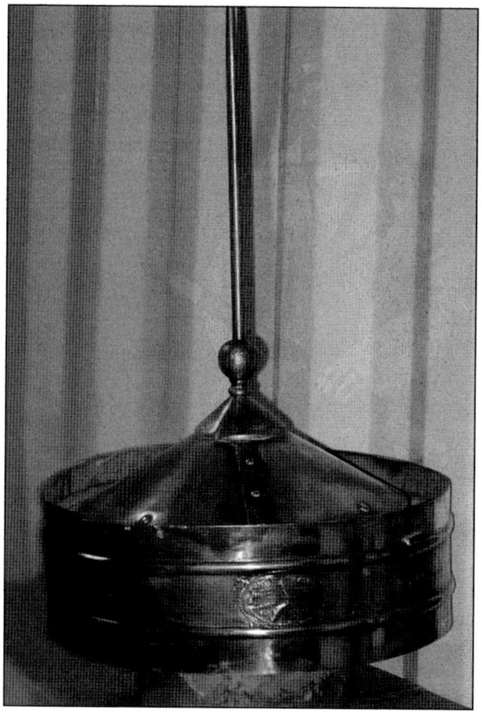

The pinnacle of a lighthouse lantern is the vent cap. Usually topped with a lightning rod, the vent cap, or a ventilator ball, would allow burned gases from the interior lantern apparatus to be expelled into the outside air. Even with sufficient airflow, soot could still accumulate on the lighthouse lens. Pictured here is a modern replica vent cap that was installed at North Point during its renovation. (Courtesy of Julie Bastin.)

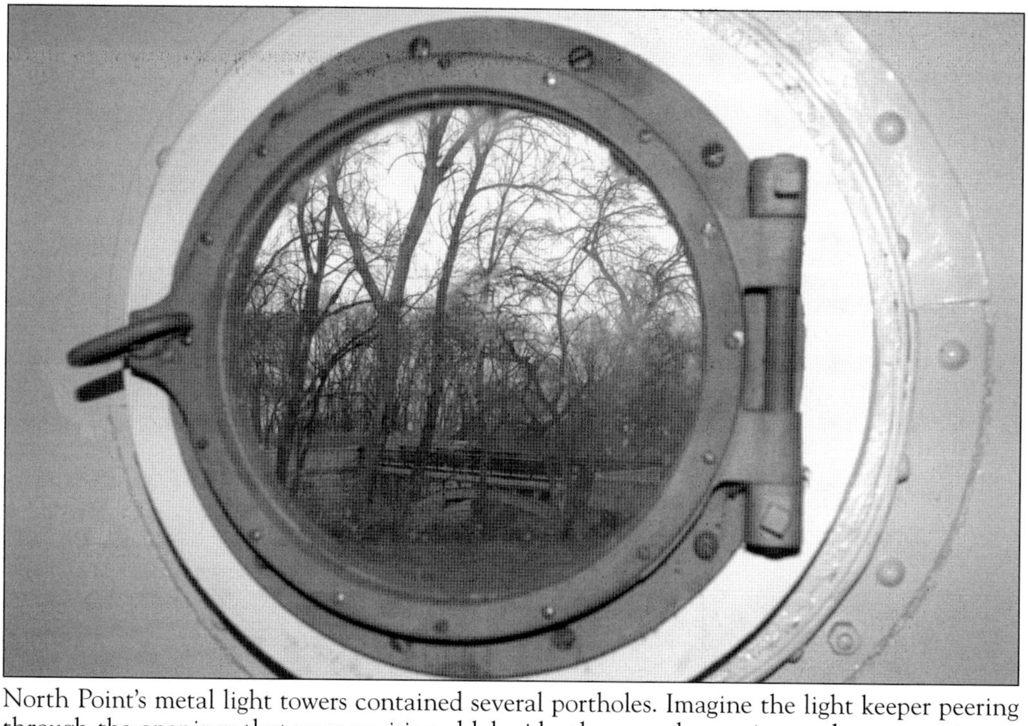

North Point's metal light towers contained several portholes. Imagine the light keeper peering through the openings that were positioned lakeside; they may have witnessed an oncoming or passing storm or a ship in distress near Milwaukee's harbor. Today, a person can still look out of North Point's portholes to get views of Lake Park, Milwaukee's lakefront, or Lake Michigan. (Authors' collection.)

Three

North Point Light Station

Crown Jewel of Lake Park

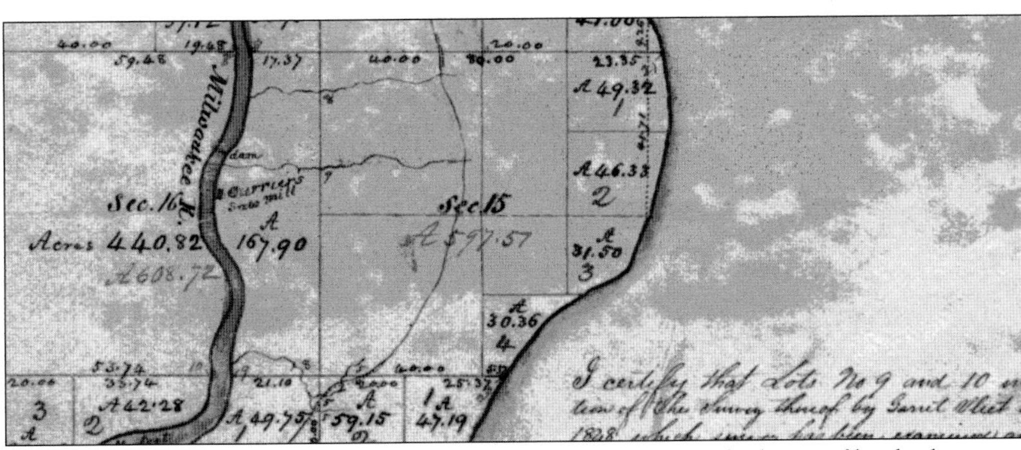

This old survey map shows the northern limit of Milwaukee Bay. The bump of land is known as North Point. The parcel that would eventually include the North Point Lighthouse is in section 15 and is 31.5 acres in size. Other than various lot sizes, little information can be gleaned from this illustration other than noting a small dam and a mill to the west along the Milwaukee River. (Courtesy of NPLHF.)

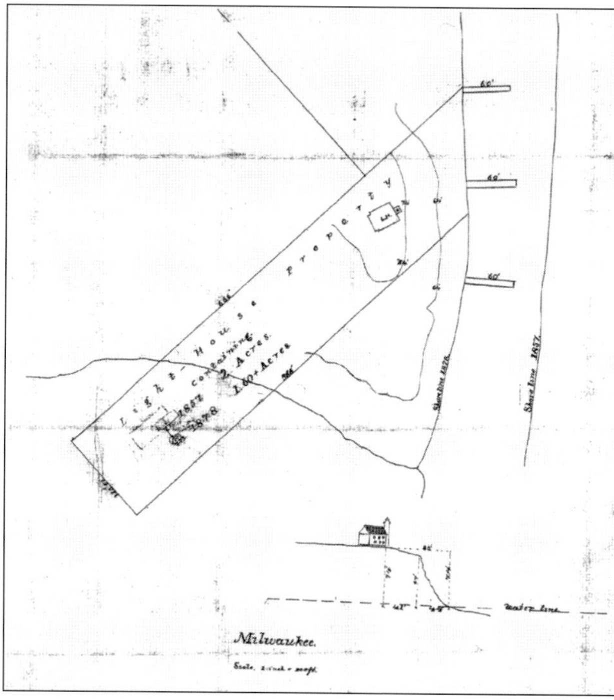

An early plotted area of the parcel of land that the North Point Lighthouse was situated on is shown here. For these two acres, $1,000 was paid to a Mr. J. Bonesteel. The original 1855 lighthouse is located on the northeastern portion of the lot. As the shoreline continued to erode over the years, the government selected a more southwestern location in the parcel for the second North Point signal. (Courtesy of NPLHF.)

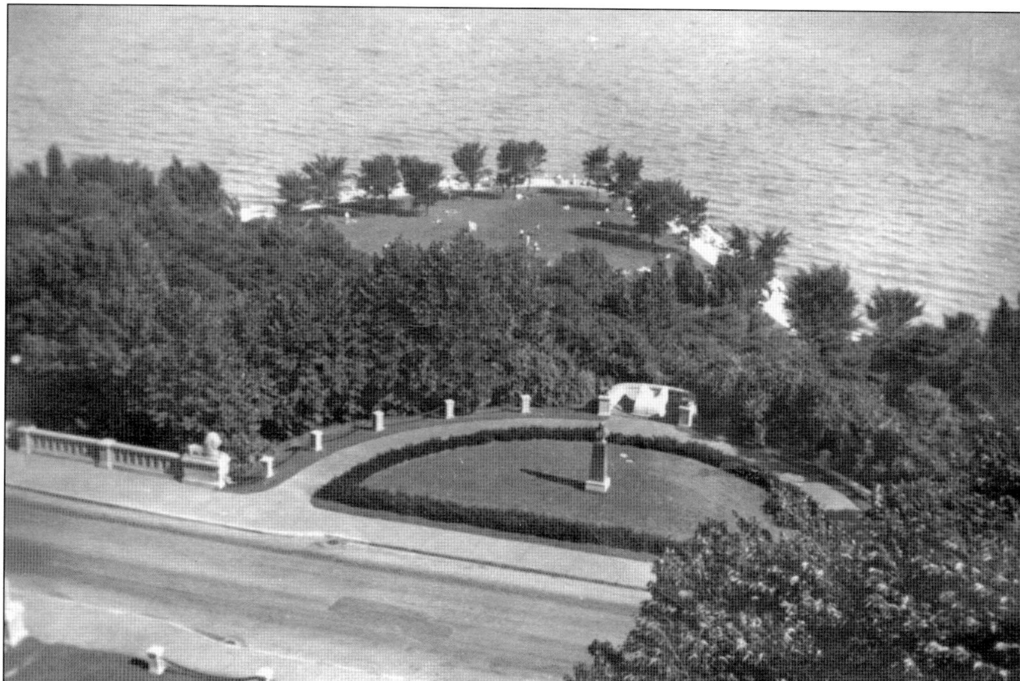

A view from the top of the lighthouse in 1946 gives a bird's-eye view of the far eastern portion of the lighthouse grounds in Lake Park. The statue and bust of Christian Wahl and remnants of the old cannon stand can be seen in the circular area adjacent to the roadway. In the distance, the land meets Lake Michigan—the actual place known on maps as North Point. (Courtesy of Ed Werner.)

The North Point Milwaukee Lighthouse was not the only southeastern Wisconsin beacon to have the name North Point. The next port south of Milwaukee was Racine. Its distinctive tall lighthouse is mostly referred to as Wind Point. Early residents and some mariners also called it North Point or Racine Point. To confuse matters more, North Point Milwaukee was also called Milwaukee Point in some logbooks. There is no mistaking either lighthouse. An archival postcard of Wind North Point is featured here. (Courtesy of Pam Cook.)

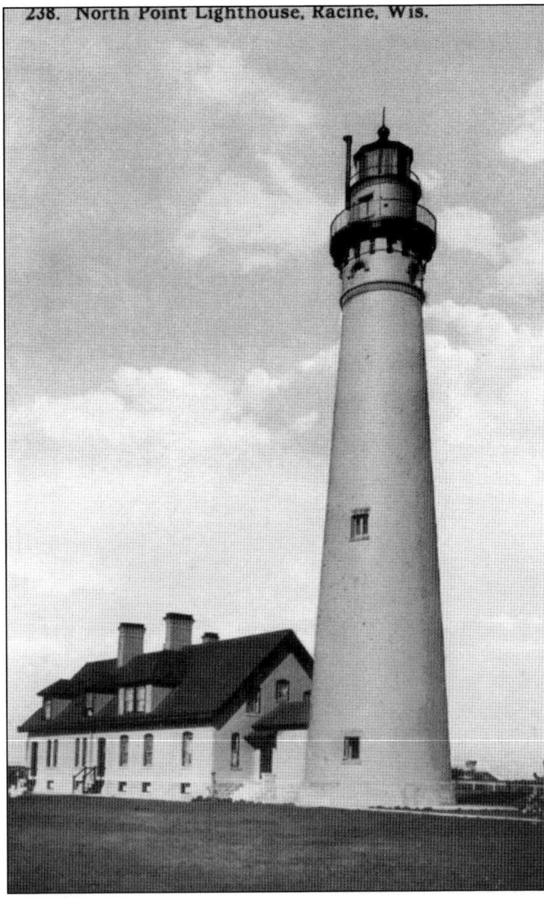

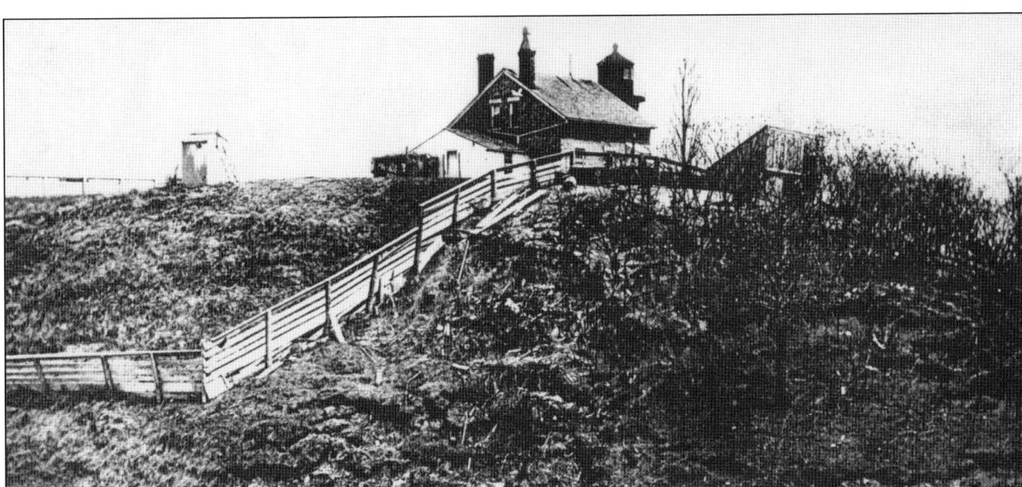

This grainy image, which dates to the mid- to late 1800s, is the lone existing photograph of North Point's inaugural 1855 brick light. All other known pictures depict the structure after its lantern and portions of the house had been removed. The fencing outlines the lighthouse grounds. The building at the rear of the house could be a summer kitchen or a storage area. An outhouse, known as a privy, is on the far left. The lighthouse was first lit in November 1855. (Courtesy of MPL.)

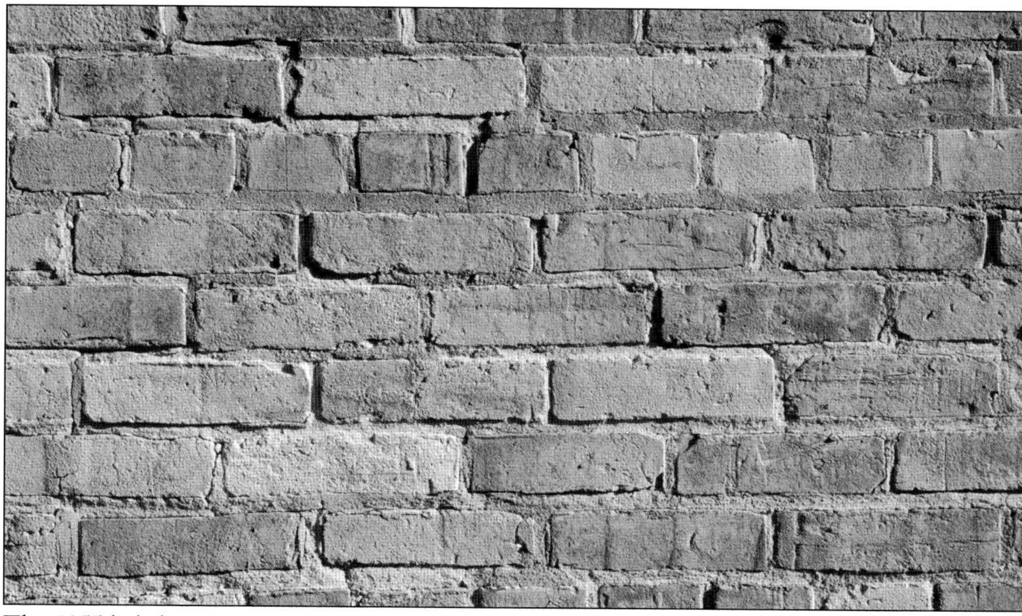

The 1855 lighthouse at North Point Milwaukee was constructed of Milwaukee cream city brick. This was a common material used in many buildings in the Midwest during that era. In fact, several notable buildings in downtown Milwaukee were constructed of cream city brick. Possessing considerable strength, good weather resistance if manufactured properly, and a pleasant color, the brick made North Point's original lighthouse quaint and attractive. (Authors' collection.)

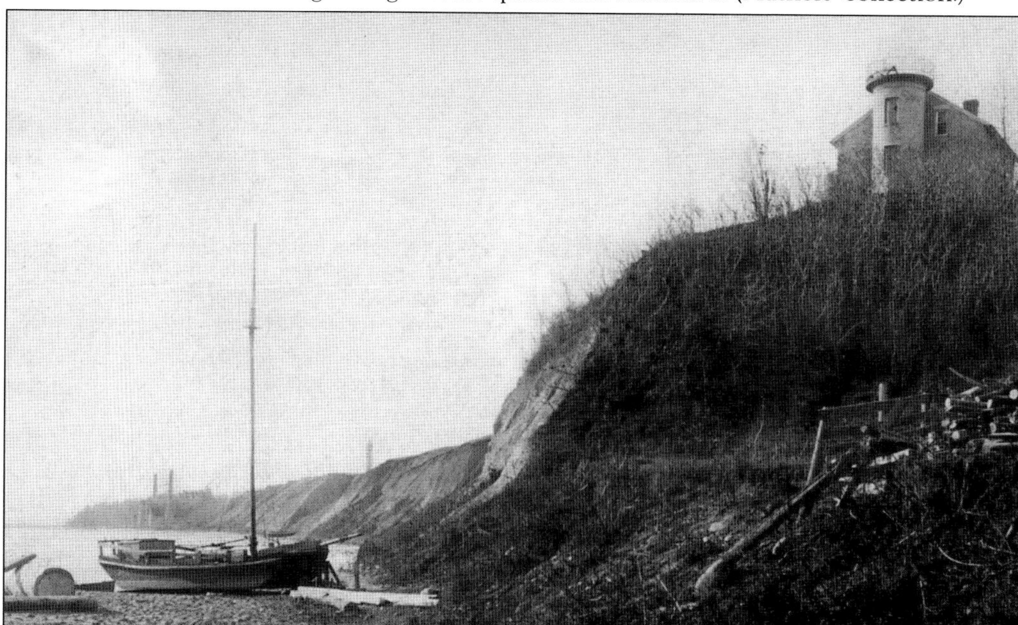

North Point's first lighthouse is pictured here around 1887 atop the eroding bluff. This vantage point gives a great sense of the steepness of the Lake Michigan shoreline and the reason it was determined that another lighthouse should be constructed several hundred feet farther inland. This image also shows wooden steps down to the lake and small boats that were used to travel to the Milwaukee harbor, located a few miles to the south. (Courtesy of MCHS.)

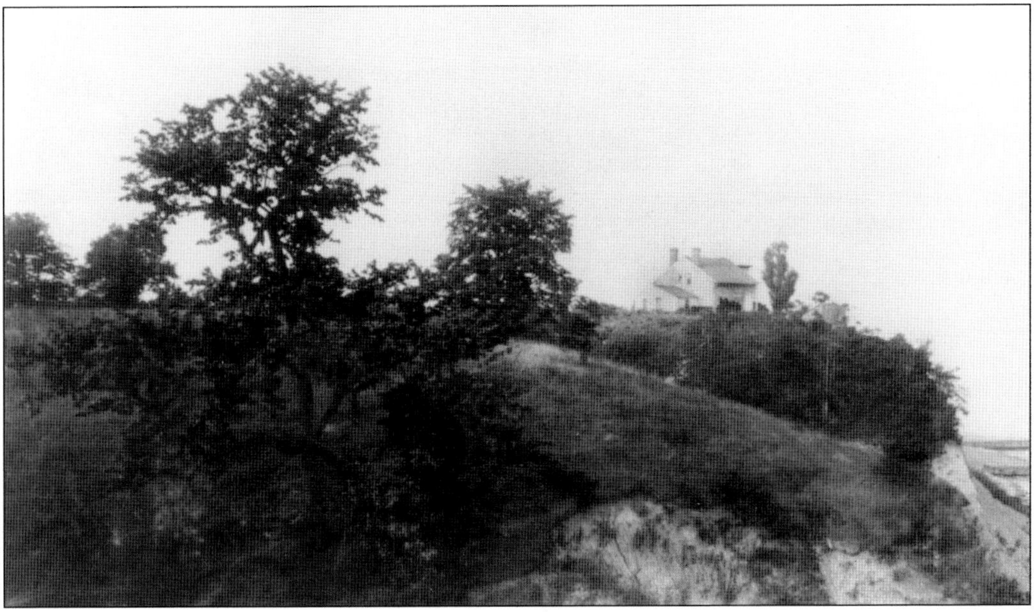

The inaugural 1855 lighthouse at North Point is shown here perched high atop a bluff overlooking Lake Michigan. Ravines in the foreground cut deeply into the landscape in this area. The location of this beacon notified mariners of Milwaukee Bay and its harbor a few miles to the south. Note the two small piers at the bottom of the bluff on the far right in the photograph. (Courtesy of MCHS.)

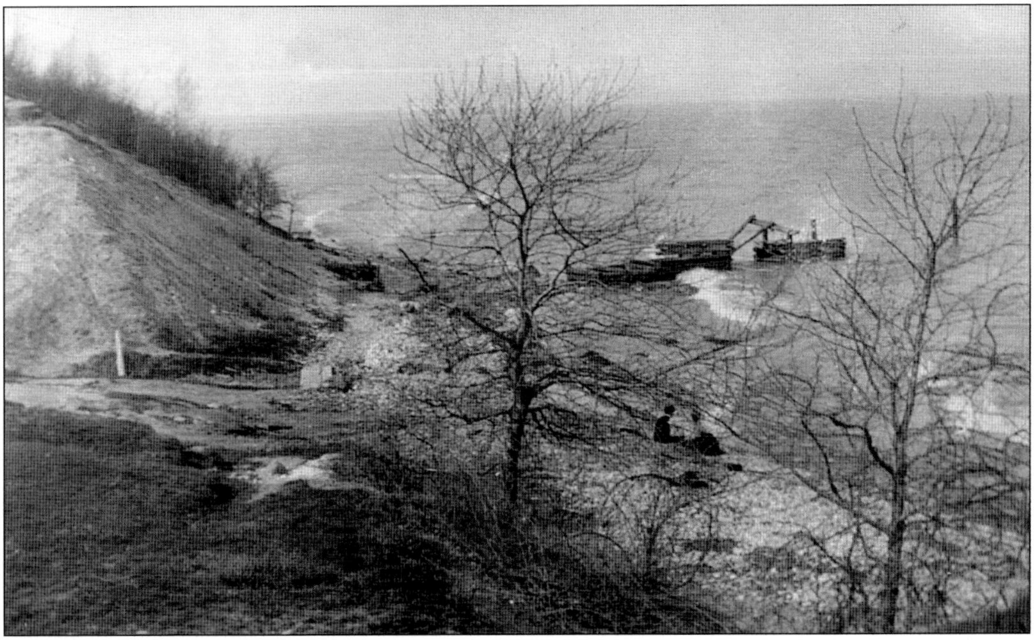

During its earliest years, there were some piers jutting out into Lake Michigan at the North Point Lighthouse. They would have been used to launch small crafts that allowed keepers from the lighthouse to head south to the Milwaukee harbor. A 1915 government document that inventories all structures at North Point states that the old landing wharfs were in very bad condition and of no value, and there were no boats anymore. (Courtesy of MCHS.)

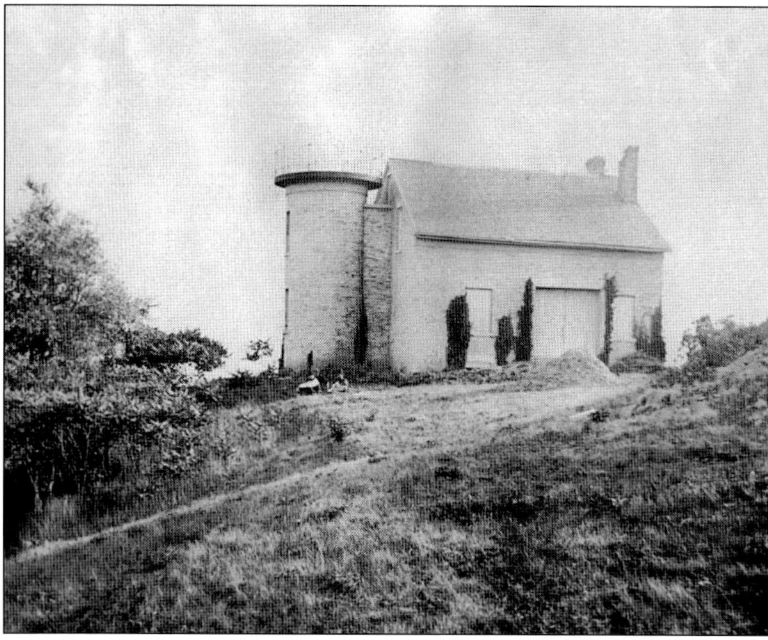

In this c. 1887 photograph, three unknown men sit near the partially dismantled original North Point Lighthouse. Lake Michigan is to the left, out of the picture, with a steep bluff straight down to the big lake. Note the lack of a lantern atop the brick tower; it would have been moved to the new lighthouse. One of the chimneys is also missing some bricks. (Courtesy of MCHS.)

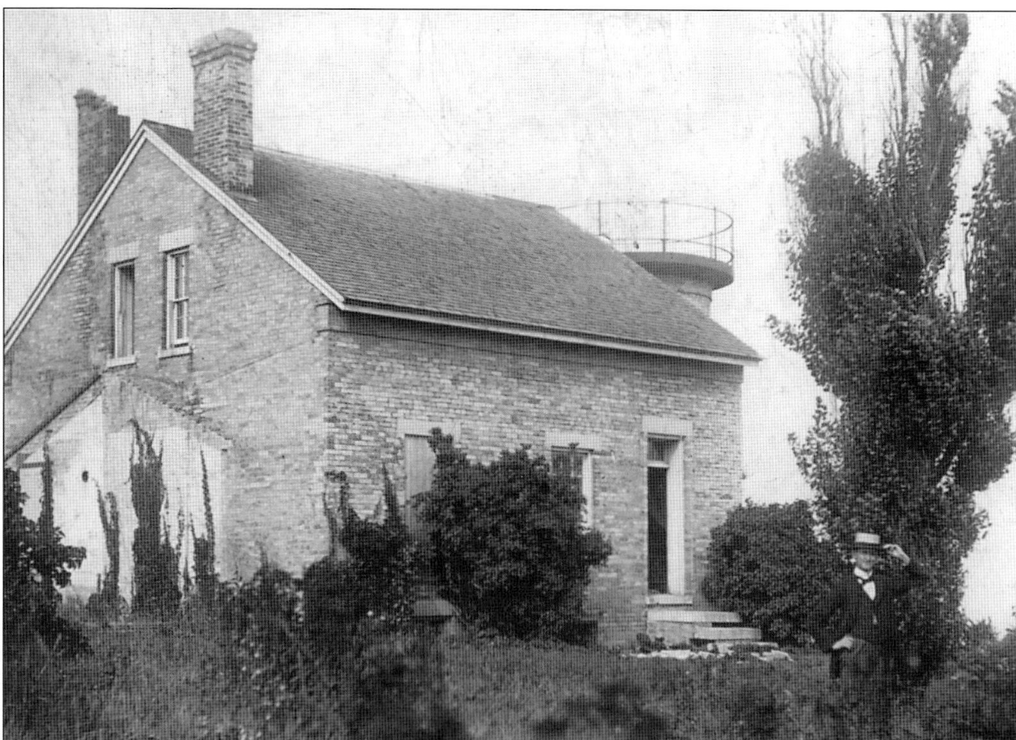

A view from the other side of North Point's 1855 lighthouse gives more information about the beacon's impending status. Lacking both a lantern, which was used in the new lighthouse erected farther inland, and parts of the buildings, its ultimate destruction is foretold. An unknown gentleman holds his hat in the lower right of the c. 1887 photograph. (Courtesy of MCHS.)

North Point's lens had a certain distinct color and pattern to its beam. Known as its distinct feature, this helped mariners distinguish it from other nearby Milwaukee harbor lights, as well as those in other cities along the Wisconsin coast. North Point's original 1855 beam was a steady white light punctuated with a white flash every two and a half minutes. The light, which shined 100 feet above Lake Michigan, was visible for 14 miles in clear weather. The flash pattern changed several times over the years. (Courtesy of NPLHF.)

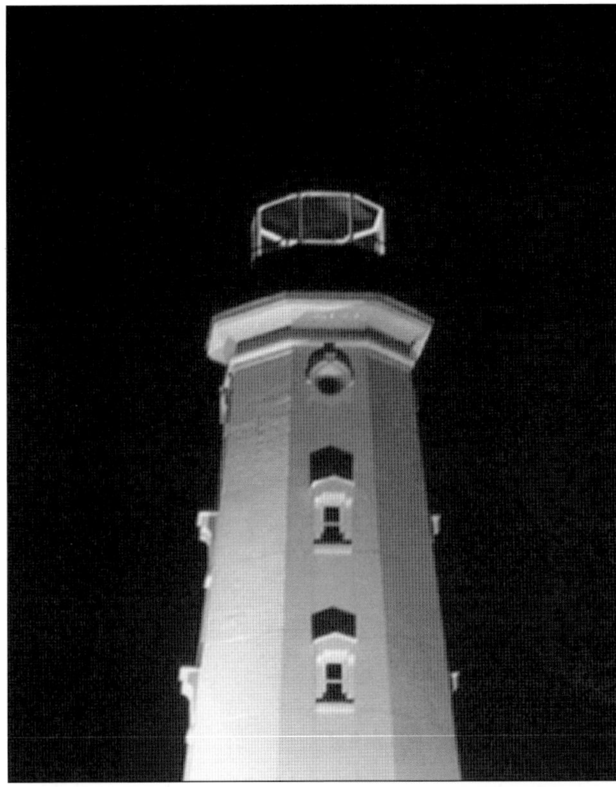

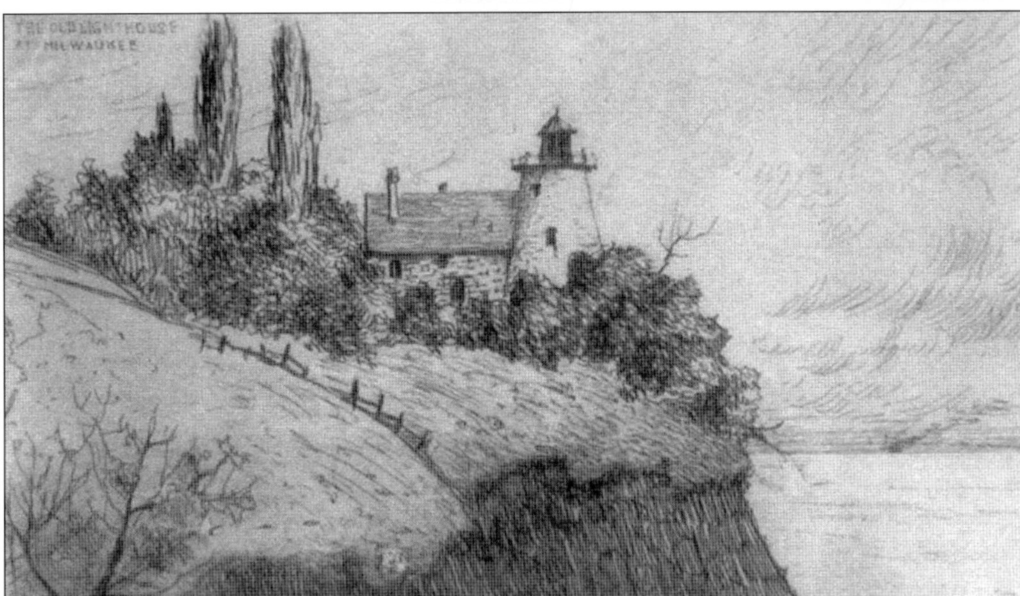

Very few photographs exist of the inaugural 1855 North Point Lighthouse while still in operation. This 1897 sketch by Milwaukee artist Paul Hammersmith nicely portrays the original short, squat 28-foot-tall lighthouse tower, meager dwelling, and the severely eroded bluff that doomed the brick lighthouse. The Lake Michigan shoreline would eventually be artificially filled below. (Courtesy of NPLHF.)

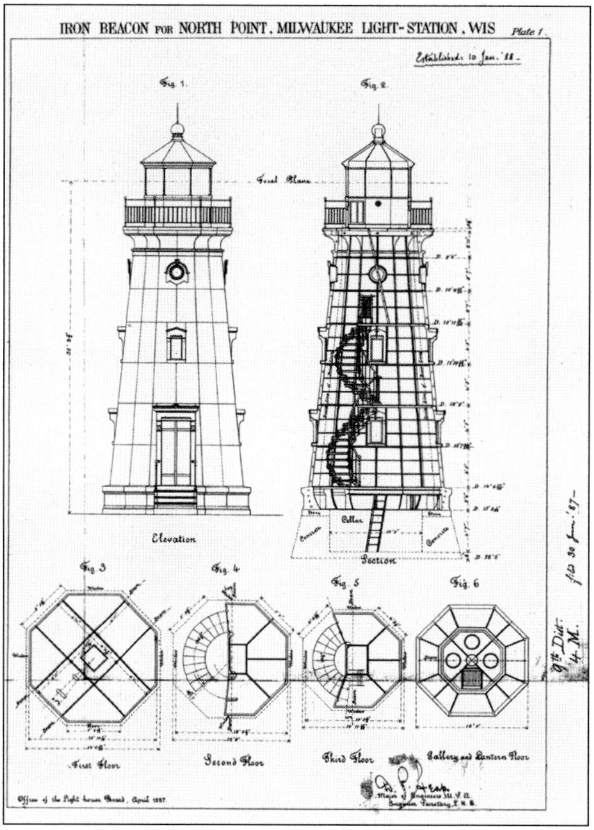

In the 1870s, the government realized that the continued severe erosion of the bluff at North Point would necessitate a major decision and a change. A second lighthouse was constructed farther inland at North Point, with the old brick building set to be abandoned and eventually demolished. In 1887, the office of the Lighthouse Board drew up this schematic for a new iron beacon at North Point Milwaukee. (Courtesy of USCG.)

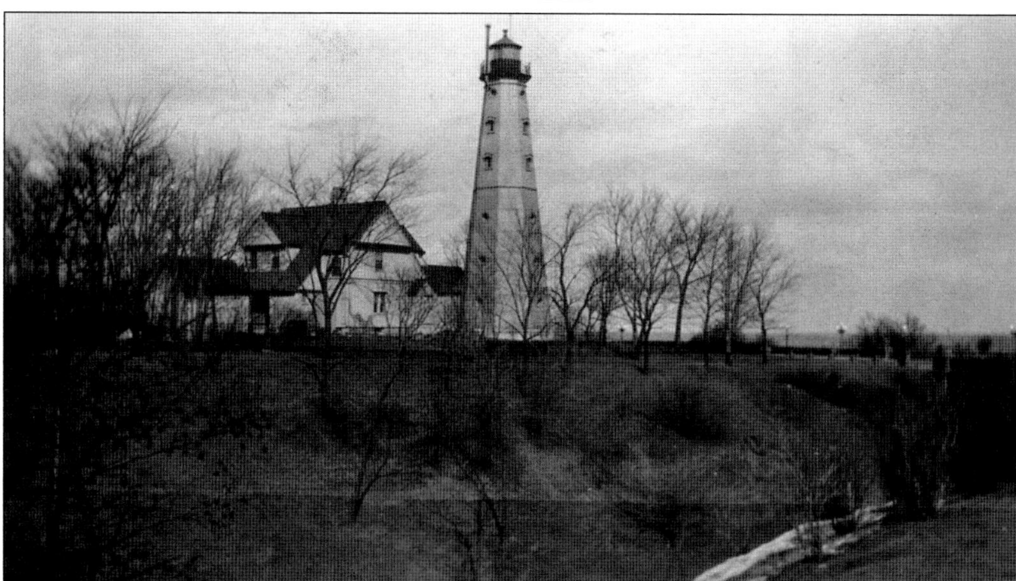

A location farther inland, away from the dangerously eroding bluff, was the government's choice for North Point's second lighthouse. Situated between two sloping ravines, the new site offered a much more stable location. The setting proved a great choice, as the lighthouse was never moved again, although the tower's height was raised in 1912. (Courtesy of the Bevry family.)

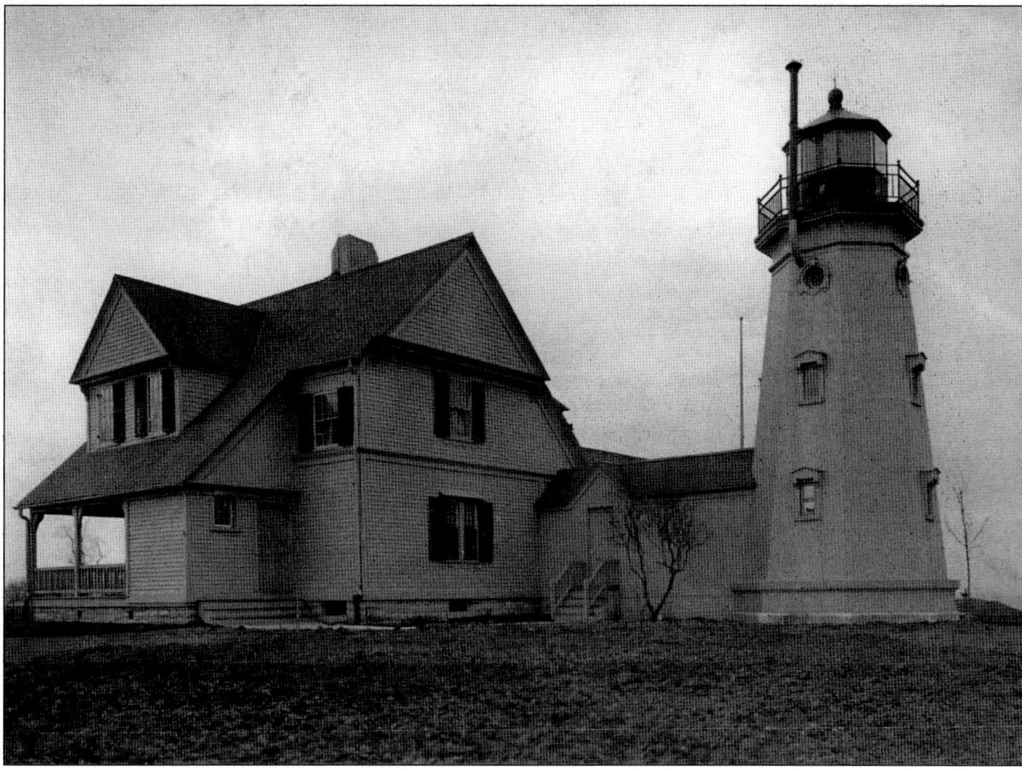

The second lighthouse at North Point is shown here. The 39-foot octagonal, cast-iron tower was completed in late 1887 and was first lit on January 10, 1888. A two-story, Queen Anne–style keeper's house connects to the tower by way of an enclosed walkway. Note the stovepipe projecting out of the upper section of the tower; a coal-burning stove was most likely used to heat the structure at that time. (Courtesy of MCHS.)

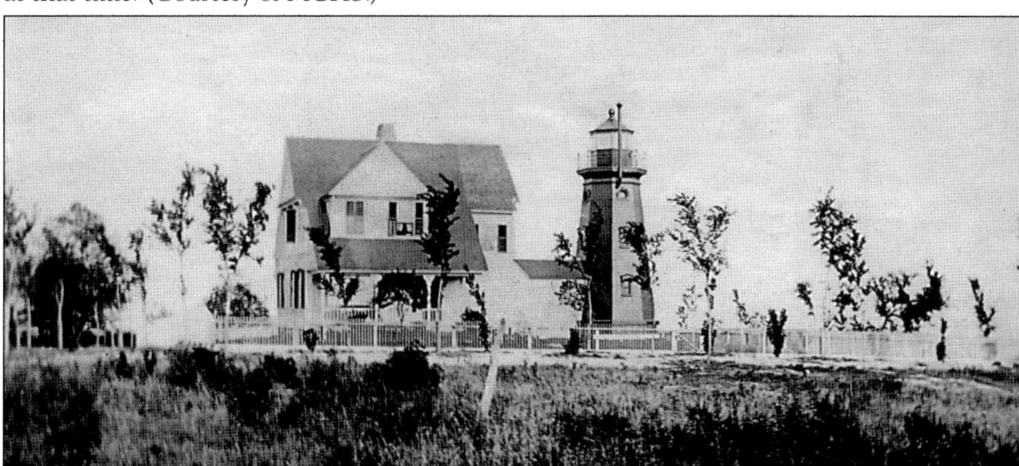

Seen here is another view of the second lighthouse at North Point that was taken from the west, probably near Wahl Avenue. Highlights are the distinctive, short, cast-iron lighthouse and the large two-story residence with its fenced-in premises. Another curious feature is the color of the tower, probably a dark brown. The metal towers at North Point were primarily light or buff colored. (Courtesy of MCHS.)

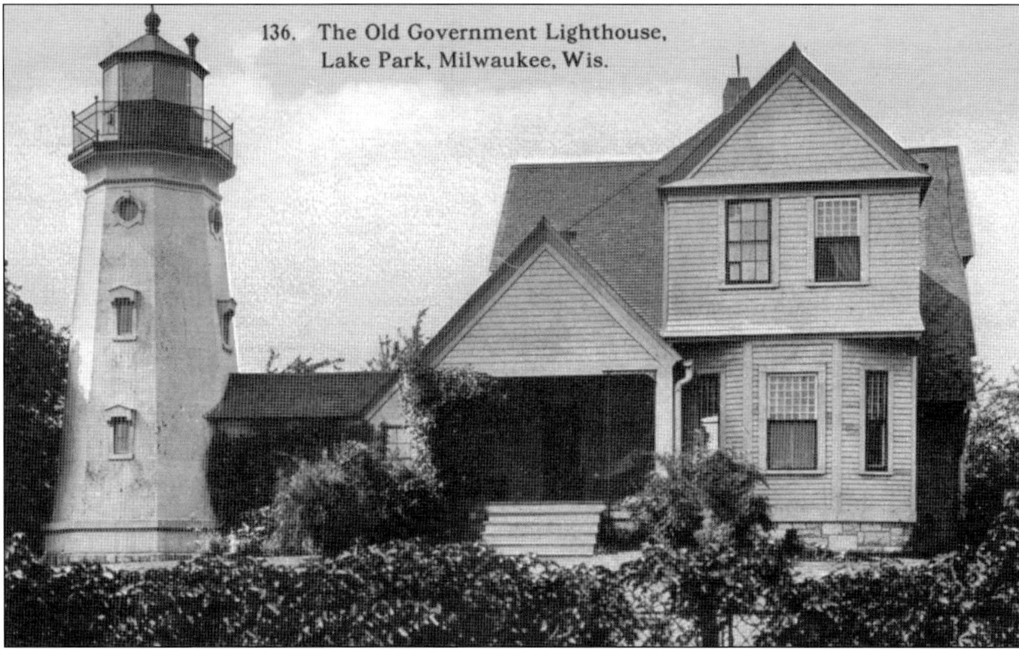

Postcards have historically been used to depict prominent buildings and classic points of interest in various cities. Tourists would send a postcard to family members to show them a special place they were visiting. This rendition of the lighthouse prior to 1912 was a black-and-white photograph that was colorized. Many different postcards exist of the North Point Lighthouse. (Courtesy of Pam Cook.)

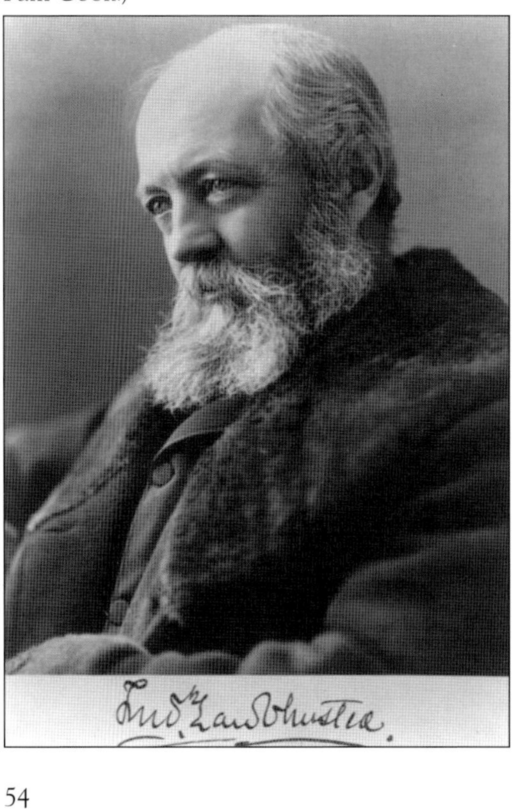

Frederick Law Olmsted is considered the chief landscape architect of Milwaukee's Lake Park. When city planners decided to set aside large tracts of land for public use and enjoyment, they solicited the services of one of America's foremost landscape architect firms, Frederick Law Olmsted & Company, located in Brookline, Massachusetts. Olmsted was also involved in the design of New York's Central Park and the layouts of Milwaukee's Riverside and Washington Parks. (Courtesy of National Parks Service.)

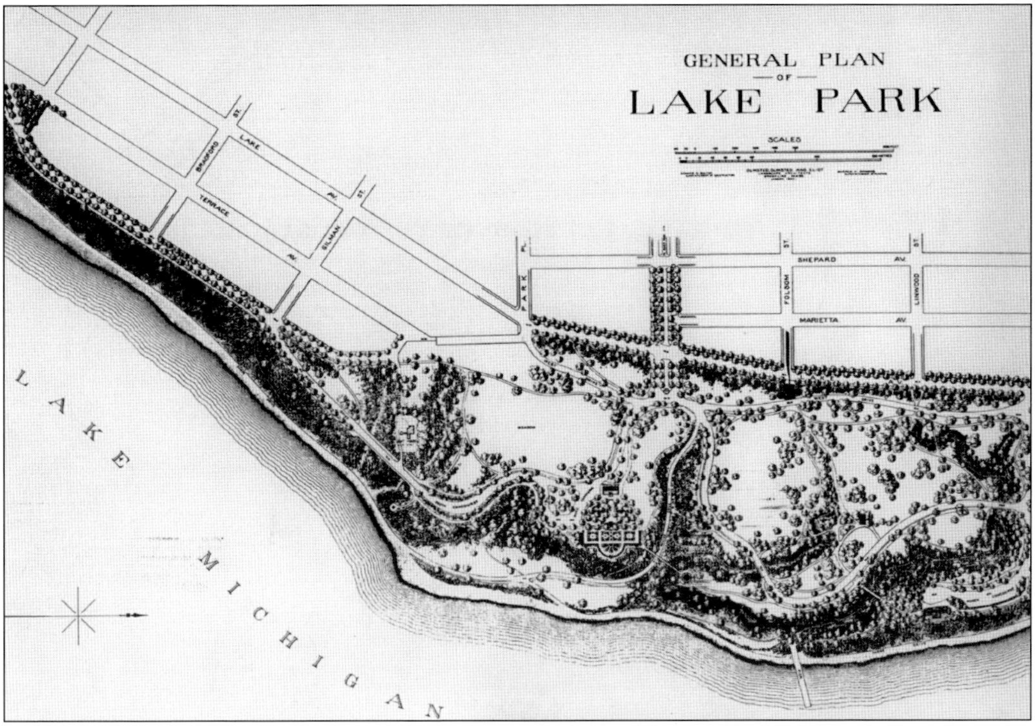

This general plan for Milwaukee's Lake Park is dated January 1892, with Olmsted, Olmsted and Eliot listed as the company hired to design the green space. Since the North Point Lighthouse was already a permanent fixture, Olmsted decided that the lighthouse would logically be a prominent focal point. In this layout, the lighthouse is in a small rectangular tract to the left of center near the meadow area. (Courtesy of MCHS.)

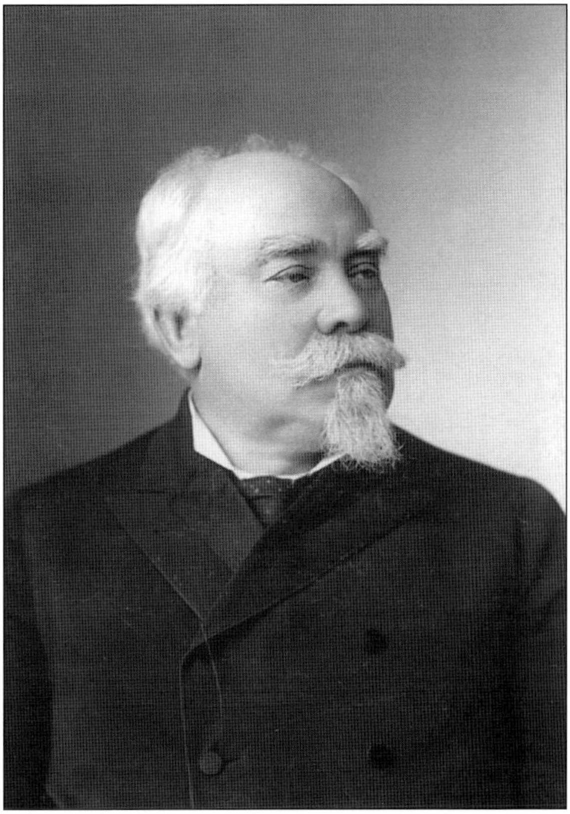

Christian Wahl was an influential and wealthy Milwaukee and Chicago businessman. Born in Bavaria, his family came to the United States in 1846. He was heavily involved in the city's park system in the late 1800s and is sometimes referred to as one of the fathers of Milwaukee's parks. He had a keen interest in the completion of Lake Park. One of the streets just west of the lighthouse is named Wahl Avenue. (Courtesy of MCHS.)

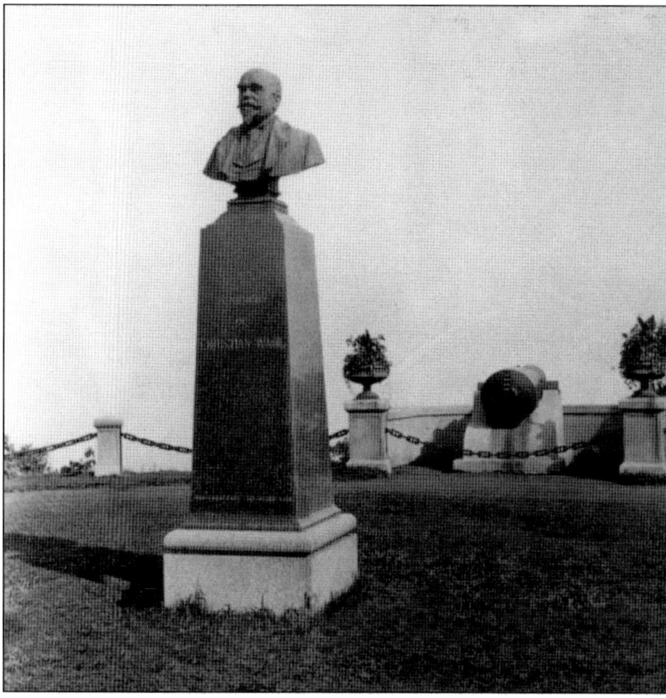

A sculpture of Christian Wahl was created in 1903 and erected just east of the North Point Lighthouse in the cannonade area of Lake Park. The granite base was topped with a bronze bust of Wahl and stood about eight feet tall. In 1960, it was moved to Wahl Park, a Milwaukee County park named in his honor, on Milwaukee's north side. (Courtesy of MCHS.)

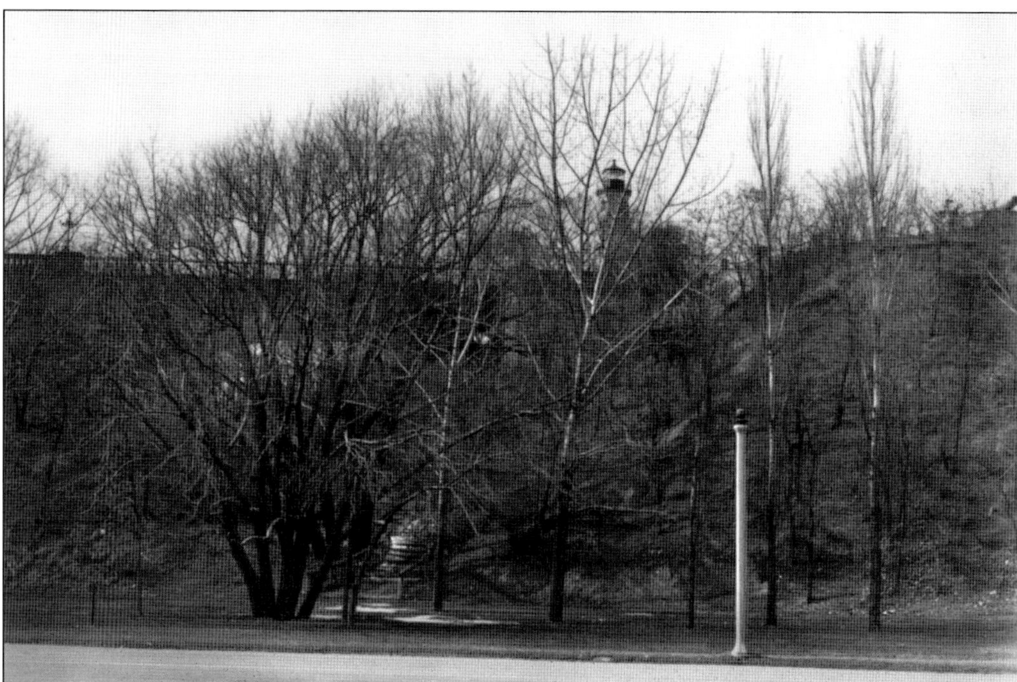

Milwaukee's lakefront was the location for placement of a few militaristic features. The land immediately east of the North Point Lighthouse, on the bluff in Lake Park overlooking Lake Michigan, featured a cannon, seen here in the upper far right. Juneau Park, in downtown Milwaukee, also had a similar feature for a time. The North Point Lighthouse can be seen through the trees. (Courtesy of MCHS.)

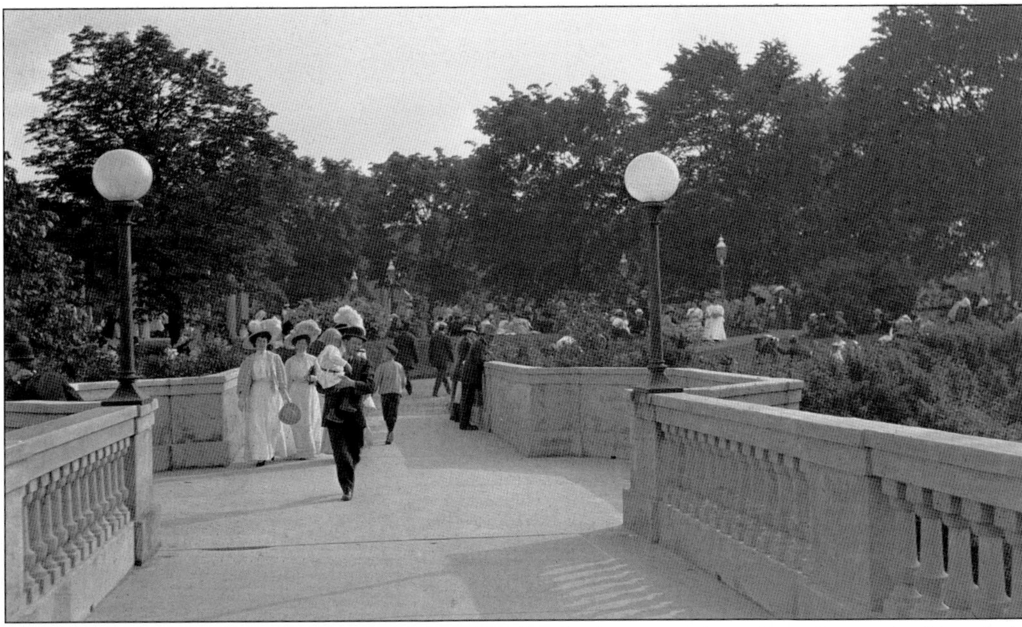

Lake Park is approximately 140 acres of public land, about a mile in length, overlooking Lake Michigan. A registered national landmark, the urban park was first envisioned by Milwaukee's Park Commission in the 1890s. The North Point Lighthouse is one of only a few lighthouses nestled in a major American city and park. Here, people traverse one of the many splendid concrete walkways in the park around 1910. (Courtesy of MPM.)

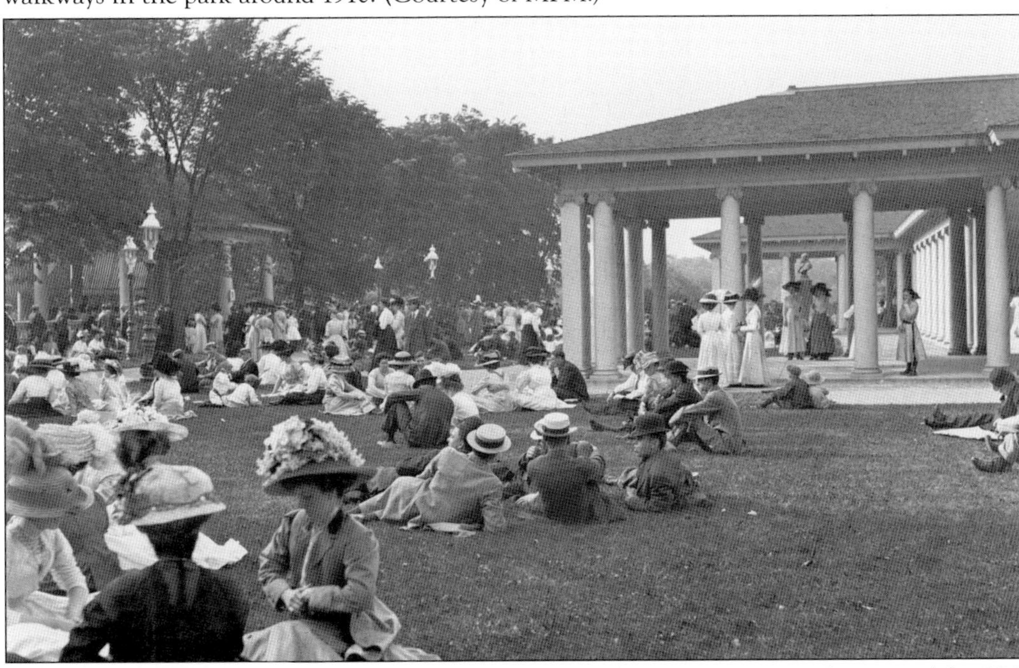

Milwaukee's Lake Park was the place to go for leisure and entertainment at the turn of the 20th century, with social and cultural gatherings commonplace here. Electric trolleys and cars ferried people to and from Lake Park. This 1909 photograph depicts sharply dressed Milwaukeeans lounging in a grassy area while taking in a concert at the park. (Courtesy of MPM.)

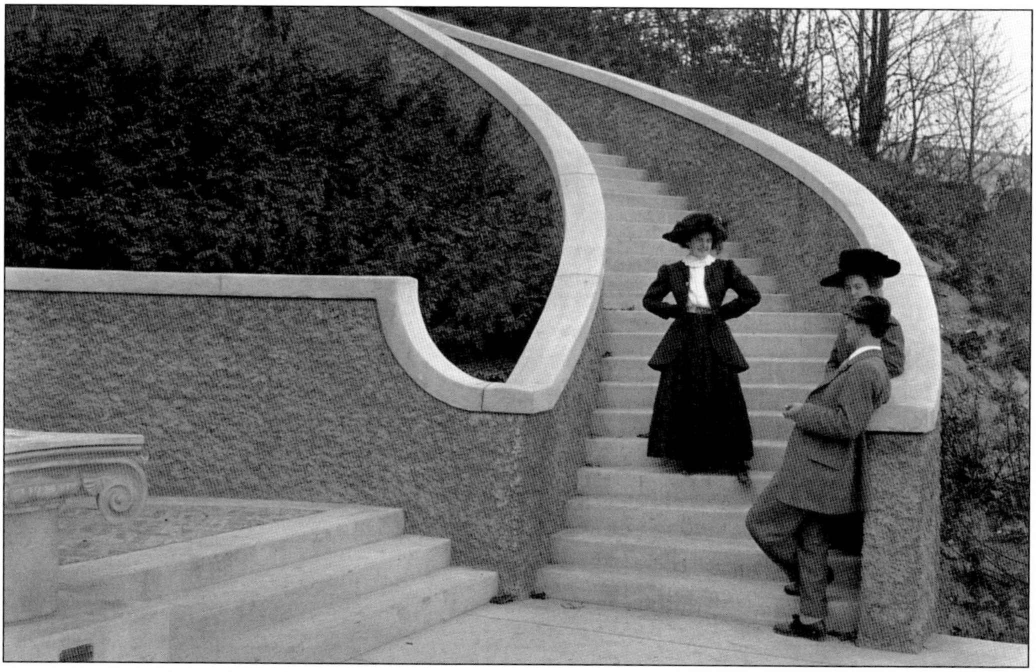

Designed by Alfred Clas, this gorgeous sweeping stairway at the Lake Park Pavilion is one of the most noticeable elements of Lake Park's design and has been a focal point for over a century. In this c. 1910 photograph, women and a man chat in their finest clothing. The park also contains some lesser-known features, including a Native American mound, a former Cold War Nike missile site, and various war remembrances. (Courtesy of MPM.)

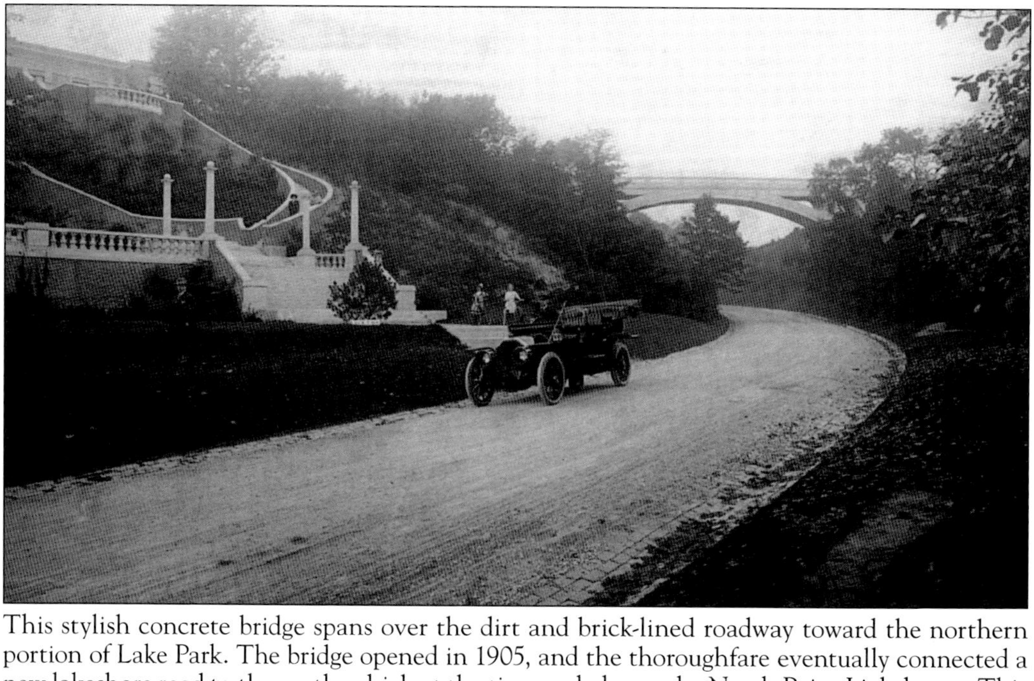

This stylish concrete bridge spans over the dirt and brick-lined roadway toward the northern portion of Lake Park. The bridge opened in 1905, and the thoroughfare eventually connected a new lakeshore road to the south, which at the time ended near the North Point Lighthouse. This c. 1910 image depicts a driver waiting near the stairway and pavilion. (Courtesy of MCHS.)

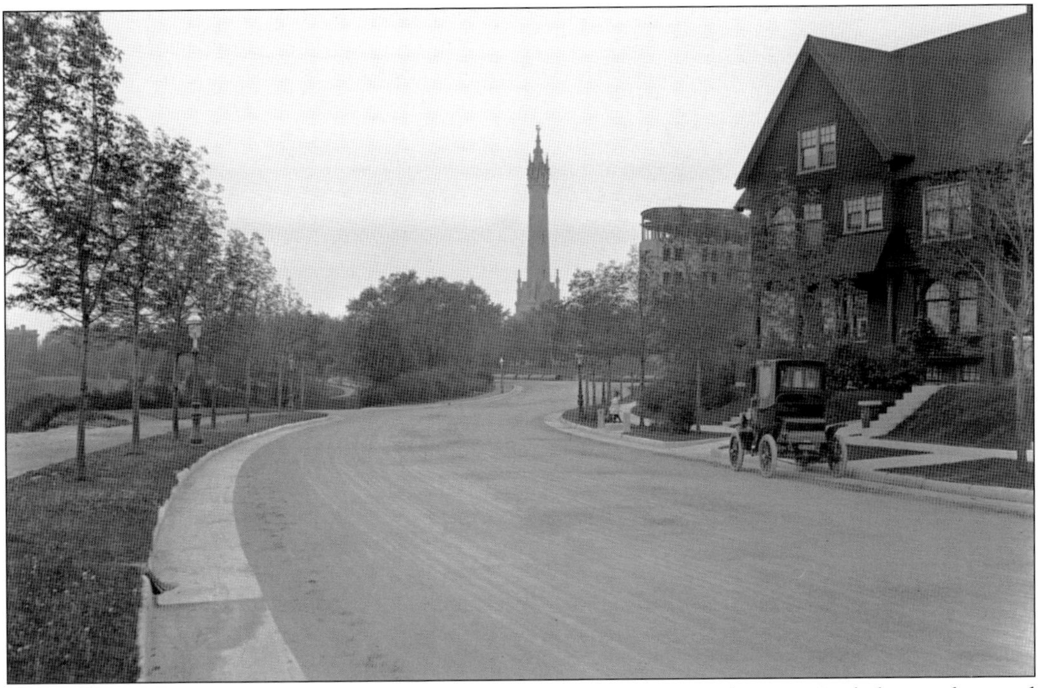

The residential neighborhood adjoining Lake Park near the North Point Lighthouse featured many elegant homes. This c. 1910 photograph shows Wahl Avenue and a view to the south. The prominent structure in the background is the 1873 Victorian-styled North Point pumping station water tower. St. Mary's Hospital, one of Milwaukee's earliest health-care facilities, is just a few blocks from North Point. Note the car on the right side of the road. (Courtesy of MPM.)

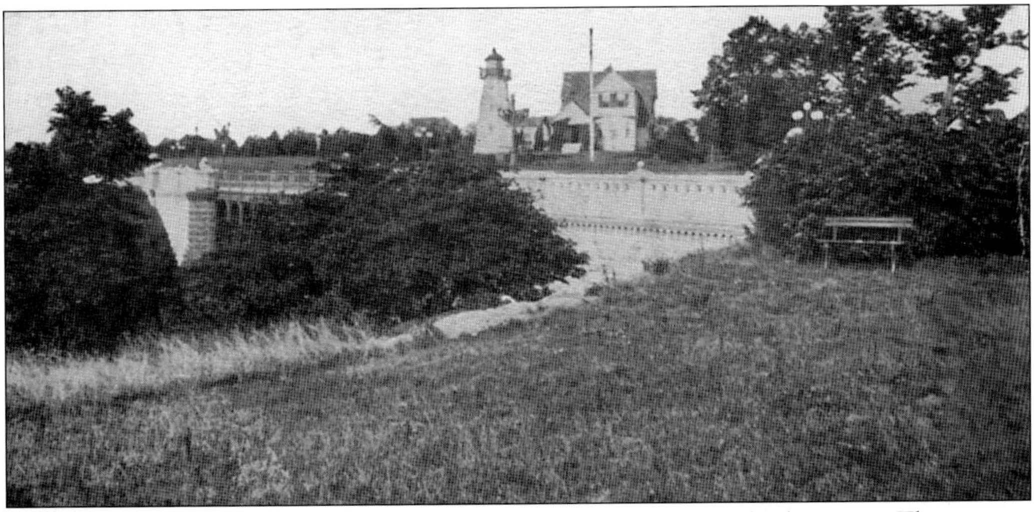

This lone bench in Lake Park provides a great setting to take a step back in time. The vantage point here would have been glorious—Lake Michigan is to the east as far as the eye can see, and the lion bridge, with its namesakes standing guard, and picturesque North Point Lighthouse can be seen to the west. One can imagine relaxing and taking in all the charm of that bygone era. (Courtesy of Pam Cook.)

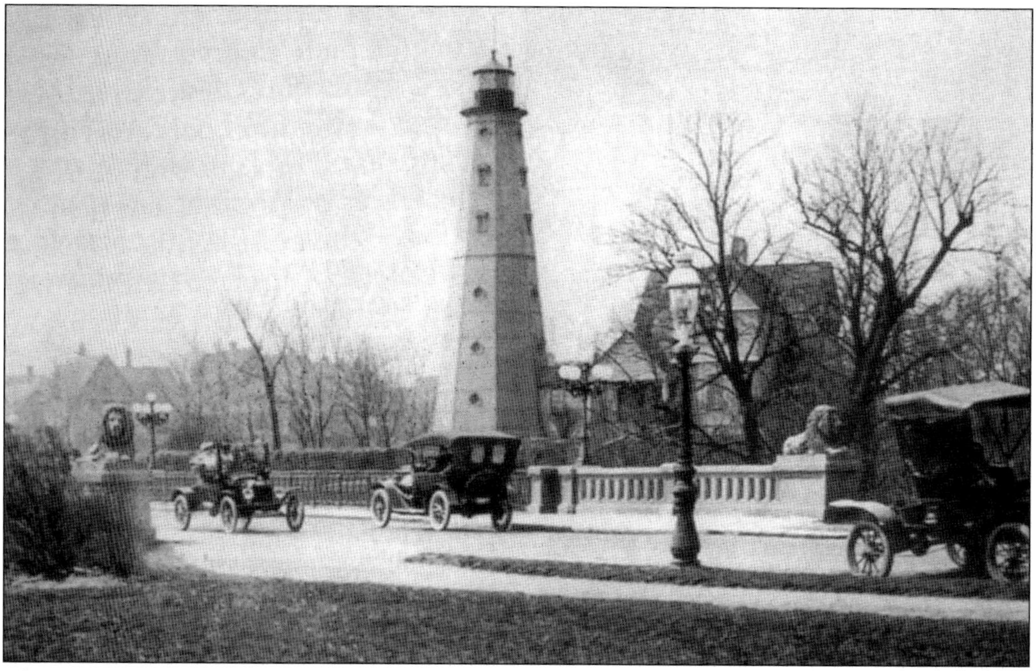

This c. 1915 photograph depicts the hustle and bustle of Lake Park and the North Point Lighthouse. Cars of various types ride back and forth through the park. The stately lighthouse sits nestled next to the street. The lion statues mark the bridge at North Point and ornate lamps line the busy roadway. What a grand scene. (Courtesy of NPLHF.)

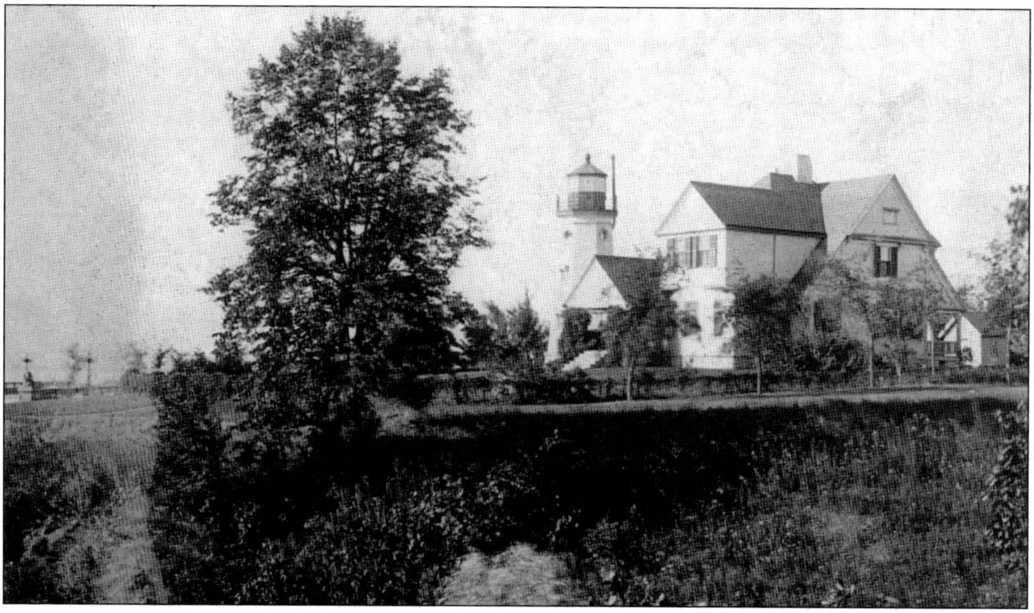

A rare view taken from the northeast of the 1888 Light Station is seen in this photograph. The house was altered in 1897 and later expanded in 1927 to accommodate a keeper, an assistant, and their families. The dwelling became a larger two-story building that included 10 rooms, a bath, a pantry, and closets. The home's entrance originally faced west; remodeling shifted the front to face Lake Michigan. The premises also contained a vegetable garden. (Courtesy of MCHS.)

When the second lighthouse was completed at North Point in late 1887, the light tower was directly connected to the keeper's house by way of an enclosed walkway. This allowed the keepers access to the tower from the inside. In inclement weather, this was undoubtedly a nice feature that allowed the attendants to stay dry and comfortable. This passageway was later removed. (Courtesy of MCHS.)

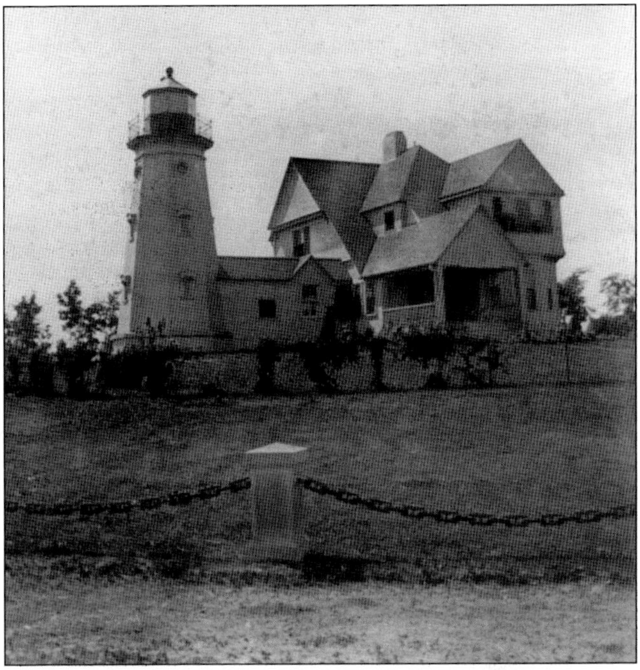

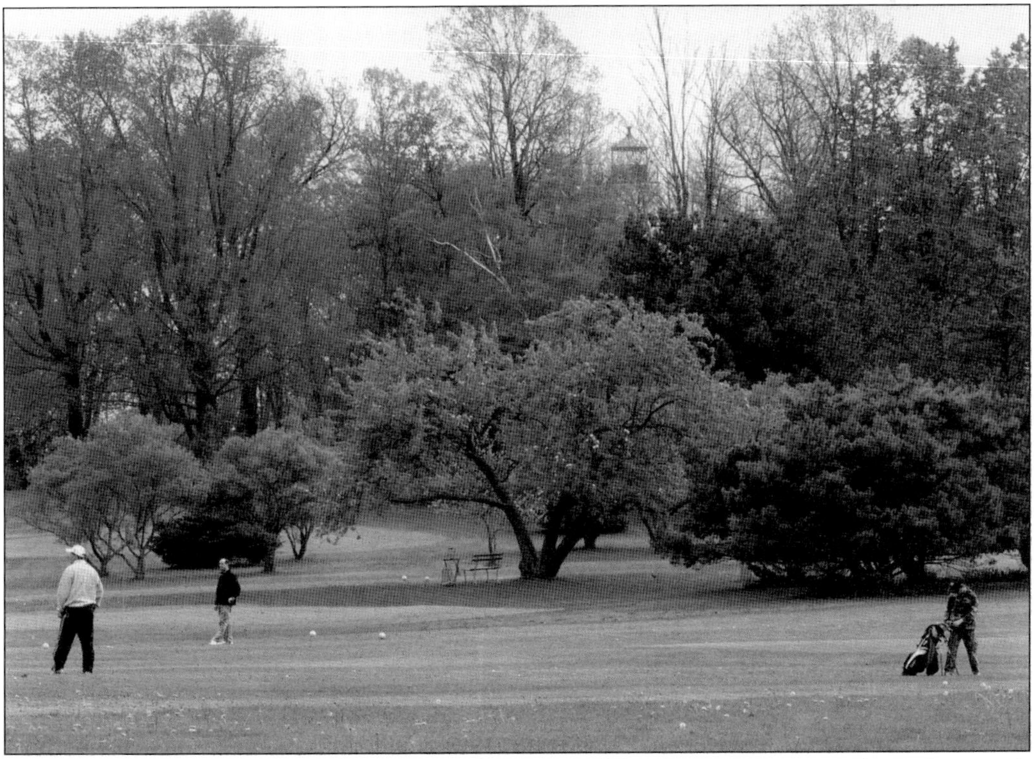

A golf course has been the North Point Lighthouse's neighbor for over a century. A meadow north of the lighthouse became a six-hole course in 1903 and expanded to 18 holes around 1930. Today, Milwaukee County continues to operate the pitch-and-putt par-three golf course. Note the lighthouse's tower in the background poking through the trees in Lake Park. (Authors' collection.)

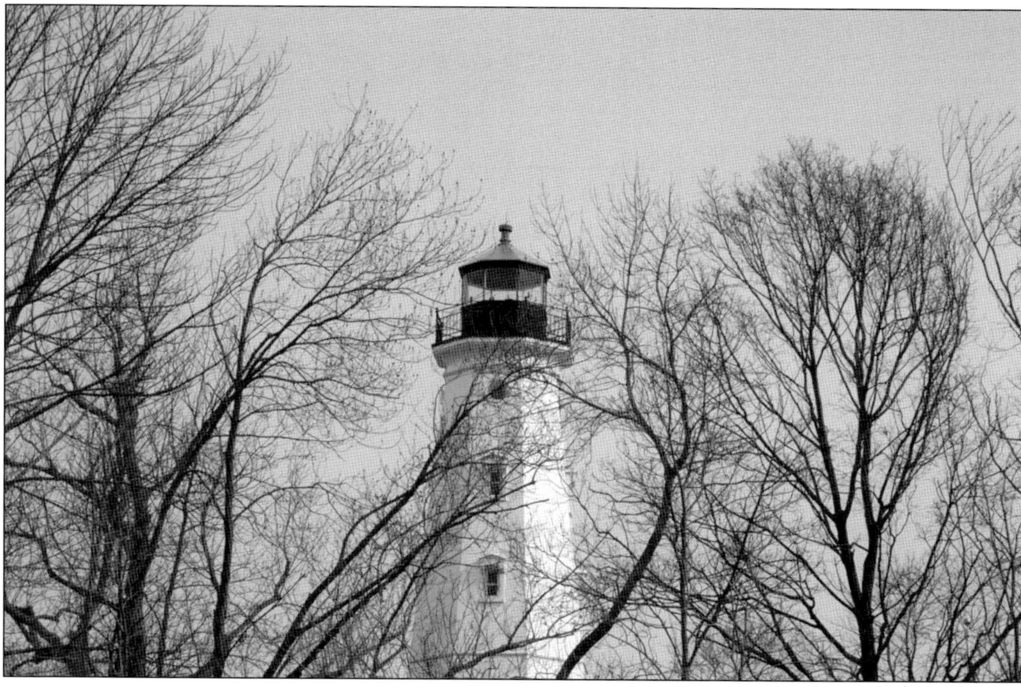

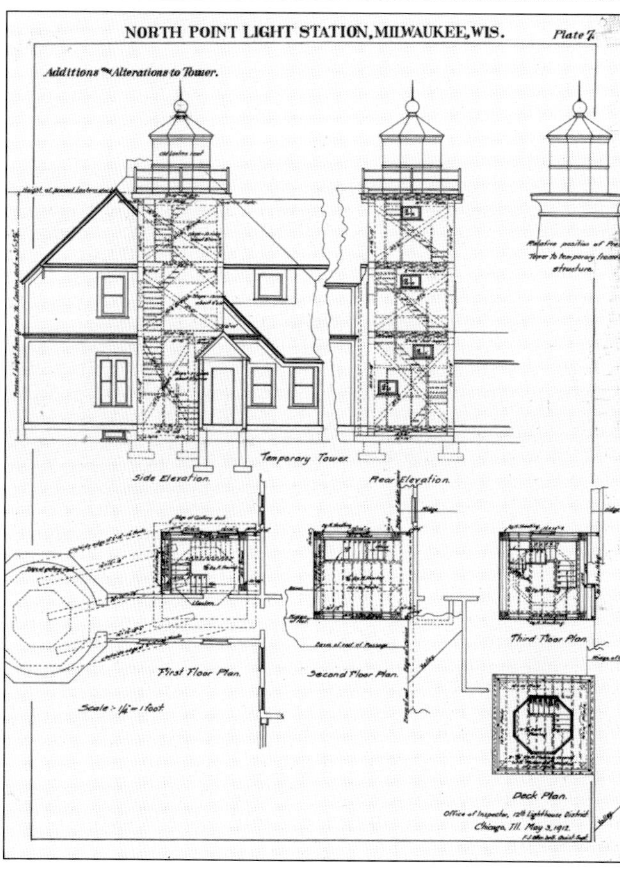

As large trees in the vicinity of the lighthouse grew taller and neighborhood housing and lighting increased, seeing an unobstructed light beam out on Lake Michigan became an issue. Mariners complained of North Point's unreliability and ineffectiveness. Without a sizeable increase in the tower's height, the North Point Lighthouse would have been routinely obscured and rendered useless. (Authors' collection.)

When the government determined that the lighthouse needed to be taller, it constructed a temporary frame tower next to the short cast-iron light. The ongoing tower additions and alterations took about five months to completed. The office of the 12th Lighthouse District Inspector in Chicago produced this drawing to guide construction in 1912. After the tower height was increased, the interim tower was dismantled. (Courtesy of USCG.)

Government officials responded to the pressing issue of a fickle light by placing the existing tower on a newly constructed base, making them a mated pair. This 1912 Department of Commerce Lighthouse Service blueprint illustrates the solution. The combined towers would be 74 feet tall and rise 154 feet above Lake Michigan, considerably higher than the original 39-foot-high lighthouse. The new lighthouse had 71 steps in the tower, along with 13 more to the lantern. (Courtesy of NPLHF.)

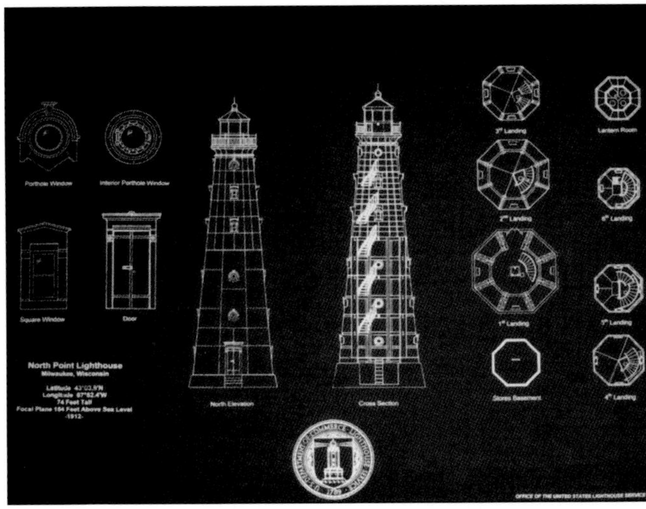

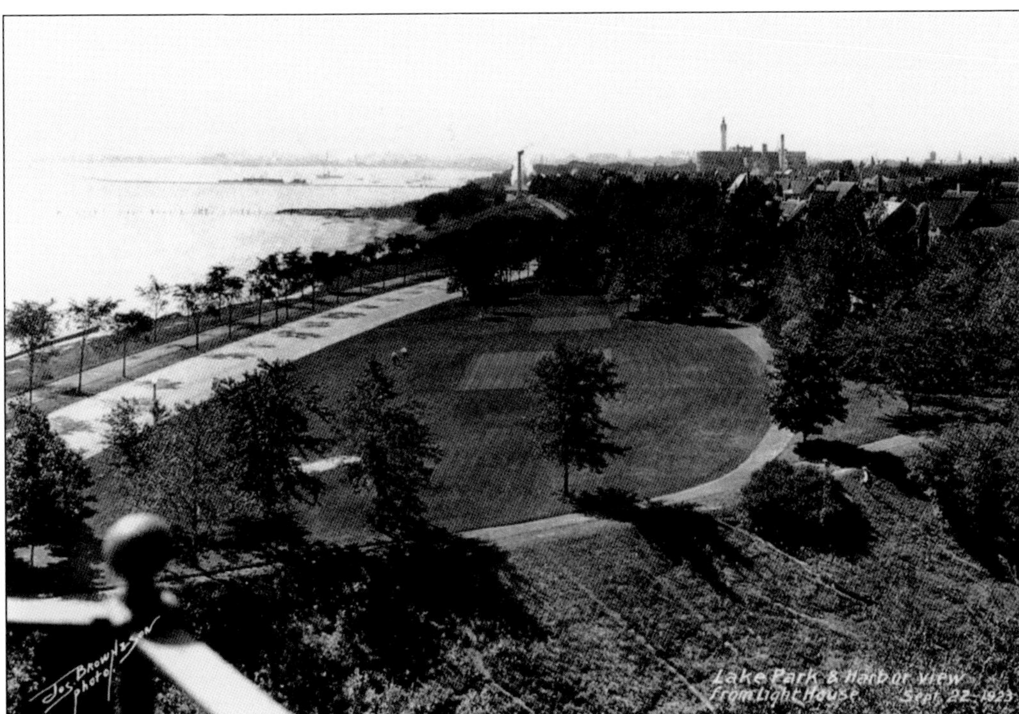

This is the view the keeper had from the top of North Point's tower in 1923. On a clear day, he would have been able to see for many miles. This vantage point, looking to the south, shows the paths in Lake Park, the North Point pumping station smokestack and water tower, and the Milwaukee harbor with part of its breakwater. (Courtesy of MPL.)

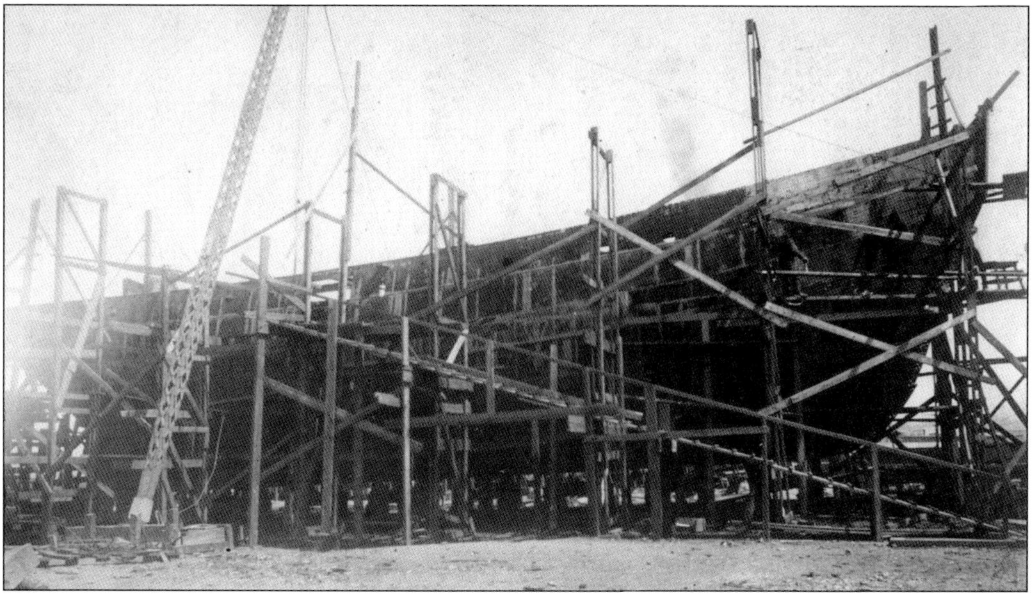

The craft that would ultimately become a lightship off Milwaukee's harbor is pictured here, with the outer steel shape of the vessel taking form. Built from 1910 to 1912 for $65,000 by the Racine-Truscott-Shell Lake Boat Company in Muskegon, Michigan, its specifications included a length of 108 feet, a beam width of 23 feet, and a weight of 368 tons. She first arrived at her post off of Milwaukee on November 20, 1912. At the same time, North Point's tower height had just been increased. (Courtesy of USCG.)

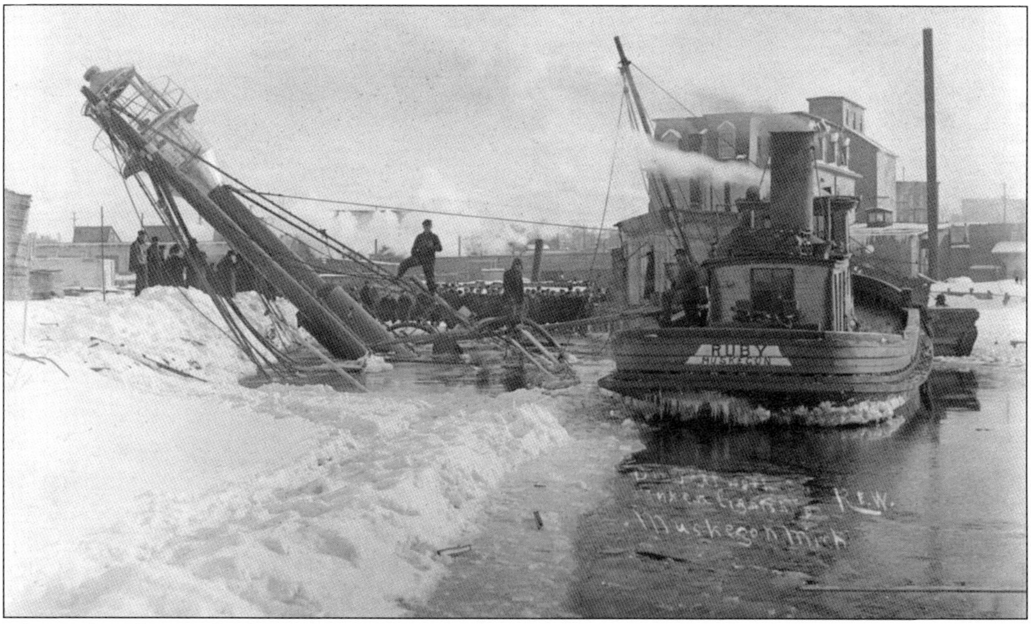

The Milwaukee Lightship's beginnings were less than ideal. The boat sank at the dock of the builder in December 1911. The stricken ship was raised in February 1912. Here, the tugboat *Ruby* assists in stabilization and raising efforts. Ultimately, the sinking had no permanent effect. The Milwaukee Lightship served at Milwaukee until 1932 and later became a relief ship. She was decommissioned in 1965. (Courtesy of USCG.)

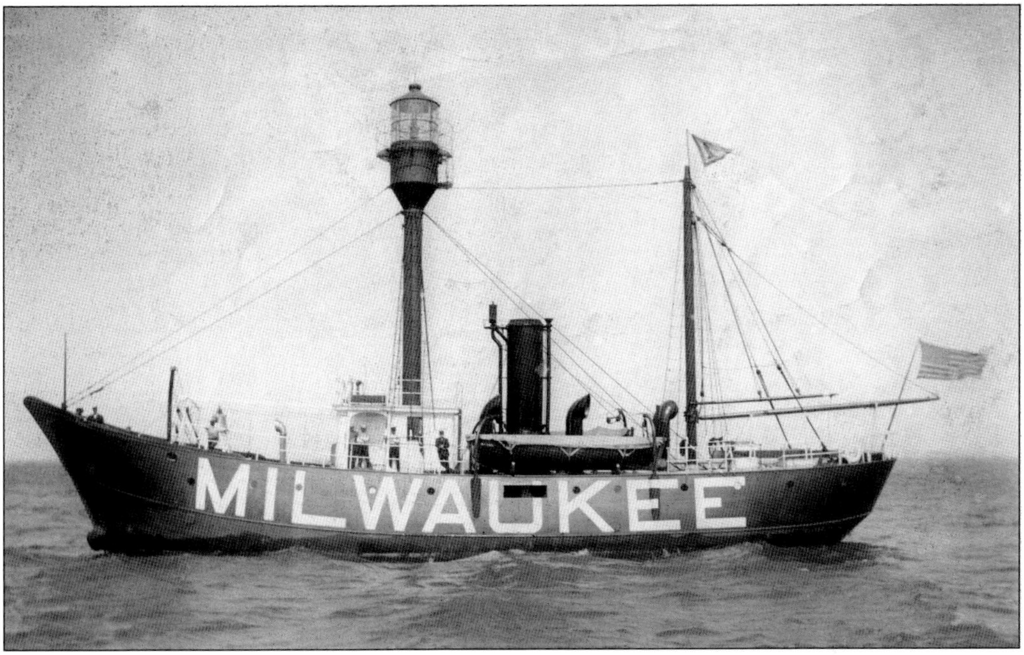

Prior to the construction of the permanent concrete Milwaukee breakwater and accompanying lighthouse (in addition to the North Point Lighthouse), mariners also relied on a floating lighthouse, the Milwaukee Lightship Vessel No. 95. Anchored about three miles from the harbor mouth, this steam-powered, sail-rigged vessel featured hardy crews who manned the station from 1912 to about 1932 in all types of weather. The Milwaukee Breakwater Lighthouse opened in 1926, making the lightship obsolete. (Courtesy of USCG.)

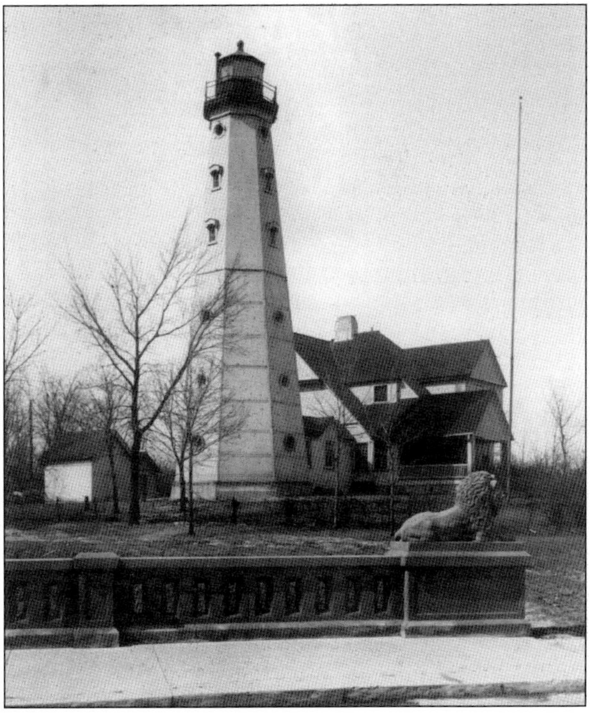

One of the stone lions in Lake Park seems to be standing guard at the North Point Lighthouse in this c. 1913 photograph. Eight lions were created by sculptor Paul Kupper. In this view, a few other small buildings can also be seen behind the newly elevated tower. Historic records indicate that, at various times, the lighthouse grounds contained a fuel storeroom, a storage shed, and a one-car garage. (Courtesy of USCG.)

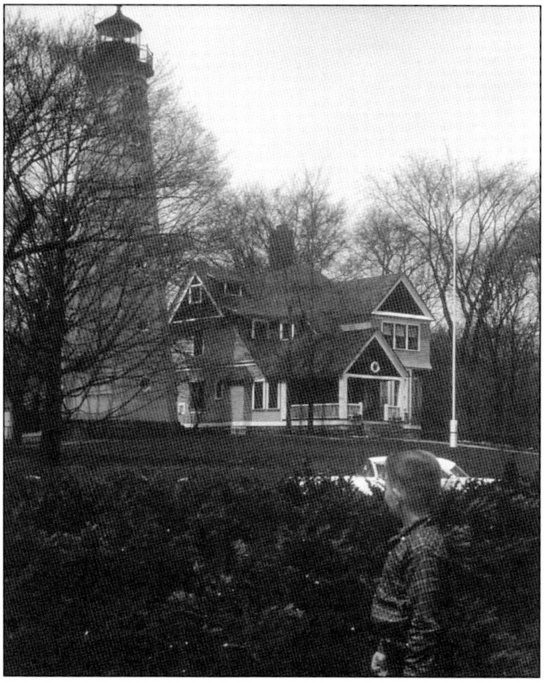

The North Point Lighthouse underwent many changes in its history. Different locations, different towers, extraordinary keepers, and other personnel were all part of the beacon's story. The tower's color also was altered at various times. The shades included white, buff, a light tan-brown, and even a dark brown hue. This young man seems to be admiring the lighthouse during the 1950s, when it was automated and light brown in color. (Courtesy of Dale Hanson.)

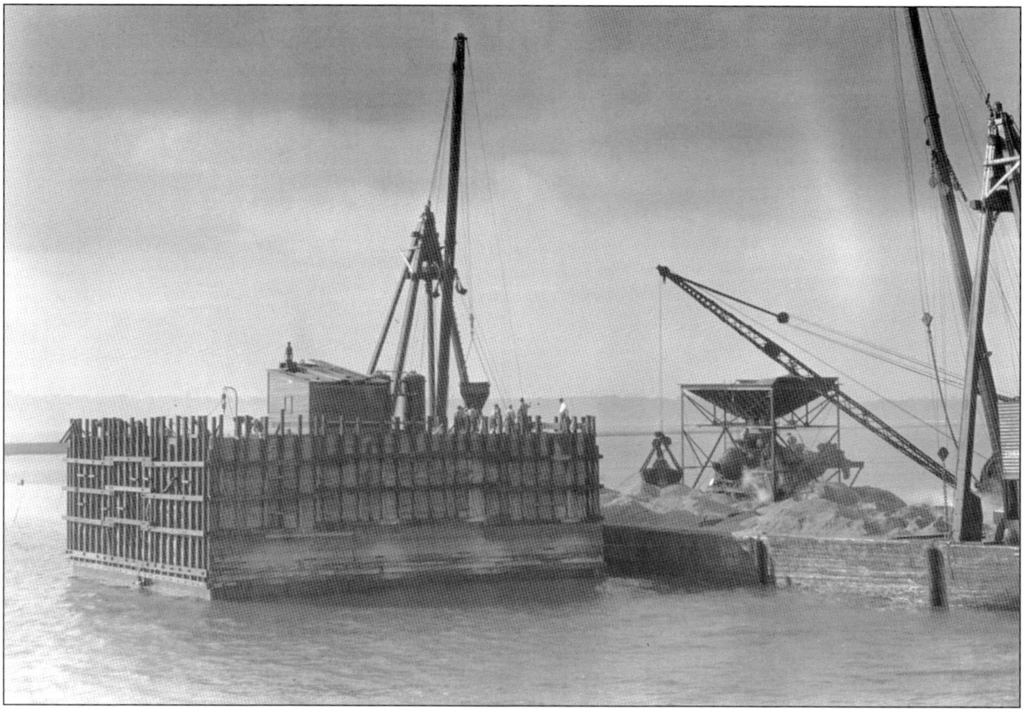

As additional harbor improvements in Milwaukee moved forward, a fully enclosed breakwater lighthouse was erected. This photograph shows some of the machinery used to assemble the concrete foundation in 1926. Construction of this lighthouse would ultimately play a major role in North Point's future. North Point and the breakwater light were merged into a single government unit in 1928. (Courtesy of MPM.)

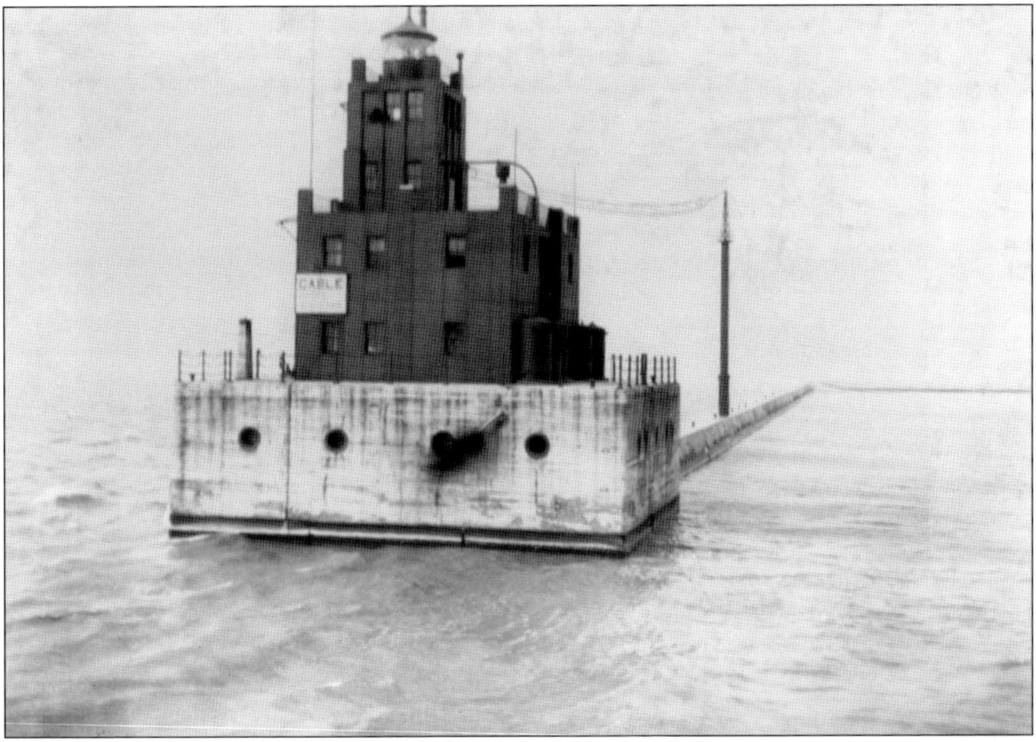

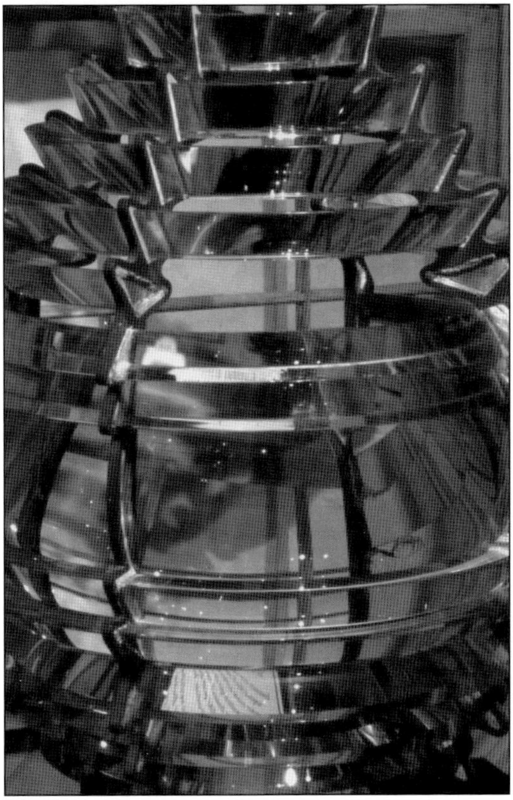

The Milwaukee Breakwater Lighthouse was constructed in 1926 and is one of the last examples of a fully enclosed breakwater beacon. Situated midway along a nearly four-mile-long breakwater, the mammoth lighthouse, its solid base, and its steel upper portion are quite massive and impressive. Even so, Lake Michigan did damage to this fortress when riled up. (Courtesy of USCG.)

The light beam at the Milwaukee Breakwater Lighthouse was produced from a fourth-order Fresnel lens—the same size as North Point's. For most of its history, the beacon had a red and flashing characteristic, visible for 14 miles in clear weather. Today, this priceless artifact is on display at the Wisconsin Maritime Museum in Manitowoc. (Authors' collection.)

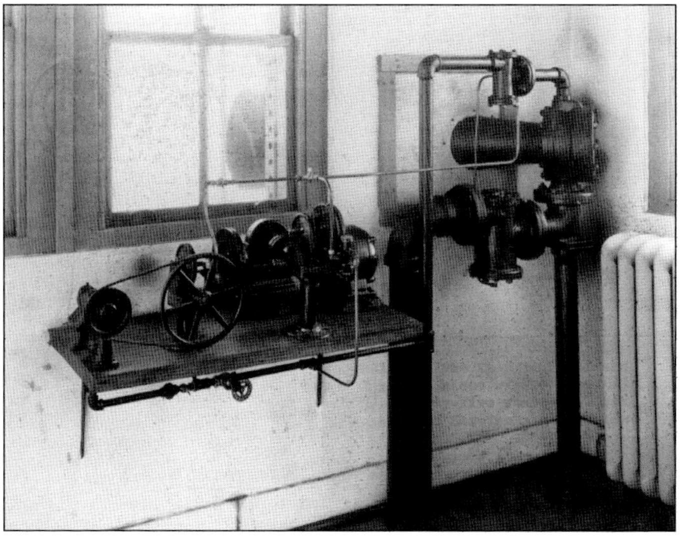

The Milwaukee Breakwater Lighthouse sported some modern technology of the time, including this foghorn, called a Type F diaphone. This 1927 photograph shows the fourth floor of the lighthouse, along with part of the horn machinery and timing device. The characteristic noise is produced by low-pressure air, a piston, a motor, and sound chambers in the unit's casing. It was a vast improvement over previous steam whistles and was incredibly loud. (Courtesy of USCG.)

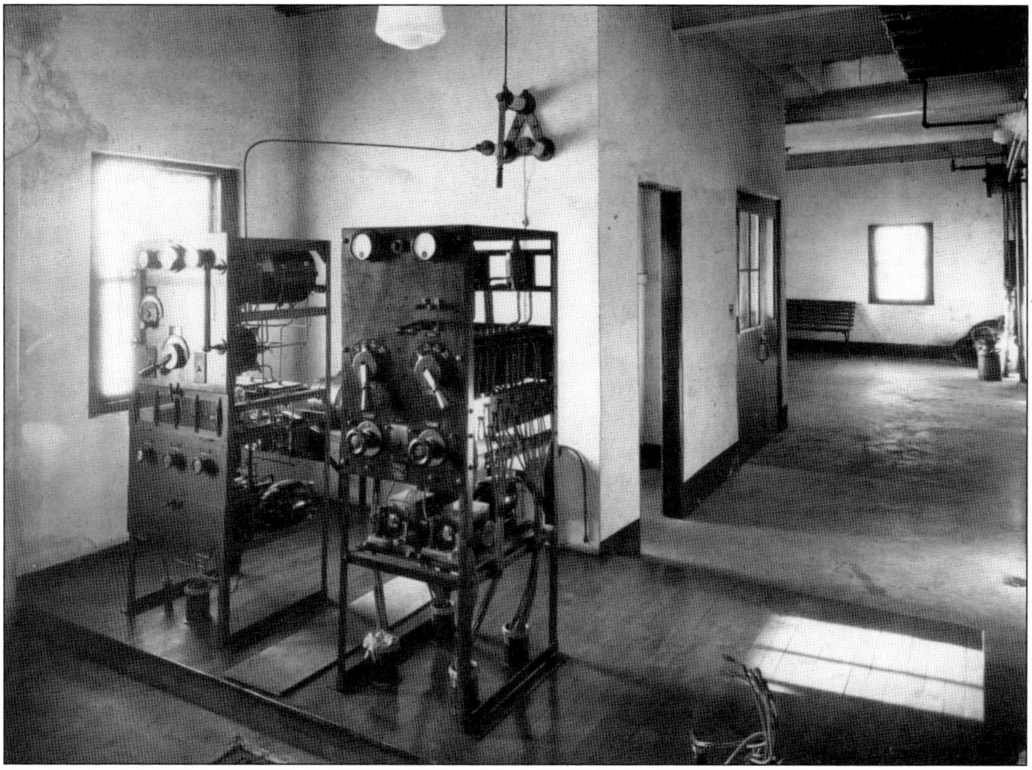

Another state-of-the-art feature at the Milwaukee Breakwater Lighthouse was the radio transmitter. The unit that actually sent the signals, along with its associated control panels, is pictured here in the basement of the lighthouse in 1927. Mariners increasingly relied on radio signals, along with visually seeing the beacons of the lighthouses, to accurately navigate the Great Lakes. (Courtesy of USCG.)

The radio beacon at Milwaukee was another important improvement for ships navigating Lake Michigan. The antenna atop a pole on Milwaukee's north breakwater is seen here. Known as an RDF (Radio Direction Finder), the system sent out a continuous beeping signal. Vessels picked up that signal and the signal from another source to triangulate their positions. Today, GPS uses satellite technology to accomplish this more accurately. (Courtesy of USCG.)

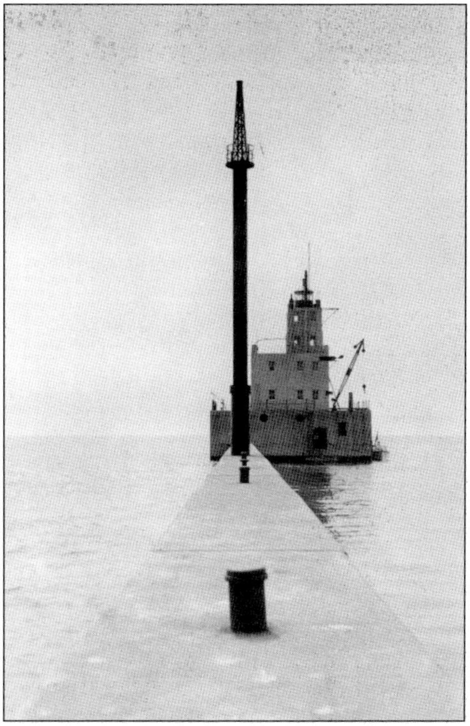

The main floor at the Milwaukee Breakwater Lighthouse is shown here in 1927. This room would have been a living area and watch room for the light keepers and Coast Guard personnel. While these quarters appear spartan, they contain simple but essential furnishings, including a calendar, a clock, a barometer, a pair of binoculars, and an all-important battery-operated radio in front of the keeper's chair. The lighthouse was also equipped with four bedrooms, a kitchen, and later an electric washer and television. (Courtesy of USCG.)

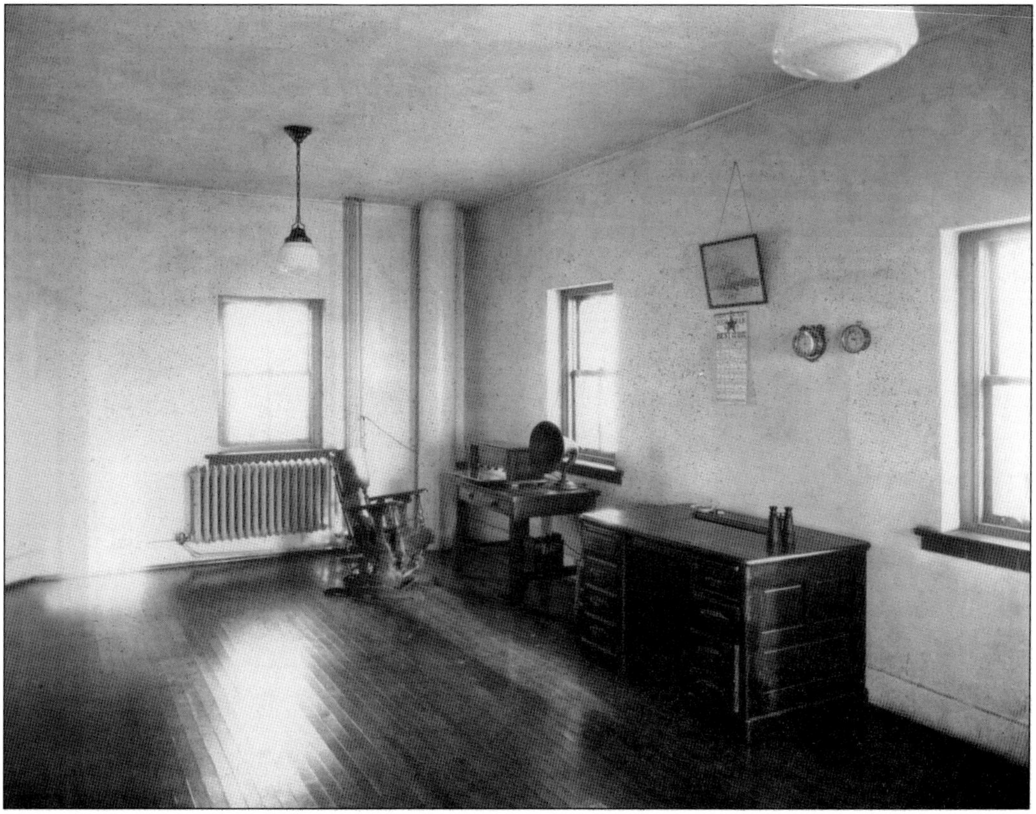

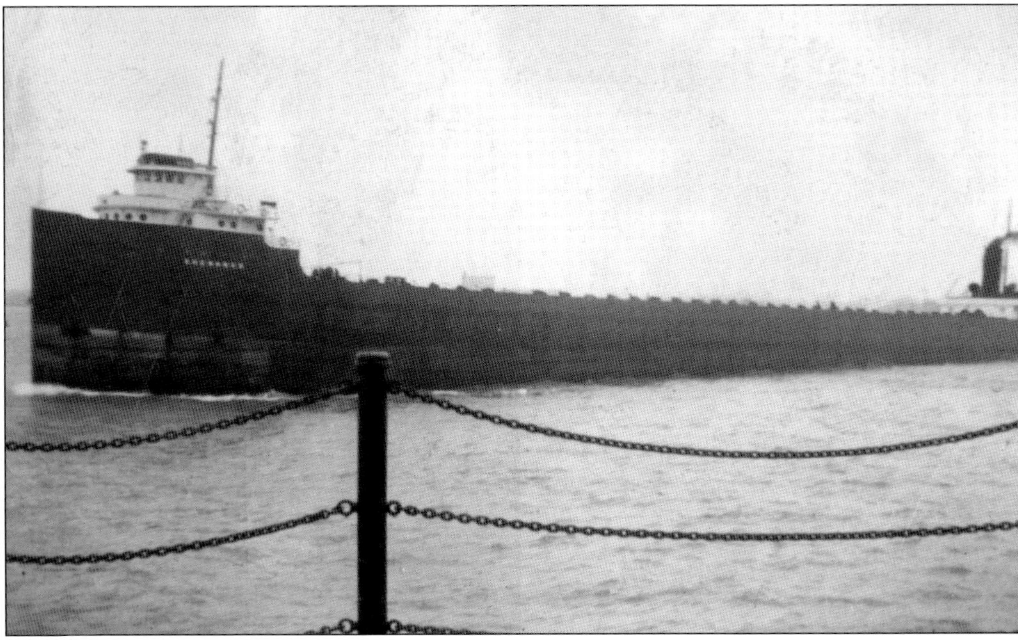

The Milwaukee Breakwater Lighthouse was an excellent location to easily monitor the bustling Milwaukee harbor. Huge freighters routinely passed by, as well as recreational vessels of all shapes and sizes. Here, a large ship, sailing high and probably empty, heads out onto Lake Michigan. A chain-link fence provides a small degree of safety for the crew stationed here. (Courtesy of Ed Werner.)

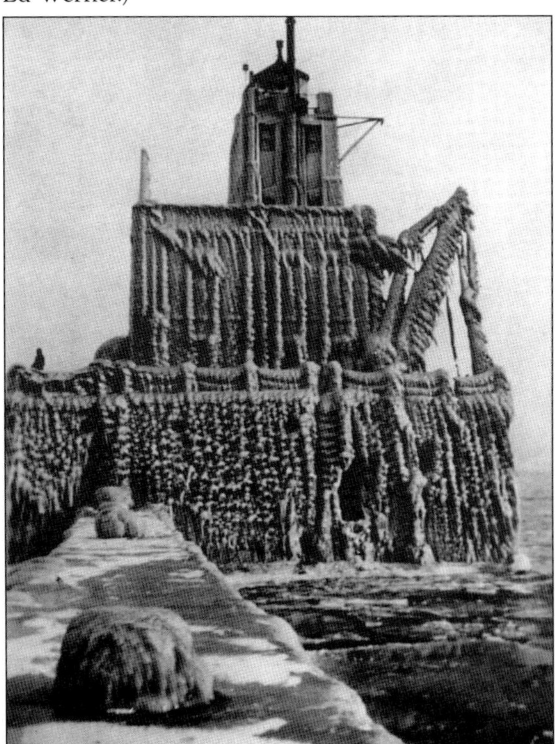

From very late autumn through early spring, treacherous weather conditions could occur on the Great Lakes, as well as at the Milwaukee Breakwater Lighthouse. There are records of the Coast Guard and North Point personnel having to chop their way in through the doorways when thick ice coated the structure. This photograph illustrates what the breakwater and lighthouse looked like after winds and spray created an icy castle. (Courtesy of Vivian Langer.)

Four

Keepers, Assistants, and Coast Guardsmen

Dedication, Duty, and Diligence

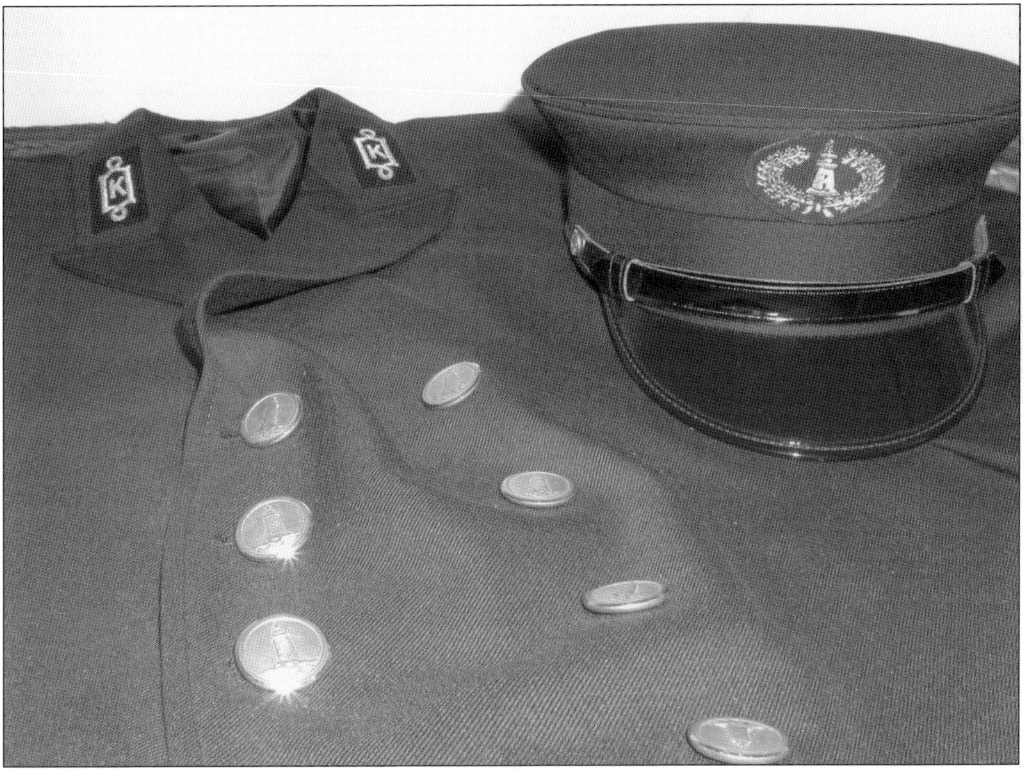

Once the federal government brought organization and regulations to the business of lighthouse keeping, the uniforms of male keepers became more consistent. An official set of clothing was established. The keeper's outer dress uniform, complete with brass lighthouse buttons and a hat, is shown here. The men who wore this uniform presented a certain standard appearance to the public with a sense of pride and prestige. (Authors' collection.)

NORTH POINT MILWAUKEE LIGHTHOUSE KEEPERS, ASSISTANTS, AND COAST GUARDSMEN		
NAME	POSITION	DATE
ANDREW SULLIVAN	KEEPER	1855 - 1856
MICHAEL BURKE	KEEPER	1856 - 1861
WILLIAM BRUIN	KEEPER	1861 - 1871
CHARLES LEWIS SR.	DECLINED	1871
ALONZO BURDICK	KEEPER	1871
DANIEL GREEN	KEEPER	1871 - 1881
GEORGIA STEBBINS	KEEPER	1881 - 1907
SAMUEL ADAMS	INTERIM	1907 - 1909
THOMAS BAILEY	KEEPER	1909 - 1917
MARTIN KNUDSEN	KEEPER	1917 - 1924
REYNOLD JOHNSON	KEEPER	1924 - 1940**
CHARLES LINSMEIER	ASSISTANT	1925 - 1934**
MICHAEL ROTTA	USCG	1928 - 1952**
HERBERT FADEL	ASSISTANT	1936 - 1942**
ALEXANDER WERNER	USCG	1946**
VARIOUS OTHER USCG	USCG	1940 - 1960s**

****Includes assignment at Milwaukee Breakwater Lighthouse. North Point automated in 1943.**

Lighthouses are lifeless bricks, mortar, and machinery if excluding their souls—the light keepers. A select group was responsible for the lighthouses at North Point from 1855 to 1943, when the station was automated. Later, Coast Guard personnel lived at North Point, though most of their duties were at the Milwaukee Breakwater Lighthouse. North Point has been in the care of some special individuals in its lifetime. (Courtesy of Phyllis and Tom Tag and NPLHF.)

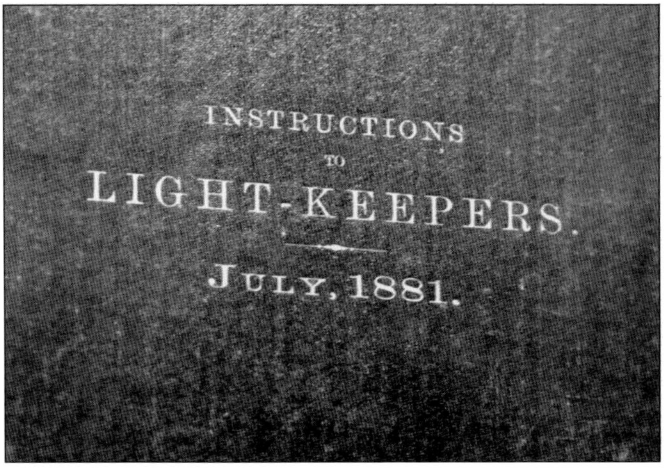

The government tried to standardize certain aspects of the responsibilities at lighthouses, so keepers were given written instructions, in the form of a booklet, for the proper operation of their light station. Considered the "Bible" for light keepers, these thorough documents featured many rules, regulations, and guidelines. They were periodically updated as policies and procedures changed. (Authors' collection.)

The lapel of the keeper's uniform used a specific system to designate rank. The chief keeper—the highest-ranking person at the lighthouse—sported the letter *K* on both lapels, while the first, second, or third assistants would have the numbers 1, 2, or 3. The cap also featured a lighthouse ornament in the middle of the hat. (Authors' collection.)

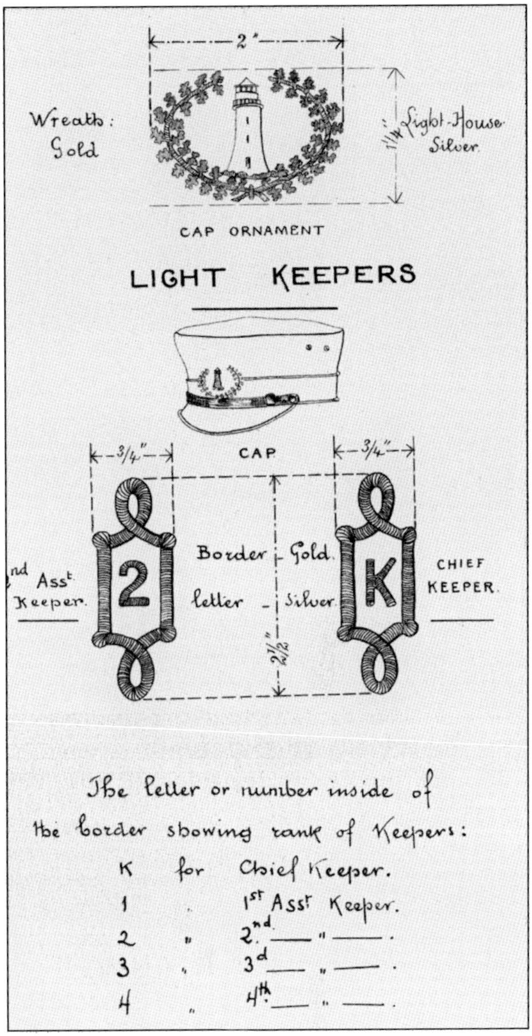

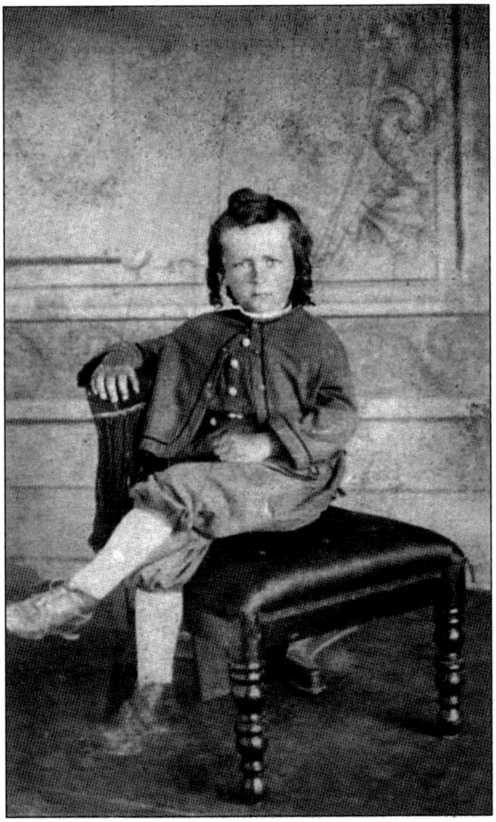

Andrew Sullivan was the first keeper at the new 1855 North Point Lighthouse. He was reassigned there after the closing of the Milwaukee Lighthouse on Wisconsin Street. The first keeper directly appointed to North Point was Irish immigrant Michael Burke, who served from 1856 to 1861. A son of Michael Burke, Thomas Henry Burke, is pictured here around 1868. (Courtesy of Kathleen Redmond.)

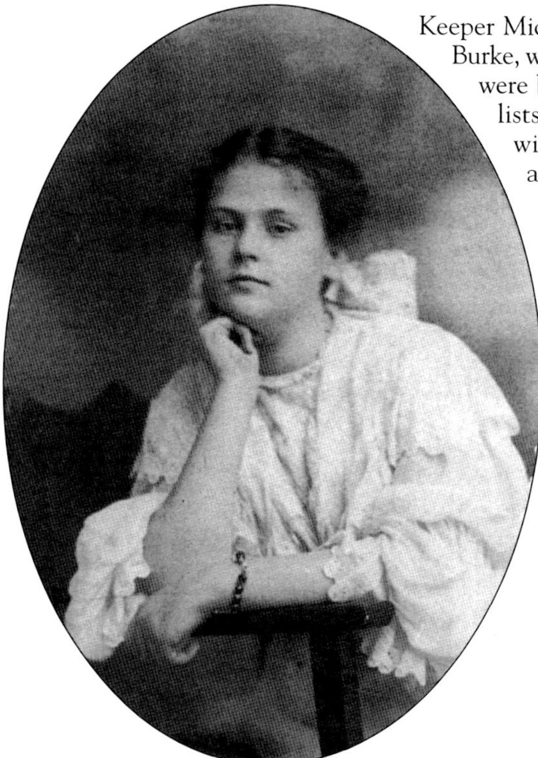

Keeper Michael Burke and his wife, Margaret McGlynn Burke, were blessed with seven children; several of them were born at North Point. The 1860 federal census lists the Burkes as living at the small lighthouse with six children. Two of their children passed away in infancy. After five years at North Point, the Burkes moved to Indiana. The lighthouse keeper's granddaughter, Kathleen Burke, daughter of Thomas Burke, is seen here in Indiana around 1909. (Courtesy of Kathleen Redmond.)

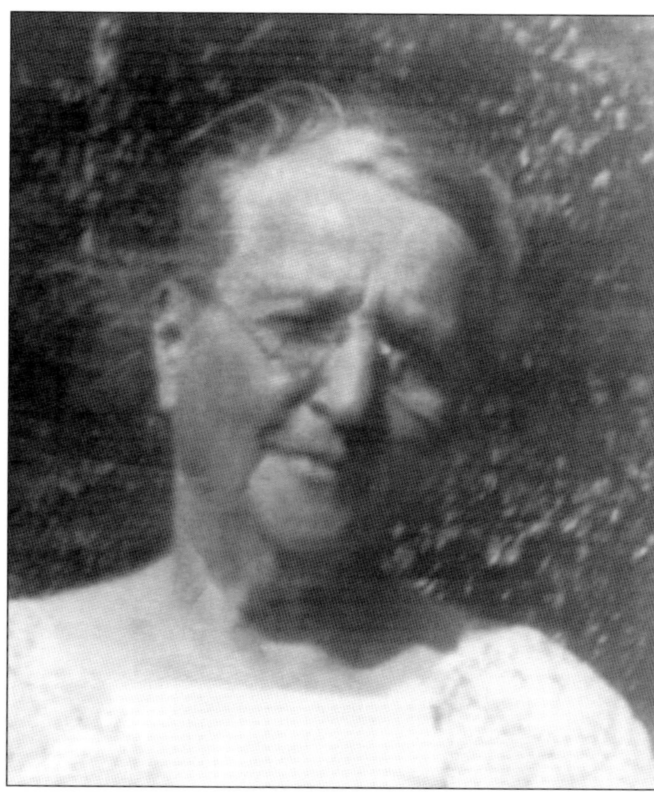

Sarah (Sadie) Burke was born at the North Point Lighthouse in August 1858. She wed at age 22, but was widowed when her husband of only 15 years, Patrick Donahue, died after a long battle with consumption. Sadie Donahue was left to raise their four sons. She is pictured here in 1936, a few years before her death at age 78. (Courtesy of the Donahue family.)

An interesting and unsolved mystery of a very brief assignment at the North Point Lighthouse involves keeper Charles Henry Lewis Sr. Records show that he was supposed to succeed William Bruin as keeper in 1871, but he declined the position for unknown reasons after only a few days. However, his son Charles Lewis Jr. enjoyed a very long tenure at the Old Port Washington Station north of Milwaukee. Census documents place them in Milwaukee by 1860, and Charles Jr. was born in Milwaukee. (Courtesy of Linda Nenn and PWHS.)

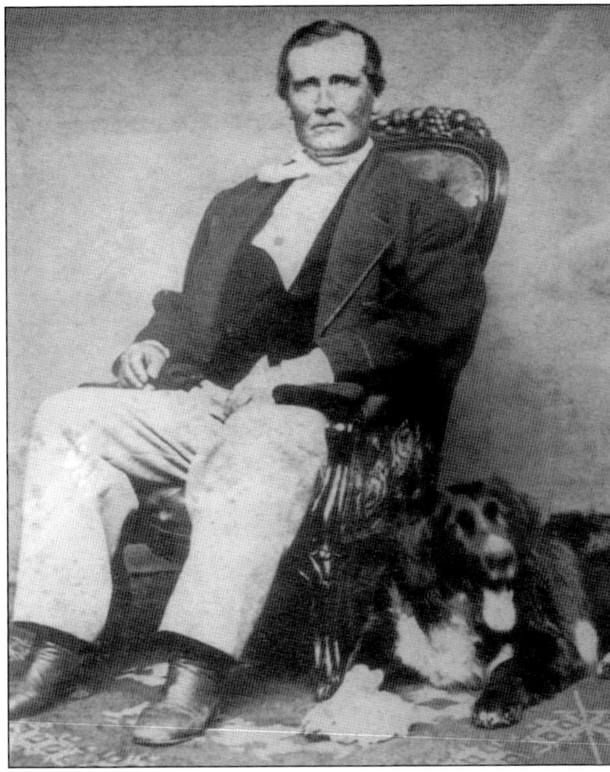

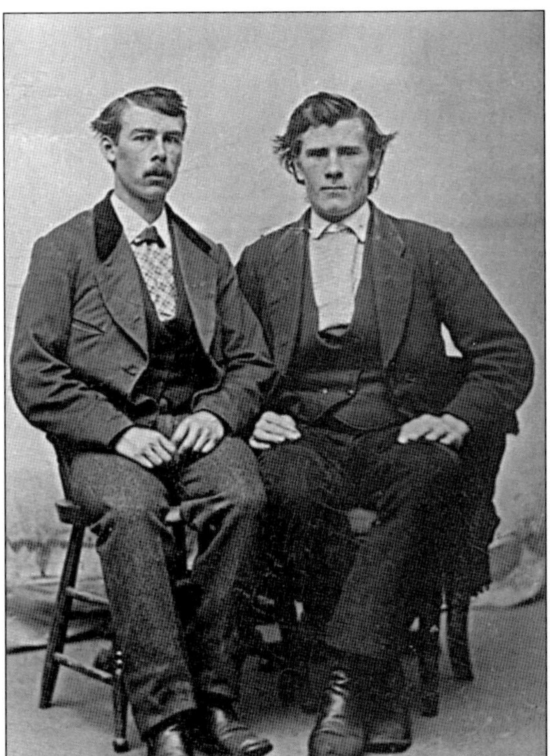

Charles Lewis Sr. (right) and his son Charles Jr. are depicted in this 1870s photograph. Many Wisconsin and Great Lakes lighthouses were staffed by members of the same family (fathers, sons, brothers, uncles, etc.) at various times, including beacons in the Bay of Green Bay and Door County, Wisconsin, among others. In many instances, lighthouse keeping was a family affair, with the spouse and children being thoroughly involved with chores around the station. North Point had no other members of the same family tending it except the father-and-daughter team of Daniel Green and Georgia Stebbins. (Courtesy of Linda Nenn and PWHS.)

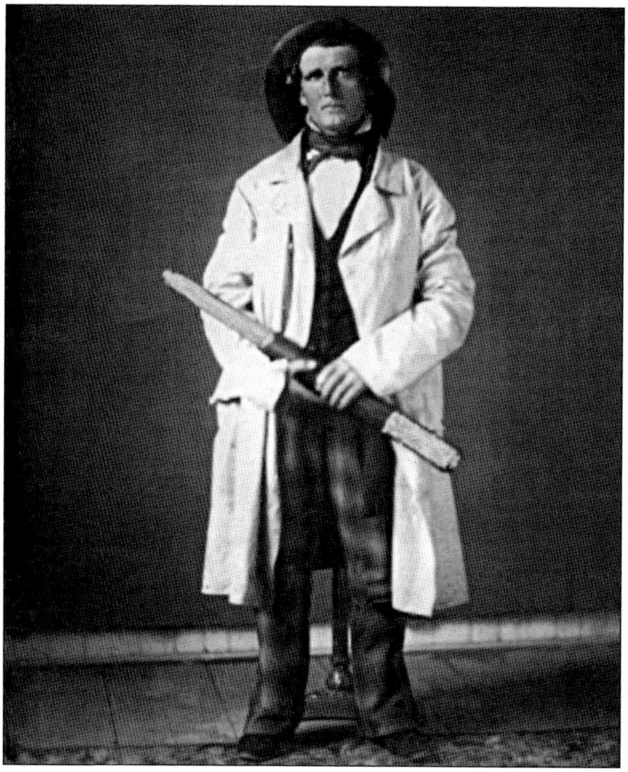

Charles H. Lewis Sr. is seen in this wonderful rare daguerreotype image from around 1845. Found in the pages of a family Bible, it depicts Lewis in some sort of seafaring outfit; he appears to be holding a mariner's telescope. A whaling captain on the East Coast of the United States before venturing to the Midwest, his whereabouts between 1871, when he was in Milwaukee, and 1874, when he was in Port Washington, are unknown. (Courtesy of Linda Nenn and PWHS.)

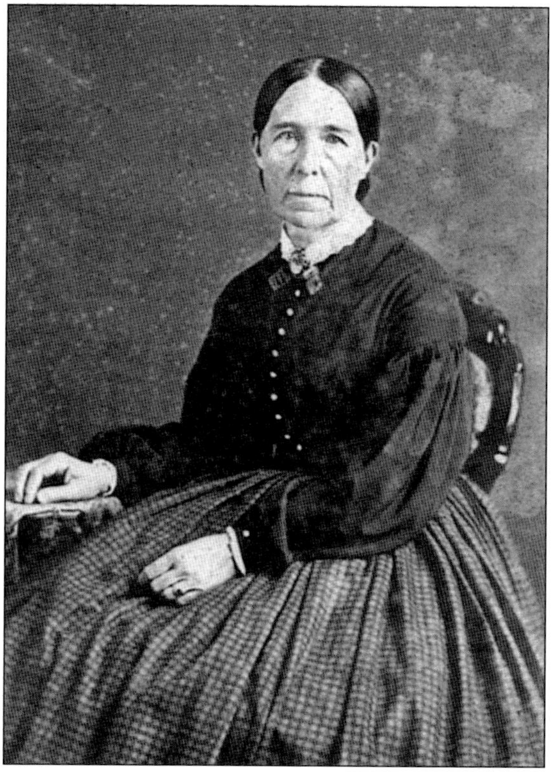

Mariah Prosser Lewis, shown here, was married to Charles Lewis Sr. When her husband became ill, she took over lighthouse duties at the Old Port Washington station. She also persuaded their son Charles Jr. to become a light keeper there. Born in New England, it is not known if Mariah ever stayed at the North Point Milwaukee Lighthouse during her husband's brief two weeks there prior to their many years in Port Washington. She died at the Port Washington Light Station. (Courtesy of Linda Nenn and PWHS.)

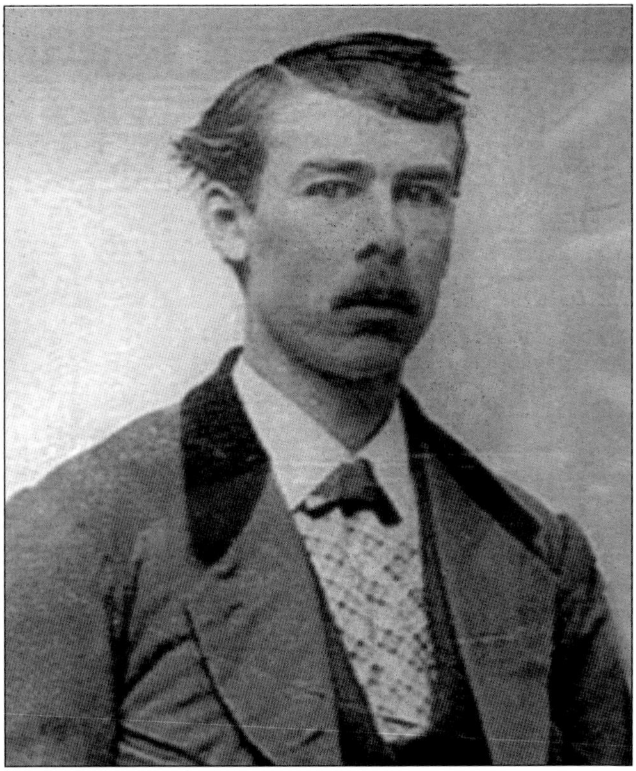

While a fleeting name at North Point, the Lewis family is synonymous with extensive lighthouse duties in Port Washington. Charles Lewis Sr. was a keeper at the Old Port Washington Light Station for six years until his death in 1880. Pictured here is his son Charles Jr., who took over upon his father's death and maintained the Old Port Washington Station and, later, the Port Washington Pier Light for over four decades. (Courtesy of Linda Nenn and PWHS.)

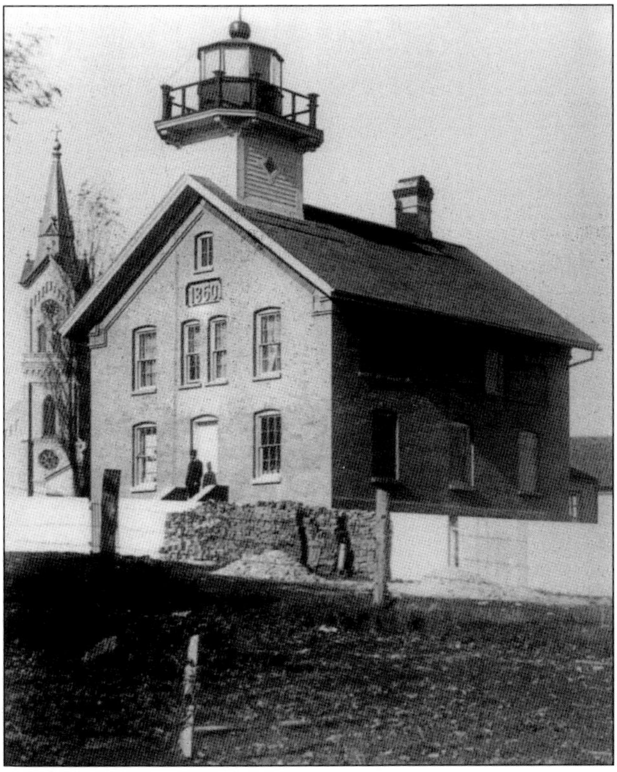

The Old Port Washington Light Station is the next lighthouse up the Wisconsin coastline; it is 25 miles north of the Milwaukee harbor. The date of its completion, 1860, is clearly visible in the brickwork on the front of the building. It was constructed just a few years after the original 1855 North Point Lighthouse. (NARA photograph courtesy of Wayne Sapulski.)

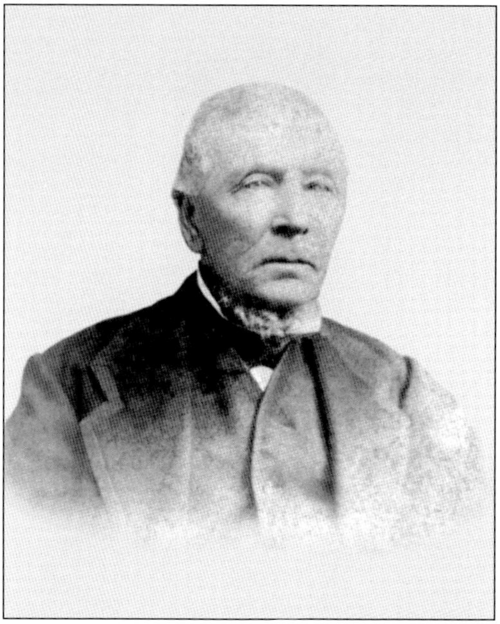

Daniel Kellogg "D.K." Green came to Wisconsin in the 1860s to farm the land. He was appointed keeper at North Point's original brick lighthouse from 1871 to 1881. When Green's poor health began to negatively affect his ability to carry out his lighthouse duties, his daughter Georgia Green Stebbins left urban New York in the early 1870s for the more rural countryside of Milwaukee, Wisconsin, to be with her parents. Georgia almost immediately began taking on some of her father's lighthouse responsibilities. (Courtesy of the Stebbins family.)

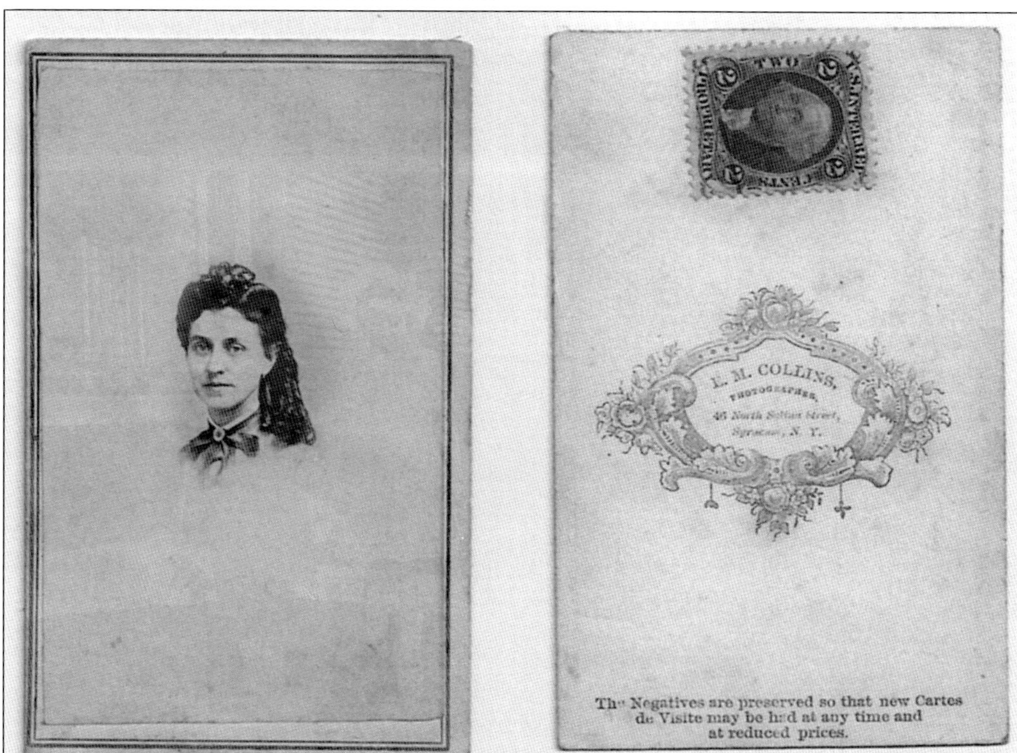

A portrait photographer in Syracuse, New York, captured this image of a youthful Georgia Anna Green prior to her marriage and arrival at Milwaukee and the North Point Lighthouse. Her dark and flowing locks, along with the tiniest hint of a smile, are striking. After she became sick, she left the metropolis of New York City and evolved into a fit and confident female lighthouse keeper. (Courtesy of the Stebbins family.)

Lemuel Dibble Stebbins was born in Bethel, Connecticut, in 1841. He became a watchmaker and jeweler in New York who one day wanted to specialize in diamonds. He married Georgia Anna Green in 1866. They had three children: two daughters, Emma and Lillian, who both died in infancy, and a son, Albert, who lived into his 60s. (Courtesy of the Stebbins family.)

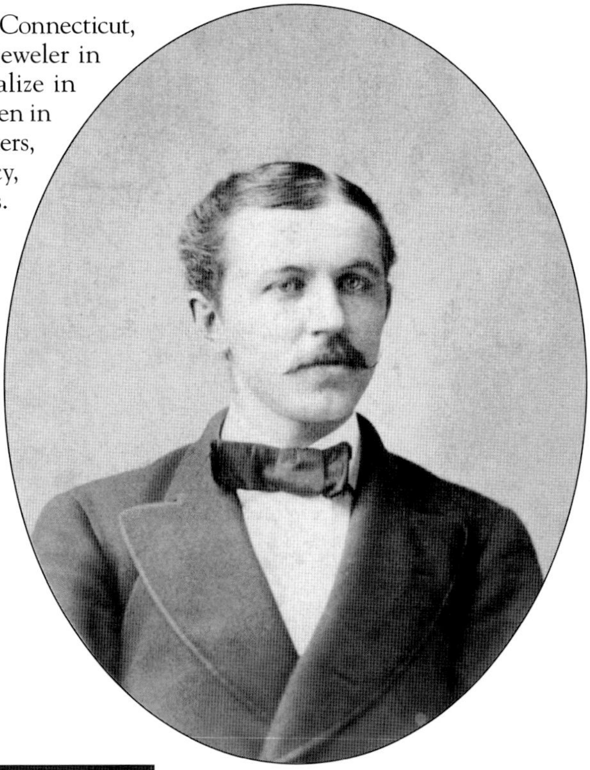

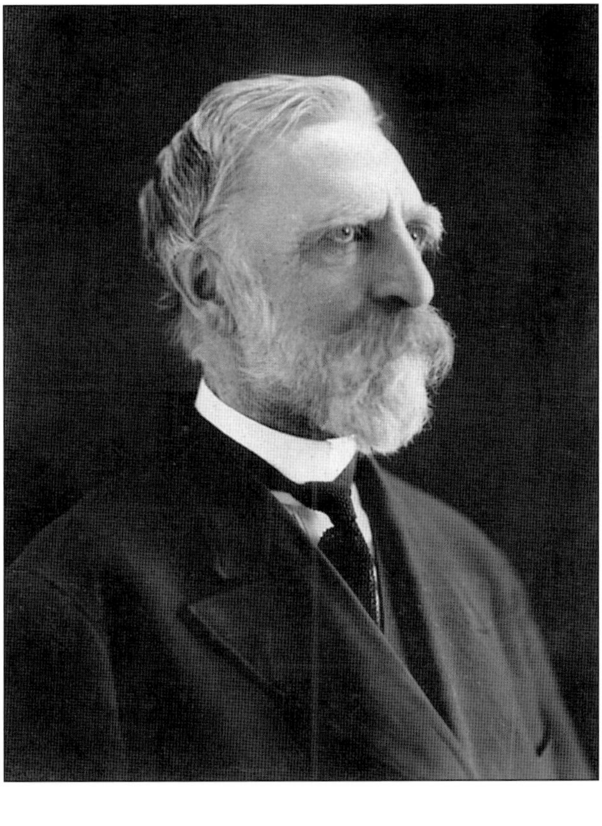

Lemuel Stebbins came to Milwaukee in the early 1870s and resided there for about 60 years. Much of that time was spent at the North Point Lighthouse. His jewelry business on Mason Street served him well for nearly 40 years until his retirement. Stebbins died in Milwaukee in 1930 at the age of 89. Georgia Stebbins preceded her husband in death by about nine years. (Courtesy of the Stebbins family.)

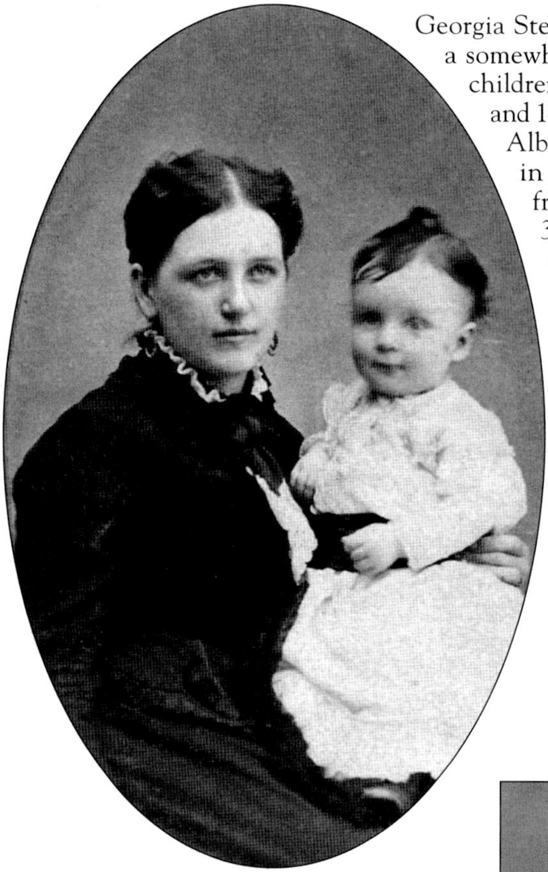

Georgia Stebbins wanted a family and must have had a somewhat difficult time after losing her first two children, both girls, in very early childhood in 1867 and 1869, respectively. Her next child, a son named Albert, was born at the North Point Lighthouse in June 1875 and is featured in this portrait from around 1877. Mrs. Stebbins was around 30 years old in this photograph. (Courtesy of the Stebbins family.)

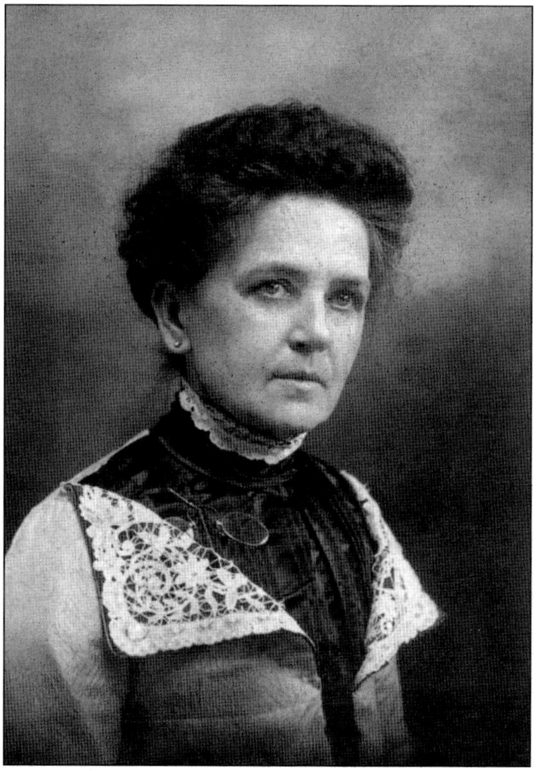

Georgia Green was born in Jordan, New York, in 1846. Suffering from tuberculosis at an early age, she temporarily left her husband, Lemuel Stebbins. She traveled to Milwaukee, where she found her father, Daniel Kellogg (D.K.) Green, the lighthouse keeper at North Point, in poor health. Lake Michigan breezes had a positive effect on her condition. Not formally recognized by the government, Georgia likely tended the lighthouse for about a decade due to her father's sickliness and then served officially the longest tenure of any keeper at North Point—over 25 years. This stunning portrait from around 1895 depicts a remarkable woman of strong will, intelligence, and determination. (Courtesy of the Stebbins family.)

Lighthouse logbooks were considered official government documents. Keeper Georgia Stebbins made daily entries concerning weather conditions, work performed, and any unusual circumstances. Most logbooks are not exciting to read and have many dull records, but occasional notes can give valuable insights into daily lighthouse life. Documentation of shipwrecks and rescues are a bonus for the lighthouse researcher. Note that at the top of the ledger, in June 1907, the station is called Milwaukee Point. (Courtesy of NARA.)

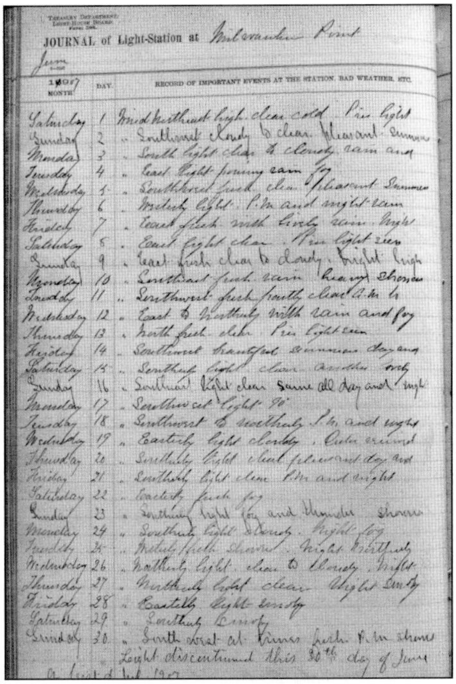
JOURNAL of Light-Station at Milwaukee Point

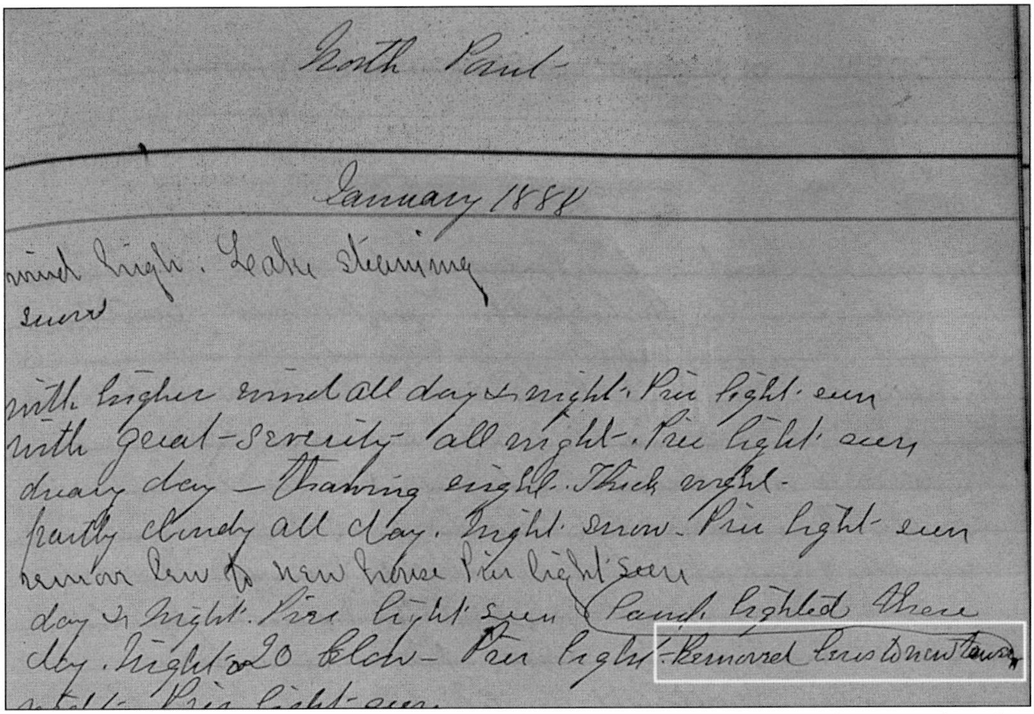
North Point-

January 1888

Researching through pages upon pages of logbook entries can be tedious and unrewarding, but every so often one stumbles upon an important piece of information. This January 10, 1888, entry from keeper Georgia Stebbins simply states, "Bernard lens to new tower. Lamp lighted there." The keeper stated a very important date in North Point's history—the new, second lighthouse had been lit for the very first time. (Courtesy of NARA.)

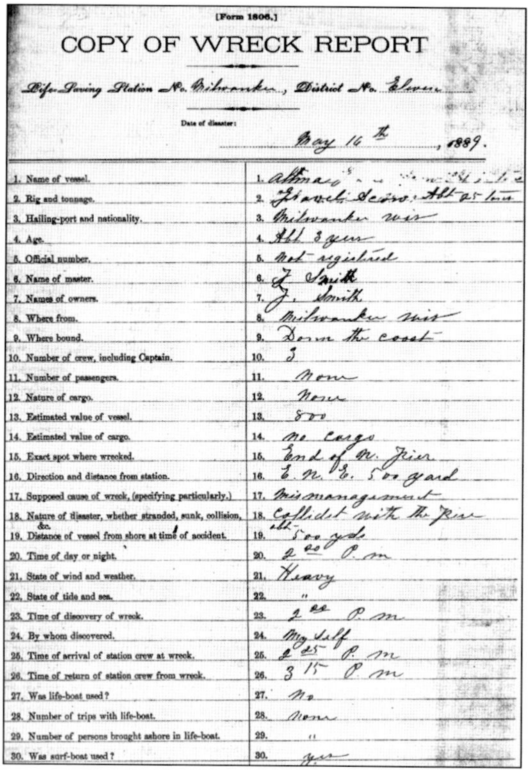

[Form 1806.]

COPY OF WRECK REPORT

Life-Saving Station No. Milwaukee, District No. Eleven

Date of disaster: May 16th, 1889.

1. Name of vessel.	1. Alma
2. Rig and tonnage.	2. Gravel Scow. Abt 25 tons
3. Hailing-port and nationality.	3. Milwaukee Wis
4. Age.	4. Abt 3 yrs
5. Official number.	5. Not registered
6. Name of master.	6. J. Smith
7. Names of owners.	7. J. Smith
8. Where from.	8. Milwaukee Wis
9. Where bound.	9. Down the coast
10. Number of crew, including Captain.	10. 3
11. Number of passengers.	11. None
12. Nature of cargo.	12. None
13. Estimated value of vessel.	13. 800
14. Estimated value of cargo.	14. No cargo
15. Exact spot where wrecked.	15. End of N. Pier
16. Direction and distance from station.	16. E. N. E. 500 yard
17. Supposed cause of wreck, (specifying particularly.)	17. Mismanagement
18. Nature of disaster, whether stranded, sunk, collision, &c.	18. Collided with the Pier
19. Distance of vessel from shore at time of accident.	19. abt 500 yds
20. Time of day or night.	20. 2 00 P.m
21. State of wind and weather.	21. Heavy
22. State of tide and sea.	22. "
23. Time of discovery of wreck.	23. 2 00 P.m
24. By whom discovered.	24. Myself
25. Time of arrival of station crew at wreck.	25. 2 25 P.m
26. Time of return of station crew from wreck.	26. 3 15 P.m
27. Was life-boat used?	27. No
28. Number of trips with life-boat.	28. None
29. Number of persons brought ashore in life-boat.	29. "
30. Was surf-boat used?	30. yes

When vessels sank on the Great Lakes, an official statement known as a wreck report was filled out. The document pictured here is the account of the damage to the gravel scow *Alma*, which hit the north pier in Milwaukee on May 16, 1889, during stormy weather. The ship was repaired but later sank just off North Point in May 1892. (Courtesy of MPL.)

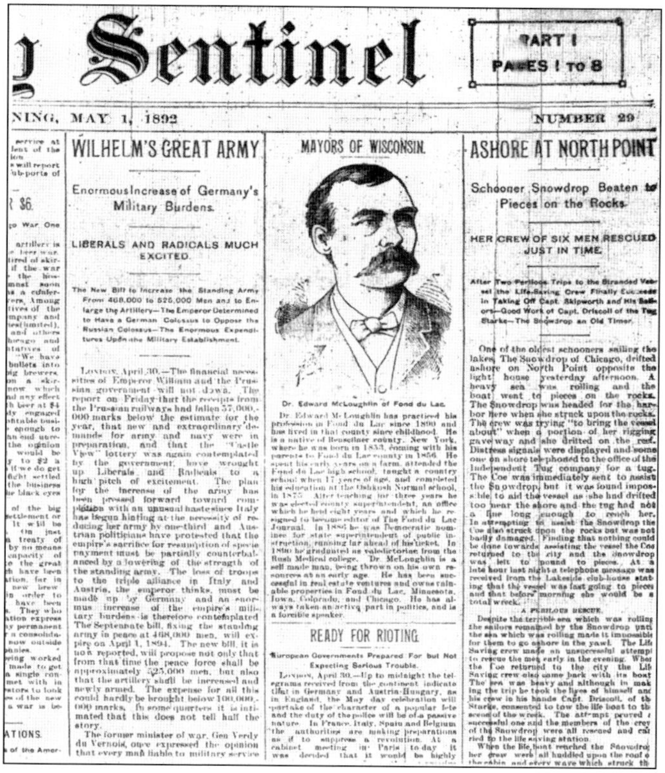

Sentinel

PART I PAGES 1 TO 8

NING, MAY 1, 1892 — NUMBER 29

WILHELM'S GREAT ARMY

Enormous Increase of Germany's Military Burdens.

LIBERALS AND RADICALS MUCH EXCITED.

MAYORS OF WISCONSIN.

Dr. Edward McLoughlin of Fond du Lac.

READY FOR RIOTING.

ASHORE AT NORTH POINT

Schooner Snowdrop Beaten to Pieces on the Rocks.

HER CREW OF SIX MEN RESCUED JUST IN TIME.

Milwaukee and North Point saw their share of shipwrecks. Several notable incidents occurred near the lighthouse. The *Milwaukee Sentinel* contained a front-page article regarding the schooner *Snowdrop* on May 1, 1892. Heavy seas damaged the vessel, and it drifted upon the rocks off the lighthouse; eventually, the ship broke into pieces. Luckily, her six-man crew was saved. Three weeks later, the scow *Alma* was also wrecked off of North Point. (Authors' collection.)

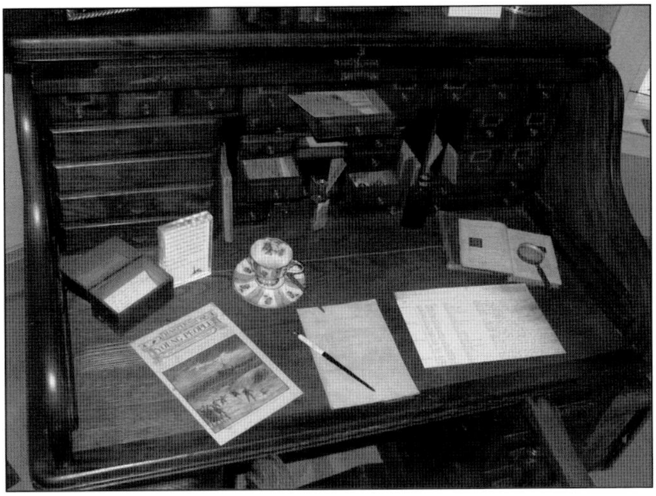

A lighthouse keeper's desk around 1900 would have looked much like the display featured today at the North Point Lighthouse. The station's logbook would be prominently displayed, along with writing implements. Nautical books and artifacts would likely be nearby. The various drawers would contain select notes and lighthouse-related objects. The lighthouse inspector would notice the organization of the desk area when he came to visit. (Authors' collection.)

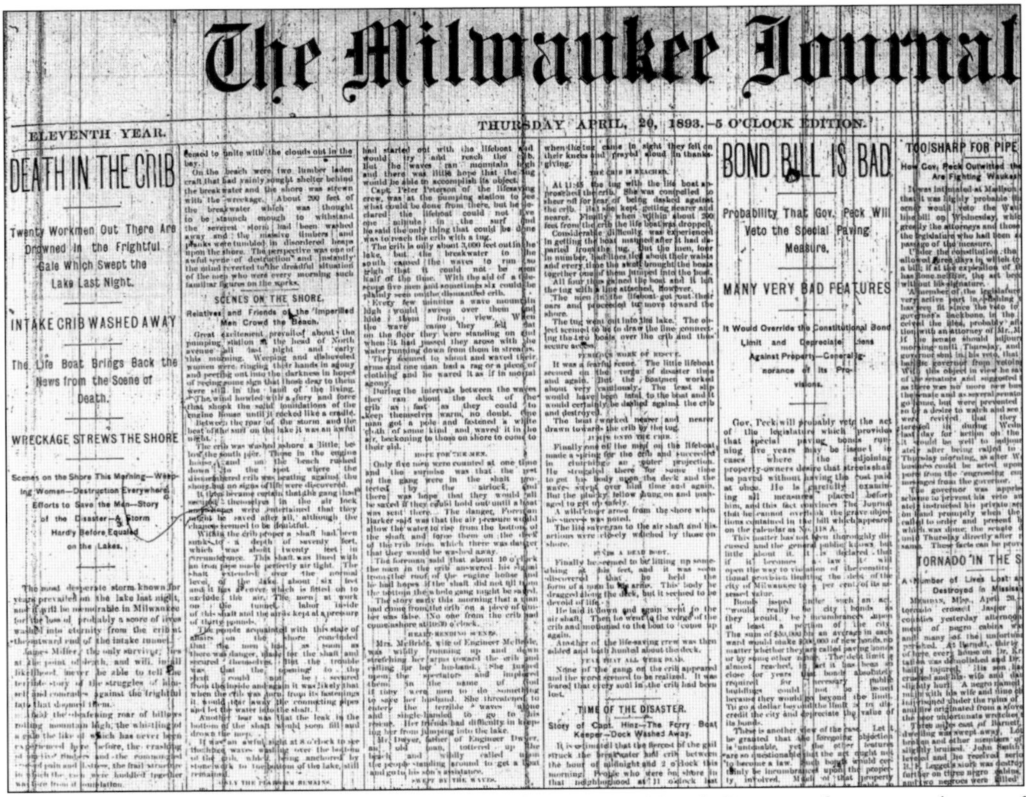

The Milwaukee Journal

ELEVENTH YEAR. THURSDAY APRIL, 20, 1893.—5 O'CLOCK EDITION.

DEATH IN THE CRIB

Twenty Workmen Out There Are Drowned in the Frightful Gale Which Swept the Lake Last Night.

INTAKE CRIB WASHED AWAY

The Life Boat Brings Back the News from the Scene of Death.

WRECKAGE STREWS THE SHORE

SCENES ON THE SHORE.

TIME OF THE DISASTER.

BOND BILL IS BAD

Probability That Gov. Peck Will Veto the Special Paving Measure.

MANY VERY BAD FEATURES

TOO SHARP FOR PIPE

TORNADO IN THE S

Keeper Georgia Stebbins was within viewing distance at North Point and witnessed one of Milwaukee's deadliest lake tragedies. In April 1893, work crews were excavating a new intake for the city's water supply off the shore of North Point in Lake Michigan. A terrible storm produced huge waves that trapped men in a chamber below the lake. One lucky soul survived and 15 workers perished. Having no telephone, Stebbins notified the Milwaukee Life Saving Service by venturing to a phone in the neighborhood. (Authors' collection.)

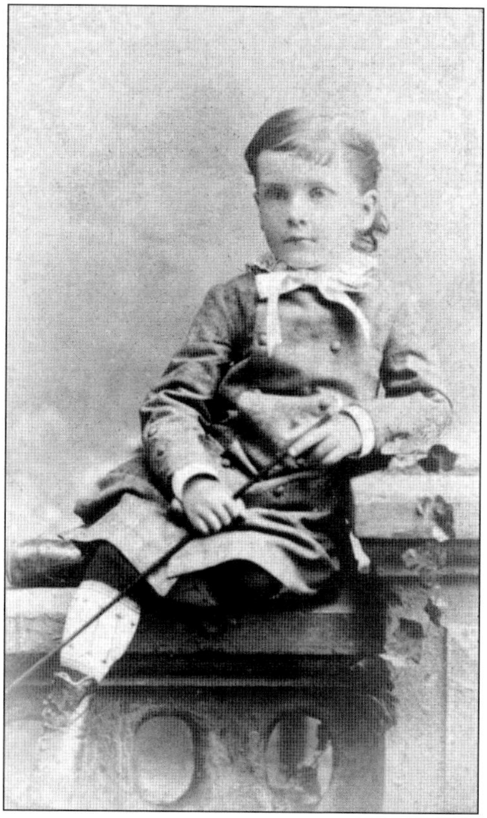

Albert Kellogg Stebbins was born at the original North Point Lighthouse in June 1875. His grandparents immigrated to the United States from Great Britain in the 17th century. Some ancestors settled in Massachusetts, with others in Connecticut and New York. Several were involved in the Revolutionary War, as well as the War of 1812. (Courtesy of the Stebbins family.)

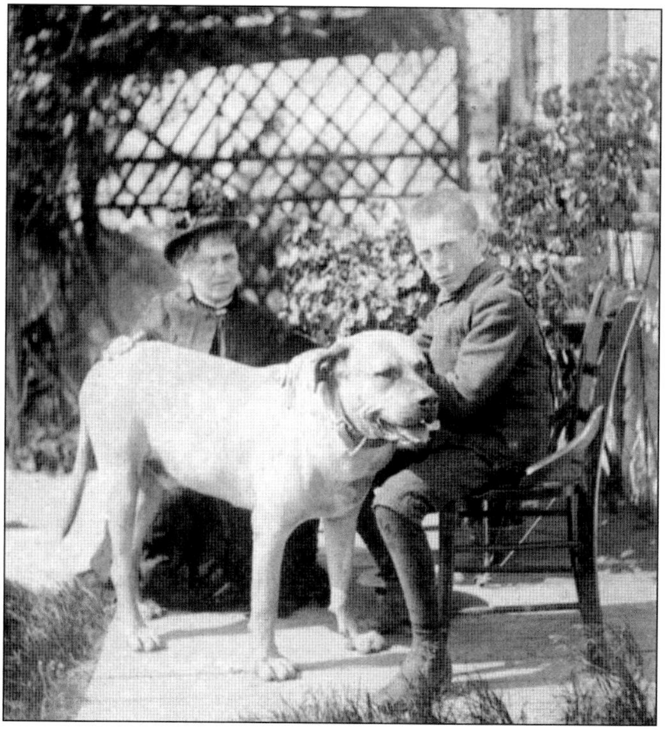

Georgia and Lemuel Stebbins's son Albert is shown here around the late 1880s with their enormous dog Tappan. They are sitting outside the rear of the first North Point Lighthouse, which was made of cream city brick. This picture was taken not long before the lighthouse was no longer in use and the second light at North Point, with a new metal lighthouse and keeper's residence, was finished and in operation. (Courtesy of the Stebbins family.)

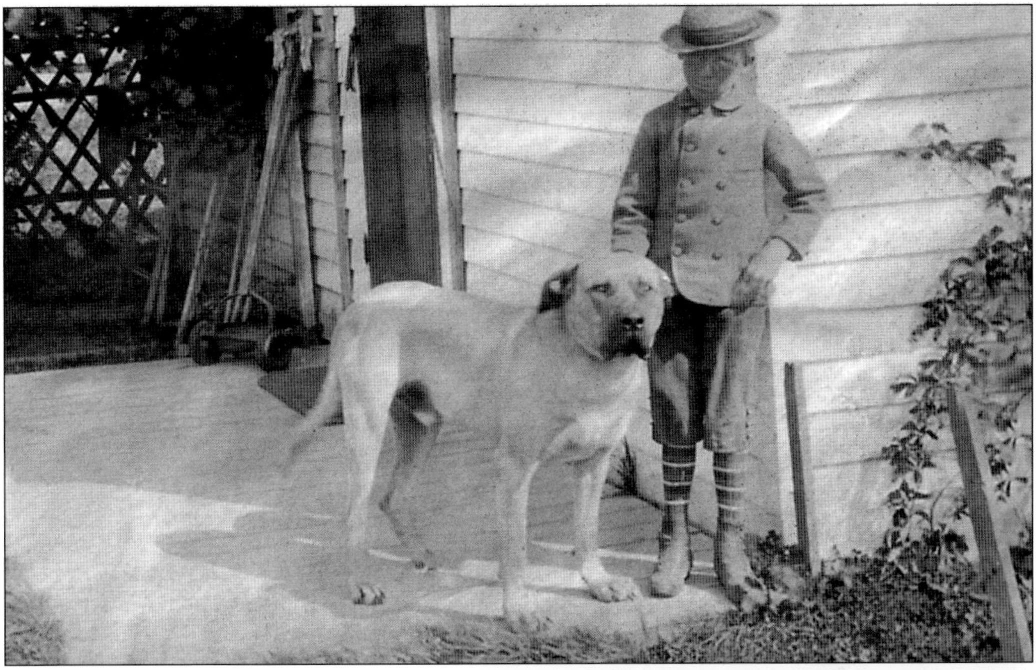

This late-1880s photograph of Albert Stebbins depicts a storage building at the rear of the original North Point Lighthouse. The massive, powerful dog is a mastiff. Albert's clothing, with his knee britches and button shoes, was typical of young male children of that era. Note the push lawn mower in the background—perhaps that was one of the youngster's chores at the lighthouse. (Courtesy of the Stebbins family.)

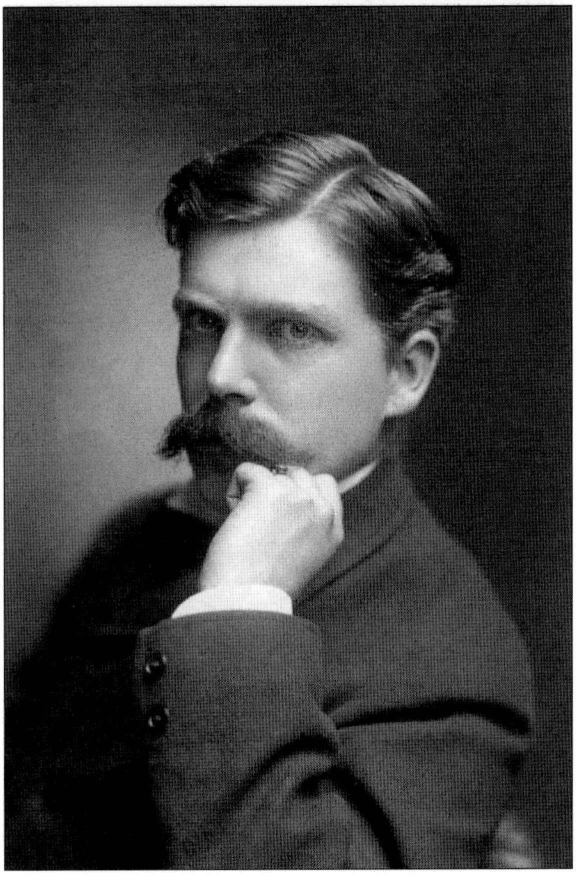

After his grade school days, young Albert Stebbins left Wisconsin for his continuing education and became a cadet at Barker Hall in Michigan City, Indiana. In 1891, keeper Georgia Stebbins wrote a letter to government lighthouse officials with a request to visit her son there. Permission was granted from the lighthouse inspector, but she ultimately decided not to leave North Point. Keeper Stebbins spent very few days away from North Point in her decades there. (Courtesy of the Stebbins family.)

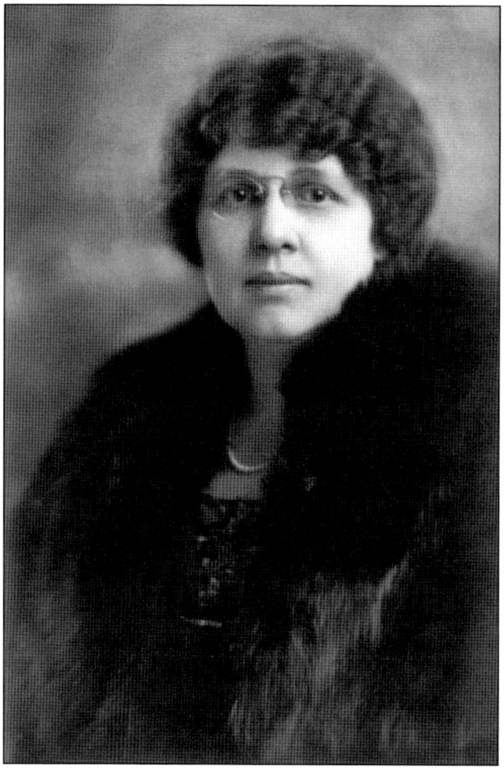

Anna Kemper Whittemore was married to Albert Stebbins in September 1897. They had two children, Rowland and Albert Jr., who were both born at the North Point Lighthouse. The sons attended St. John's Military Academy. Anna and Albert were members of St. Paul's Episcopal Church in Milwaukee. Their status in Milwaukee society was quite high. Frequently entertaining friends in their Farwell Avenue home, Anna also dabbled in poetry and wrote a short patriotic poem entitled "Women of America." (Courtesy of the Stebbins family.)

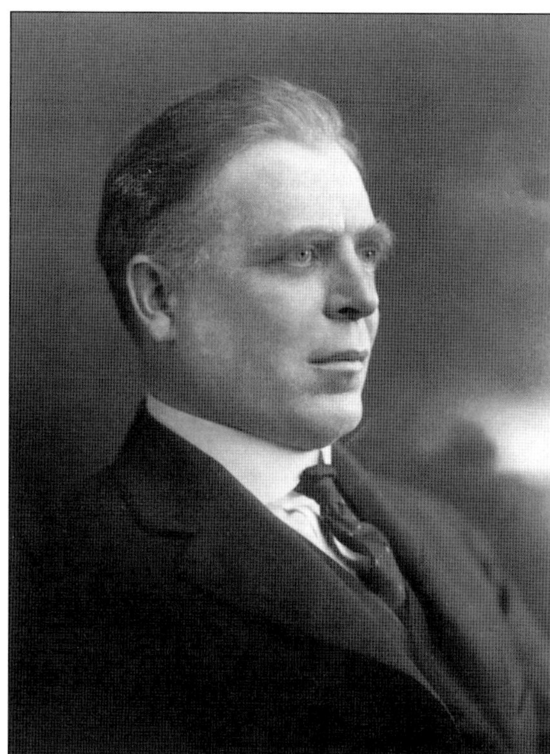

Following his time as a student at the Milwaukee High School, Albert Stebbins Sr. received an appointment to attend the US Military Academy at West Point, New York. However, defective vision prevented him from continuing military training there or a possible military career. Stebbins ultimately returned to Milwaukee, attended law school, formed a partnership, and became a prominent Milwaukee attorney. (Courtesy of the Stebbins family.)

Government rules required keepers to visit the light every four hours. The lens was visible from Georgia Stebbins's bedroom window, and she was able to awaken hourly on her own to check on the lamp. The clockwork apparatus that rotated the lens had to be wound routinely. Stebbins climbed these stairs thousands of times over the years. (Authors' collection.)

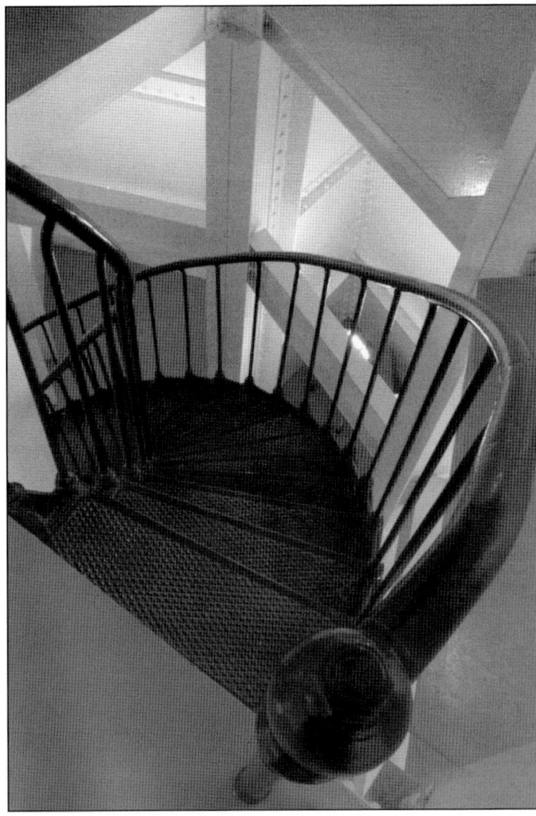

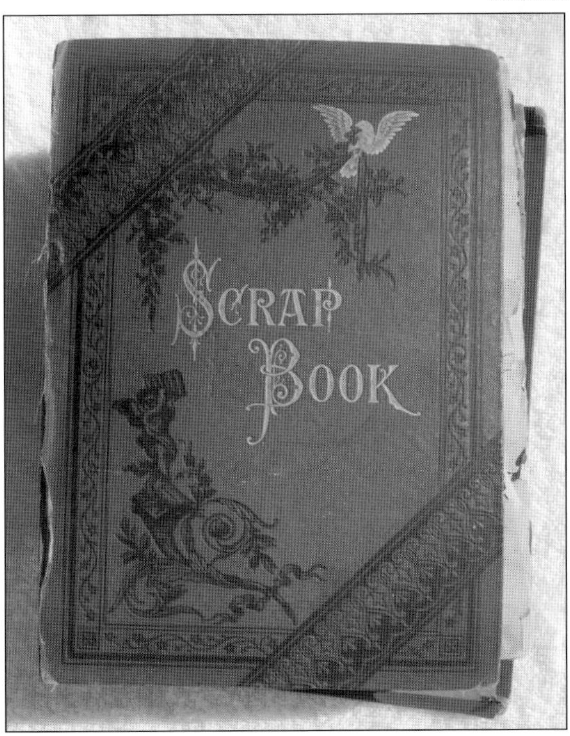

Keeper Georgia Stebbins kept a scrapbook while at the North Point Lighthouse. The book pictured here contained newspaper clippings pertaining to the lighthouses, including some vintage photographs, school papers involving her son Albert, a few recipes, and other miscellaneous family information. This artifact is an excellent tool to allow the researcher to look back to a different age. The album resides at the lighthouse in the safe hands of the North Point Lighthouse Friends. (Courtesy of the Stebbins family.)

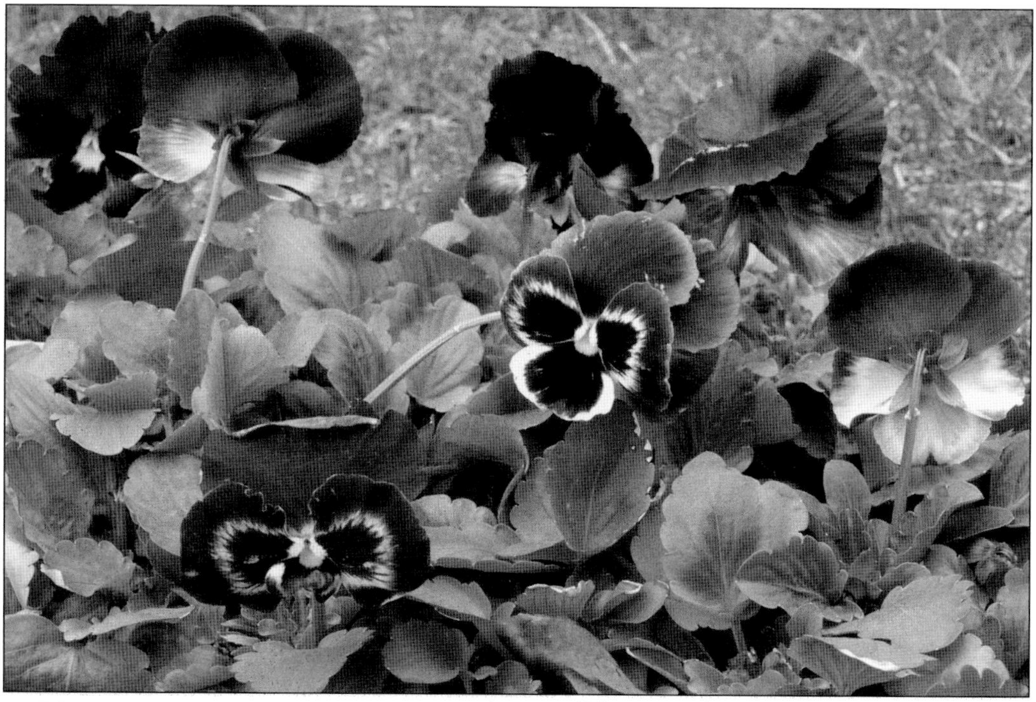

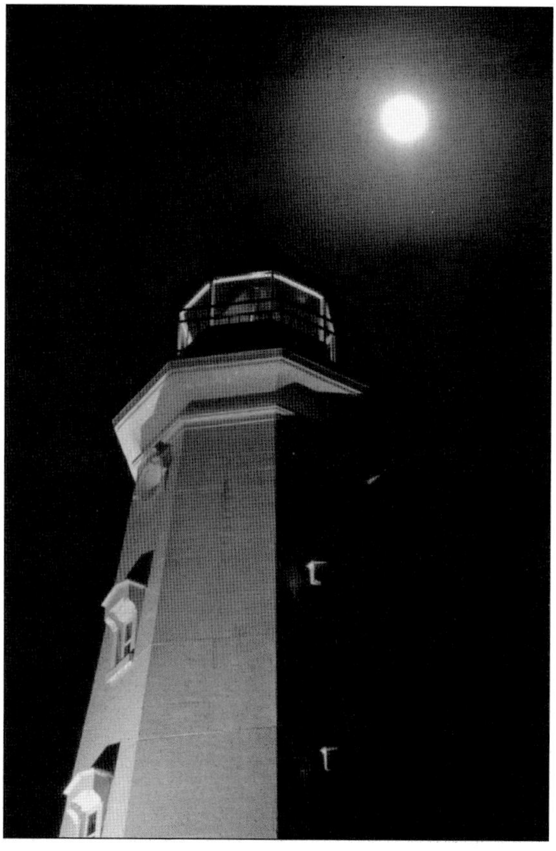

The grounds at North Point were well maintained by keeper Georgia Stebbins. Newspaper accounts mention her flower gardens of pansies and verbenas and the neatly managed lawn. Her scrapbook also contained gladiolus bulb labels from a florist in Queens, New York. The impeccably maintained lighthouse and keeper's home complimented their surroundings and together were termed "the jewel of Lake Park." (Authors' collection.)

Occasionally, interesting notations are found in the official book of a light station. A very brief entry in the lighthouse logbook was penned by Georgia Stebbins on the night of January 28, 1888. Gazing skyward, the lighthouse keeper noticed a celestial phenomenon. In the log, she simply wrote, "Total eclipse of the moon. Clear beautiful night." It must have been quite a sight. (Authors' collection.)

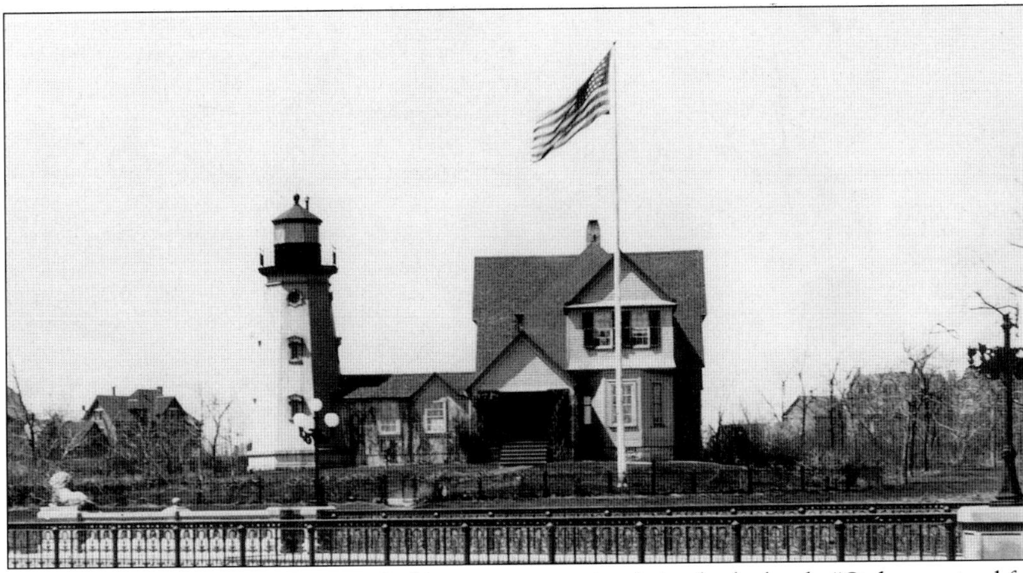

On June 19, 1907, keeper Georgia Stebbins wrote succinctly in the logbook, "Order received for discontinuance of light June 30." Stebbins's final entry was simple as well, "Light discontinued this 30th day of June 1907. Correct Statement. Georgia A. Stebbins, Keeper." No other notation was made. This proud light keeper of over 30 years ended her North Point tenure quietly with no fanfare. North Point looked much like this photograph when Mrs. Stebbins retired. (Courtesy of MPL.)

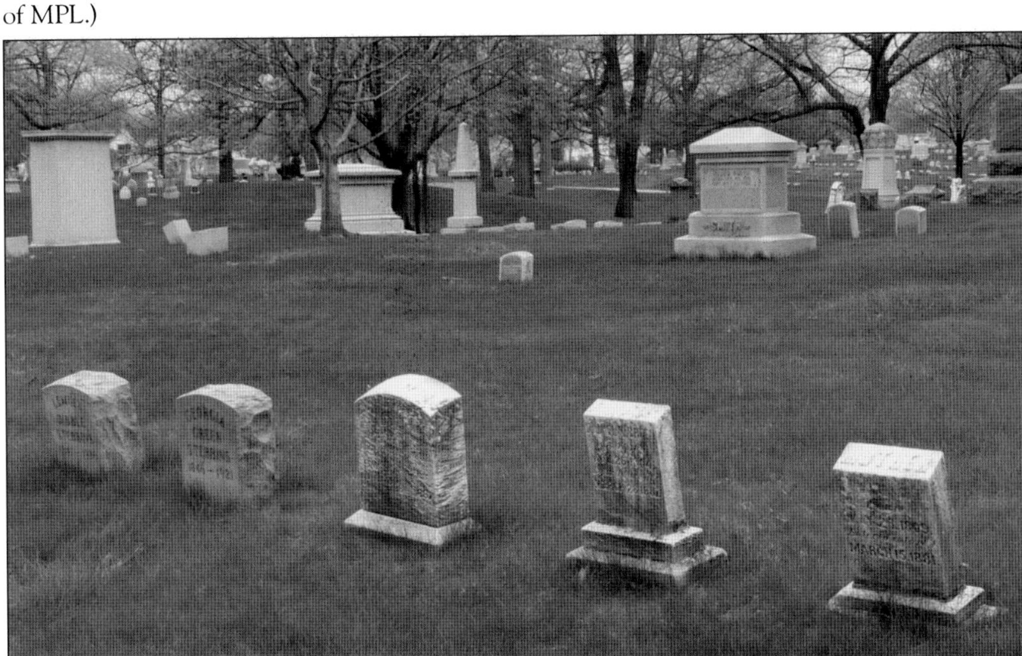

The Forest Home cemetery on Milwaukee's south side is the final resting place of some of the Stebbins family. Wife and husband Georgia and Lemuel Stebbins, as well as Mrs. Stebbins's parents, Daniel Kellogg Green and Catherine Sawyer Green, are buried here. Georgia died in 1921 at age 74. Many of Milwaukee's founding families are also interred at Forest Home. (Authors' collection.)

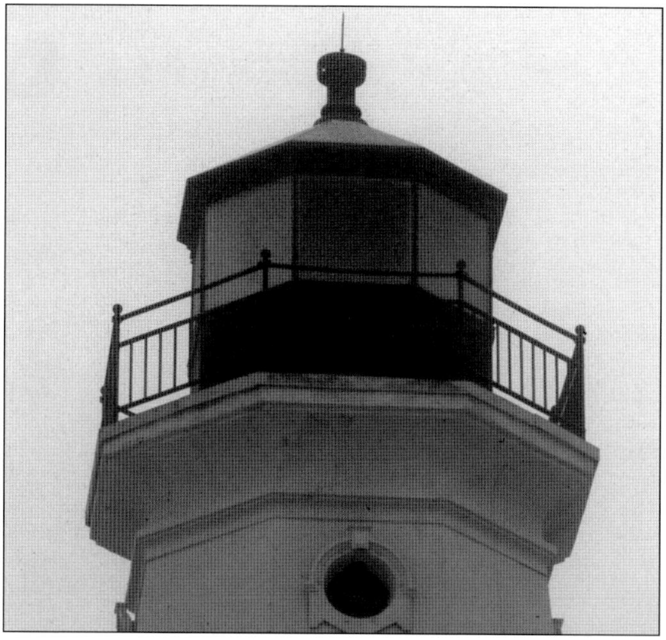

North Point was at a crossroads in 1907. The government decommissioned the light, but maritime reaction was overwhelmingly negative. Milwaukee business interests temporarily funded the costs of the lighthouse for two years. The Lighthouse Service thought of moving the light or raising its height. A proposed lightship in Milwaukee's harbor was in the planning stages. The North Point Lighthouse survived and was officially reopened in 1909. A taller tower was completed in 1912. (Authors' collection.)

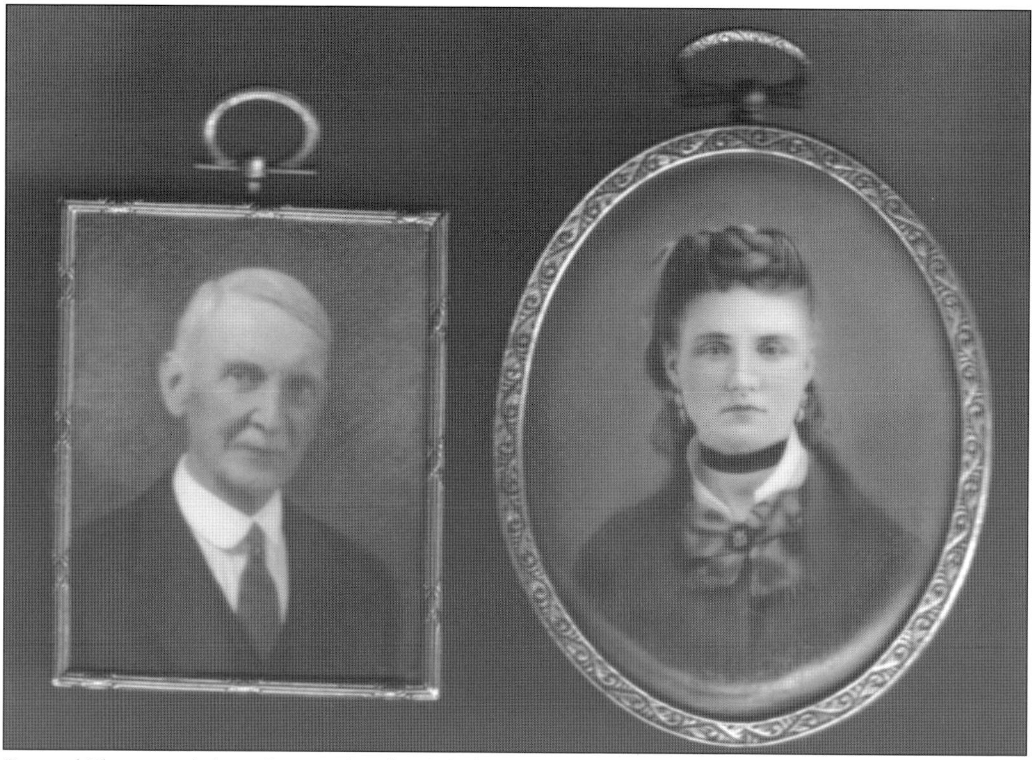

Samuel Plummer Adams Jr. was the chief clerk in the Milwaukee office of the Lighthouse Division of the US Geological Survey. An engineer by profession, he and his wife, Fannie Cate Powers, kept the North Point beacon functioning during the interim time between 1907 and 1909, when there was no official keeper. They spent one winter and two summers at North Point. (Courtesy of Barbara Valovic.)

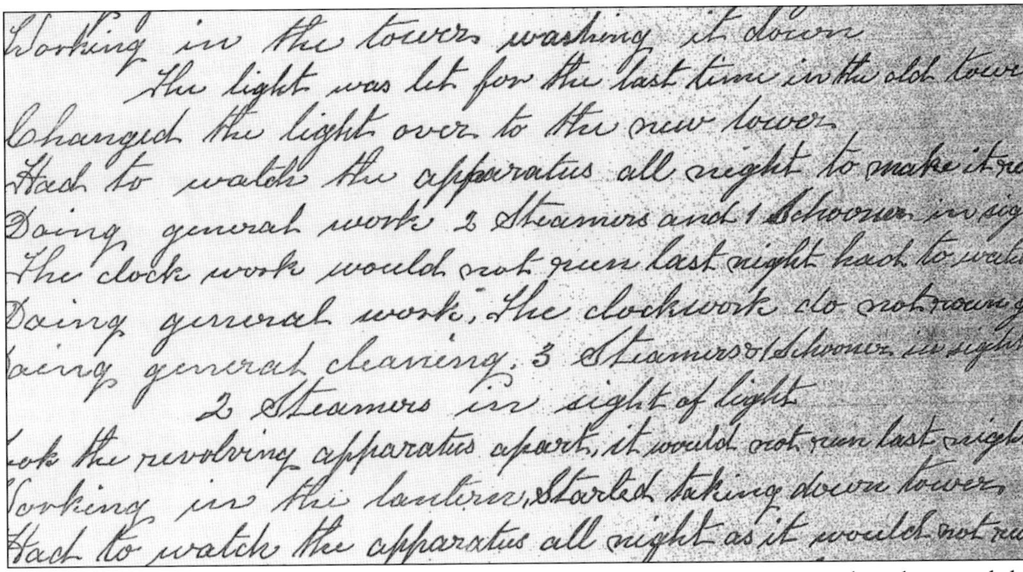

Working in the tower washing it down
The light was lit for the last time in the old tower
Changed the light over to the new tower
Had to watch the apparatus all night to make it ru
Doing general work 2 Steamers and 1 Schooner in sig
The clock work would not run last night had to watc
Doing general work, The clockwork do not run
aing general cleaning, 3 Steamers & 1 Schooner in sight
2 Steamers in sight of light
ok the revolving apparatus apart, it would not run last night
orking in the lantern, Started taking down tower
Had to watch the apparatus all night as it would not ru

The September 1912 logbook of keeper Thomas Bailey mentions routine general work around the station and the number of schooners and steamer vessels observed on Lake Michigan. He also details the conversion from the old 1888 tower to the new, taller 1912 lighthouse. Of particular note is the recording of the failure of the revolving lens apparatus to work properly on several nights and his efforts to fix it. (Courtesy of NPLHF.)

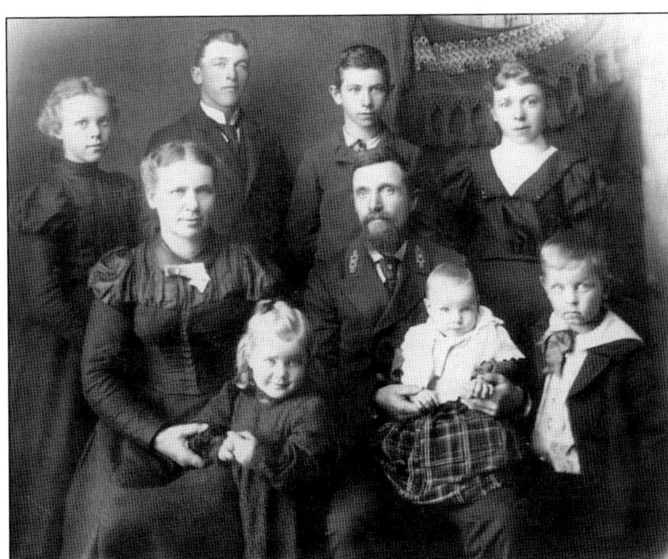

North Point's next keeper, Martin Knudsen, married in 1875 on Washington Island, Wisconsin. The young lighthouse keeper, dressed in his official government issued attire (center), is pictured here with his family in the 1890s. His wife, Theresa Koyen Knudsen, is at his side. The Knudsen children include Edward William, Agnes Margrete, Martin Arthur, Myrtle Marie, Mildred Theresa, and Harold Peter. The Knudsens also adopted a foster son named Haldor Arni Gudmunsen. (Courtesy of WIA.)

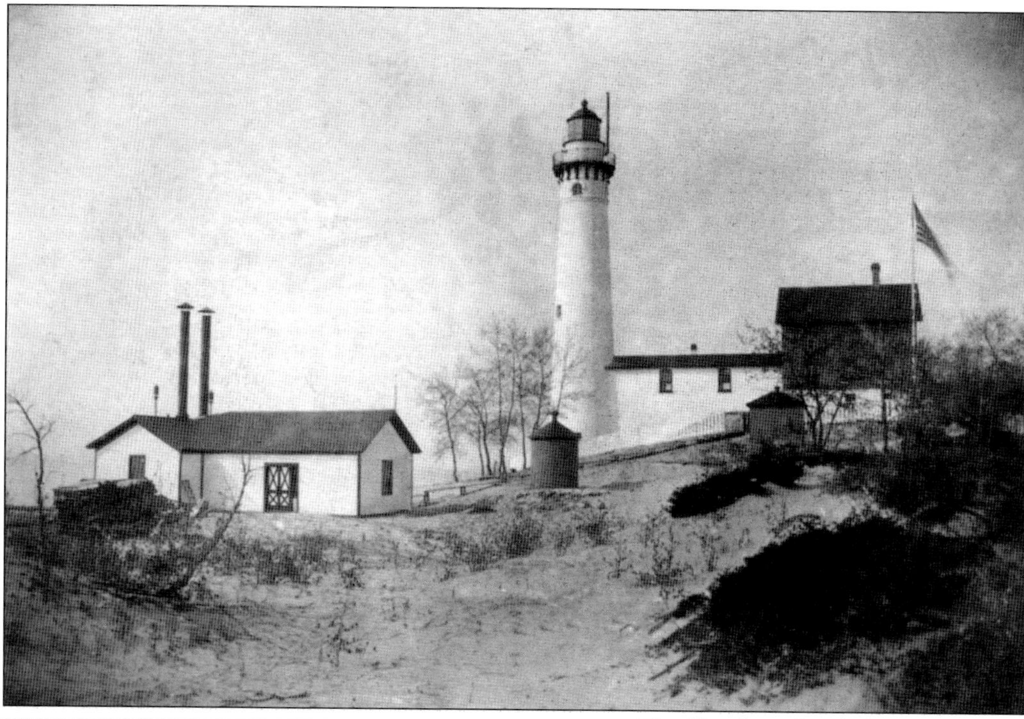

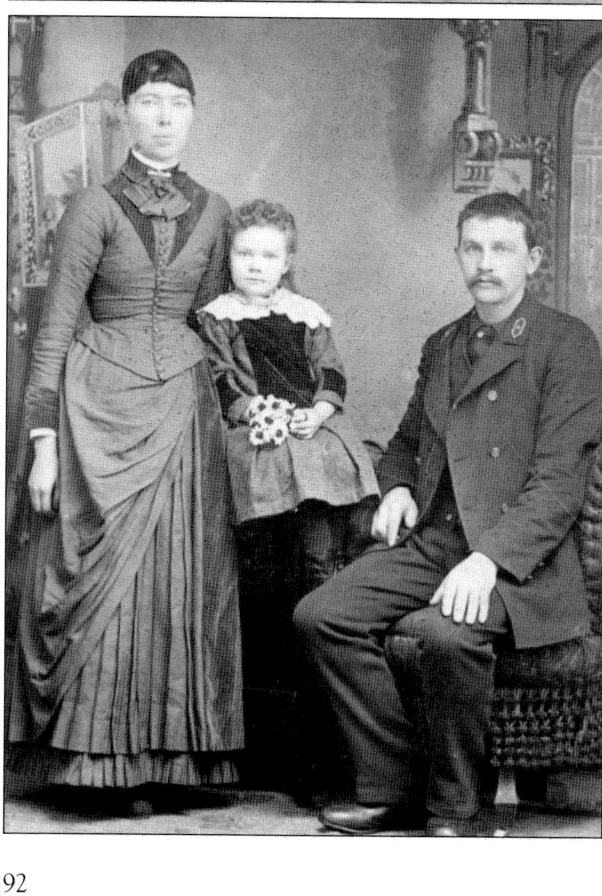

The Knudsen family had a connection to the South Manitou Island Lighthouse on northern Lake Michigan. North Point keeper Martin Knudsen and his brother Nelson were both stationed there in the 1880s. During some of those years, they served together on the island. Both Knudsens eventually attained the ranking of chief keeper, the highest possible position at South Manitou. (Courtesy of Connie Sena.)

Nelson "Nels" Knudsen, younger brother of Martin Knudsen, also had a long career in the lighthouse service, serving 28 years. It was not uncommon for brothers, fathers and sons, and other relatives to take up the light-keeping profession. Nels tended five different lighthouses in Wisconsin and Michigan. He is pictured here around 1888 with his wife, Emma, and daughter Mary. (Courtesy of WIA.)

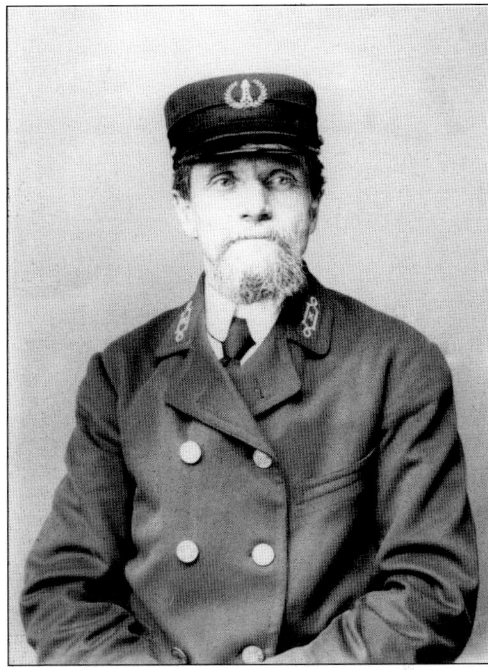

One of the most celebrated lighthouse keepers on the Great Lakes was Martin Nicolai Knudsen. In addition to his time at North Point, his assignments included the Racine North Breakwater Light, as well as Pilot Island, in the treacherous "Death's Door" strait in Door County, Wisconsin. His total lighthouse tenure added up to over four decades. A heroic rescue at Pilot Island in 1892 cemented Knudsen's place in light-keeper history. (Courtesy of Racine Heritage Museum.)

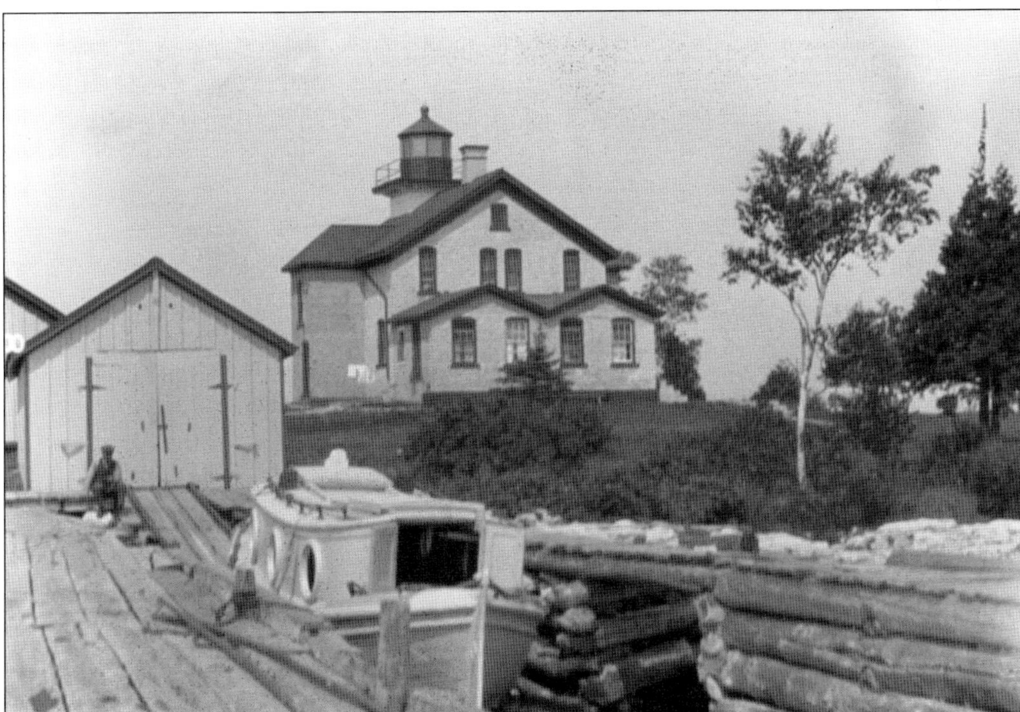

Pilot Island is a small three-and-a-half-acre rock pile. Located on the far eastern edge of the Porte des Morts Passage, between Lake Michigan and the bay of Green Bay, its lighthouse and deafening foghorn made for one of the most historic light stations in Wisconsin history. Martin Knudsen went to the aid of the shipwrecked three-masted schooner, the *A.P. Nichols*, on October 28, 1892. Six people were saved by his valiant efforts. (Courtesy of MPM.)

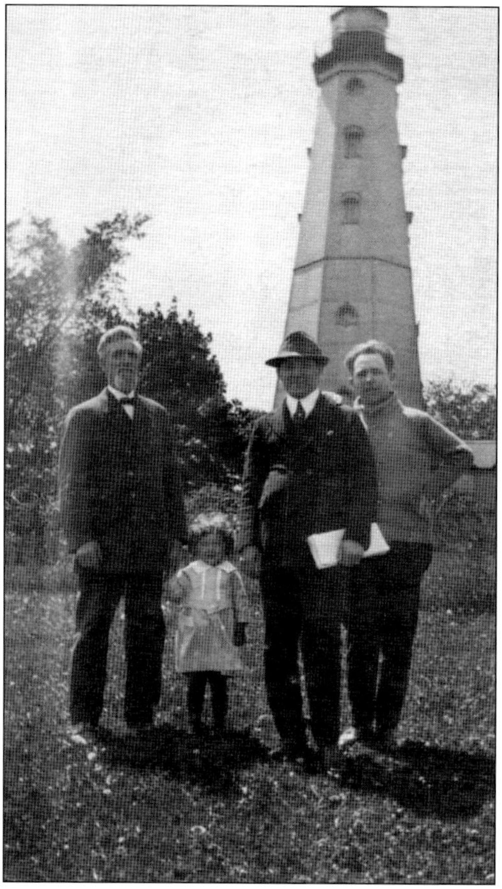

Martin Knudsen's last keeper position was at the North Point Lighthouse. His 44 years of dedicated service ended here when he retired on June 1, 1924, at the age of 70. Some of his family had come to visit when this photograph was taken. Always looking proper and in charge, Knudsen proudly stands with the North Point tower in the background. (Courtesy of WIA.)

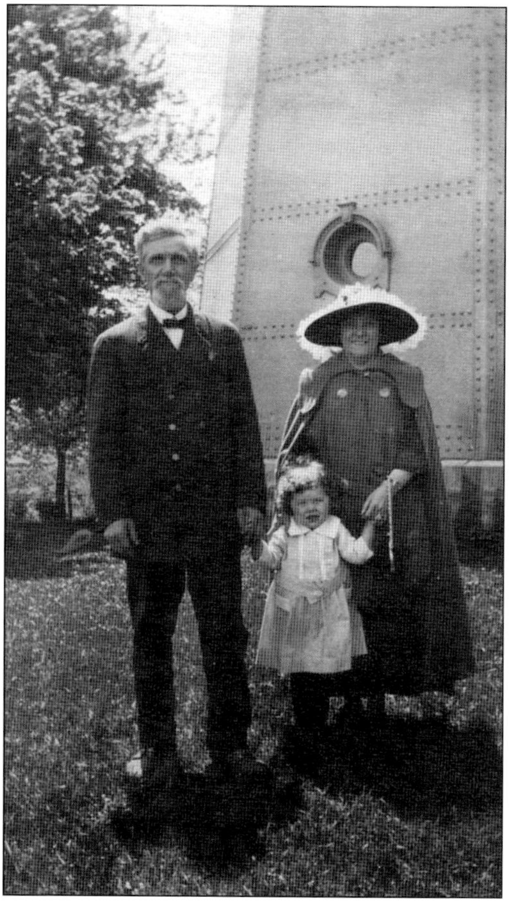

Lighthouse keeper Martin Knudsen is pictured here in front of the North Point tower around 1920, probably with his wife, Theresa, and a grandchild. It was fitting that Knudsen would end his long, distinguished tenure as a keeper at North Point. His retirement in 1924 was well deserved, and North Point was well tended. Both benefited as a grand man served a grand lighthouse. (Courtesy of WIA.)

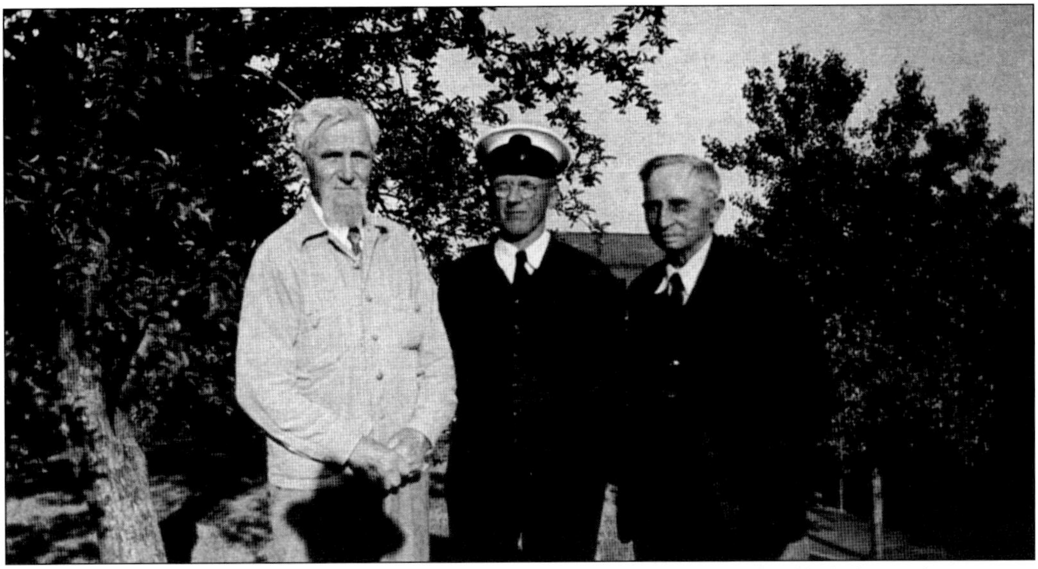

The Knudsen family must have heard the call of the Great Lakes and had lighthouse keeping in the blood. In addition to Martin (left), his younger brothers Peter (right) and Nelson Knudsen served at several Wisconsin and Michigan lighthouses. Martin's son Edward (center) was also a keeper at various lights in Racine, Kenosha, and Door County. The Knudsen light keepers are pictured here in Kenosha. (Courtesy of WIA.)

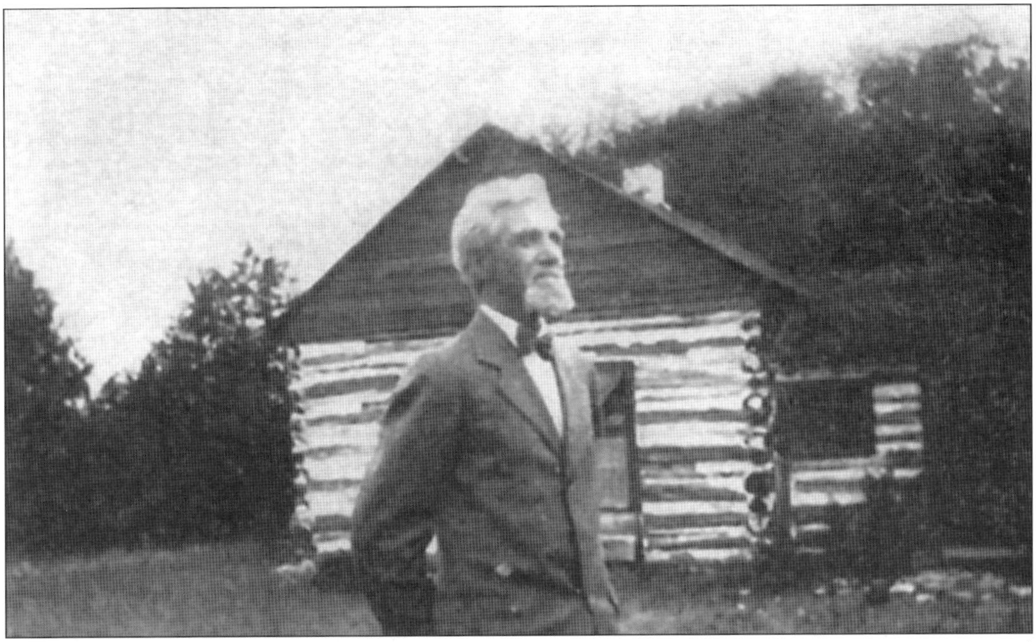

Martin Knudsen (sometimes spelled Knudson) was born in Denmark in 1854. His parents, Marie and Peder, immigrated to the United States in 1857. Martin enjoyed the water and learned to sail at a young age. His family's time in Door County—and particularly Washington Island—was formative. A Door County drowning witnessed by young Martin profoundly affected him. Here, Knudsen is shown with his distinctive facial hair in Door County, Wisconsin. (Courtesy of WIA.)

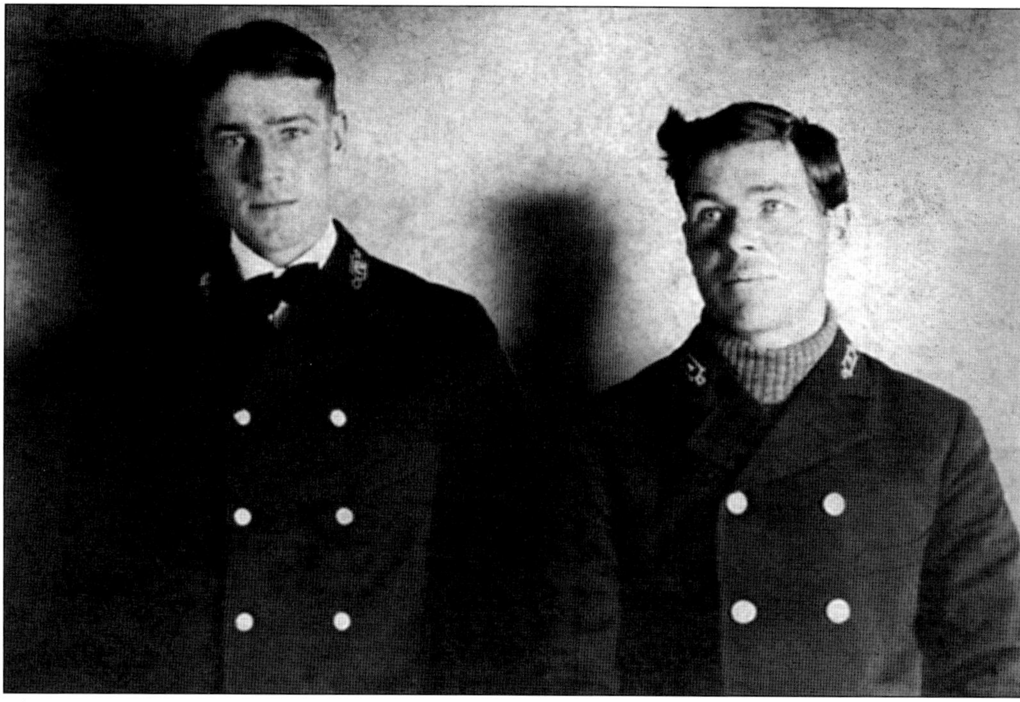

This c. 1900 image portrays two Lighthouse Service colleagues, Reynold Johnson and Nels Nelson, in their official uniforms; one is a first assistant and the other is a second assistant. They shared overlapping years together at the North Manitou Island Lighthouse, in the northern waters of Lake Michigan, before Johnson came to North Point. Perhaps their shared Scandinavian ancestry was another connection between the two young keepers. (Courtesy of Dale Hanson.)

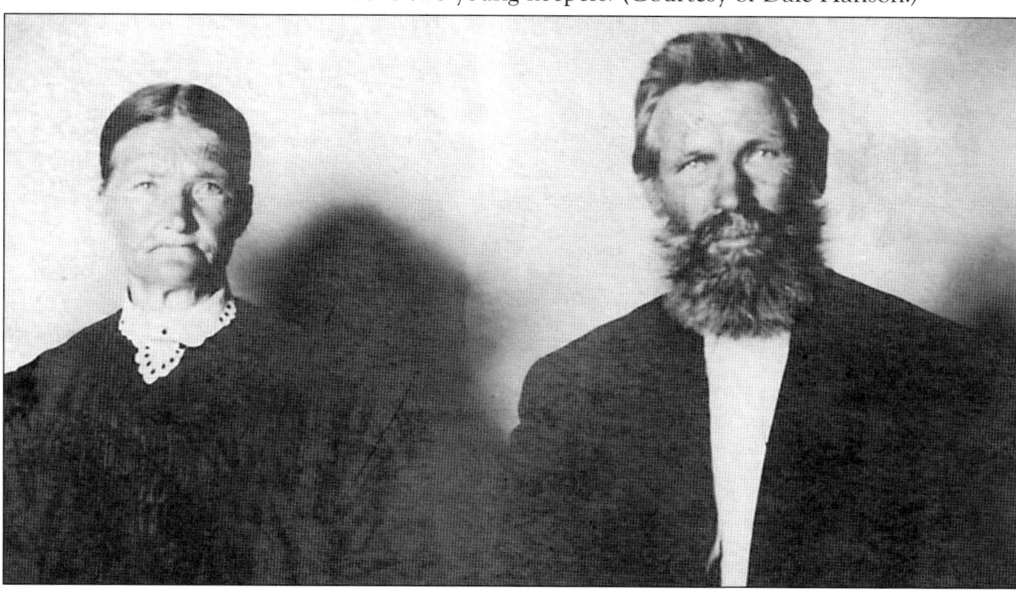

North Point keeper Reynold Johnson was of Scandinavian heritage. His parents, Venla Christina and John Peter Johnson, are seen here. Both were born in Sweden in the 1840s. They immigrated to the United States and settled in the state of Michigan. Reynold became a US citizen in 1902. (Courtesy of Dale Hanson.)

Succeeding a legendary keeper like Martin Knudsen at North Point was not easy. The Lighthouse Service selected a person with experience and great credentials, Reynold Johnson. Johnson already had 20 years of experience at two Michigan lighthouses, North Manitou Island and Grand Traverse. He eventually totaled more than 35 years of lighthouse service, with 16 of them at the North Point and Milwaukee Breakwater Lights. (Courtesy of Dale Hanson.)

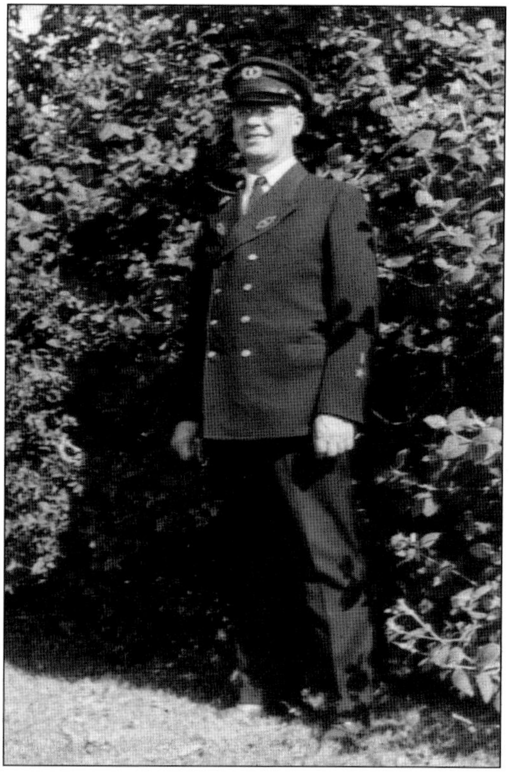

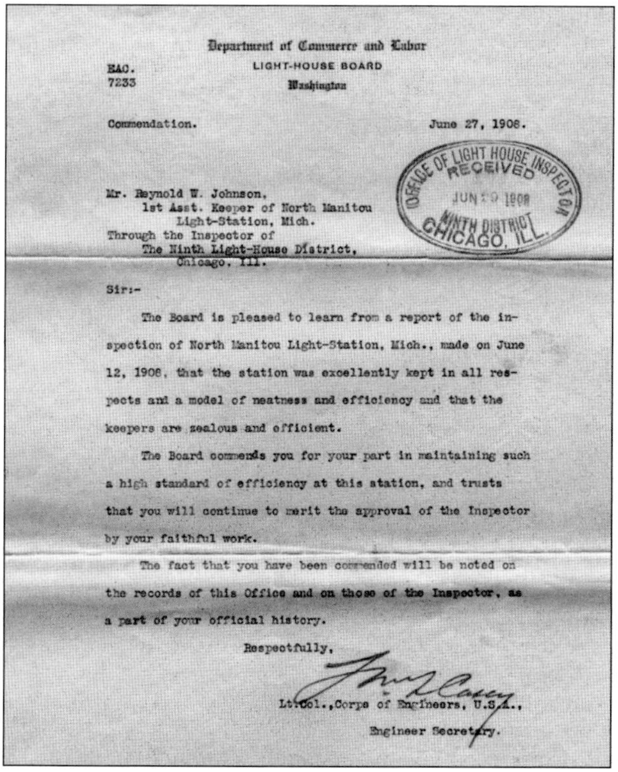

Department of Commerce and Labor
LIGHT-HOUSE BOARD
Washington

EAC.
7233

Commendation. June 27, 1908.

OFFICE OF LIGHT HOUSE INSPECTOR RECEIVED JUN 29 1908 NINTH DISTRICT CHICAGO, ILL.

Mr. Reynold W. Johnson,
1st Asst. Keeper of North Manitou
Light-Station, Mich.
Through the Inspector of
The Ninth Light-House District,
Chicago, Ill.

Sir:-

The Board is pleased to learn from a report of the inspection of North Manitou Light-Station, Mich., made on June 12, 1908, that the station was excellently kept in all respects and a model of neatness and efficiency and that the keepers are zealous and efficient.

The Board commends you for your part in maintaining such a high standard of efficiency at this station, and trusts that you will continue to merit the approval of the Inspector by your faithful work.

The fact that you have been commended will be noted on the records of this Office and on those of the Inspector, as a part of your official history.

Respectfully,

[signature]

Lt.Col., Corps of Engineers, U.S.A.,
Engineer Secretary.

Prior to his years at North Point, Reynold Johnson was an assistant at the North Manitou Lighthouse on northern Lake Michigan. Johnson's lighthouse service was marked with several commendations no matter which lighthouse he was stationed at. Here is a 1908 document, from the Department of Commerce and Labor Lighthouse Board, congratulating him on a job well done. The letter was first received by the lighthouse inspector in Chicago. (Courtesy of Dale Hanson.)

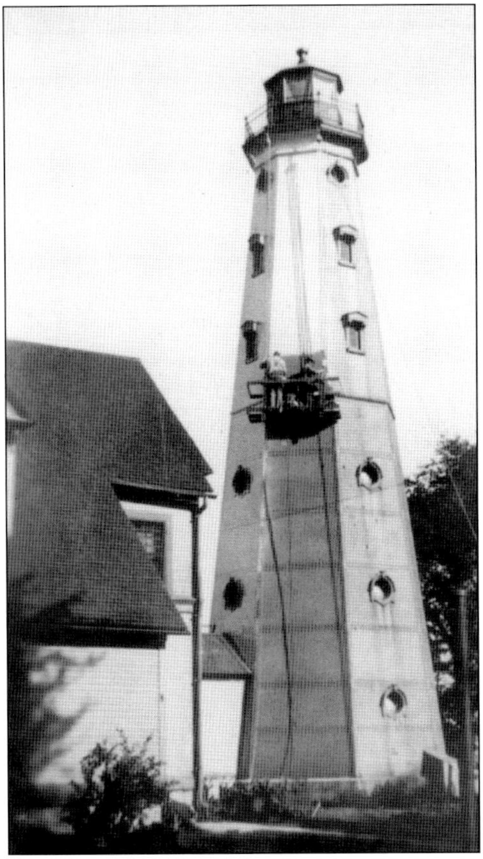

Painting at North Point, both inside and out, was a common and perhaps unending task. The outside tower was a particularly difficult undertaking. This unique photograph shows two men suspended on a painting platform midway up the tower. Their stand, connected by sturdy lines attached to the base of the gallery, was moved along each panel of the octagonal tower until the job was completed. (Courtesy of Dale Hanson.)

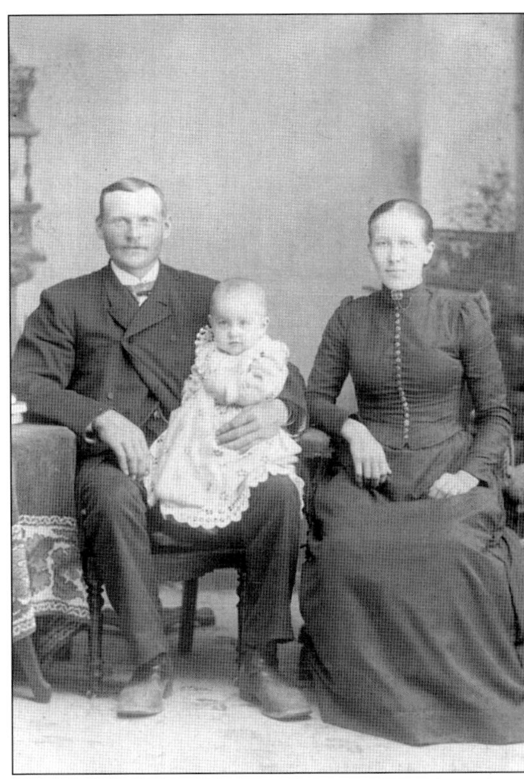

Reynold and Catherine Mason Johnson's infant daughter Evelyn is pictured here with her paternal grandparents in her baptismal dress around 1906. As a grown woman, Evelyn married sailor Yngve "Hans" Hanson at the North Point Lighthouse in 1935. The newlyweds traveled to Sweden for their honeymoon. They met five years earlier on a lake boat excursion to Chicago that was sponsored by a Swedish club. When they met, Yngve was a mate on the *Seaforth*, a 433-ton yacht owned by Herman Falk, president of the Falk Corporation of Milwaukee. (Courtesy of Dale Hanson.)

Keeper Reynold Johnson proudly poses for a *Milwaukee Journal* newspaper photographer in 1940 at the North Point Lighthouse. He is standing in the tower with the Fresnel lens, the lighthouse's most important component. Lighthouse keepers were consistently hardworking, dedicated, and fiercely loyal individuals. Many times, their livelihoods depended on high performance. Johnson was a perfect example of a highly competent keeper. (Courtesy of *Milwaukee Journal*.)

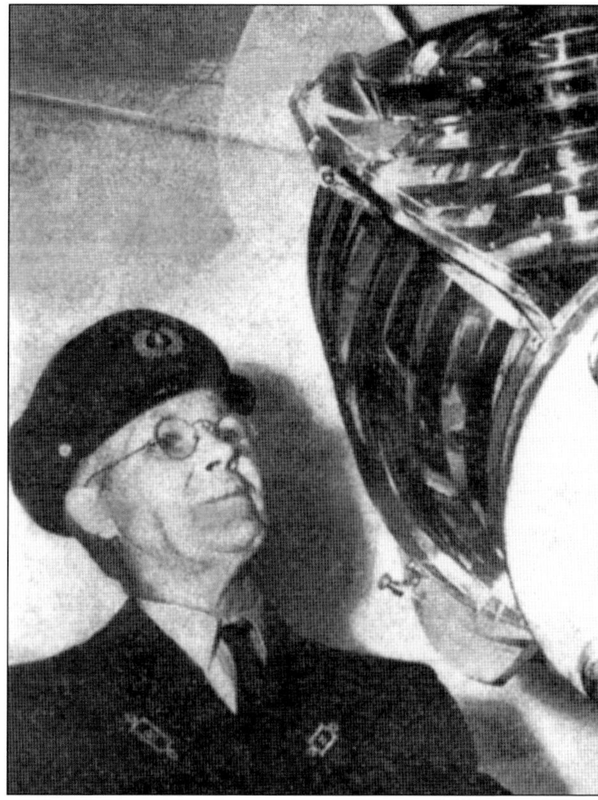

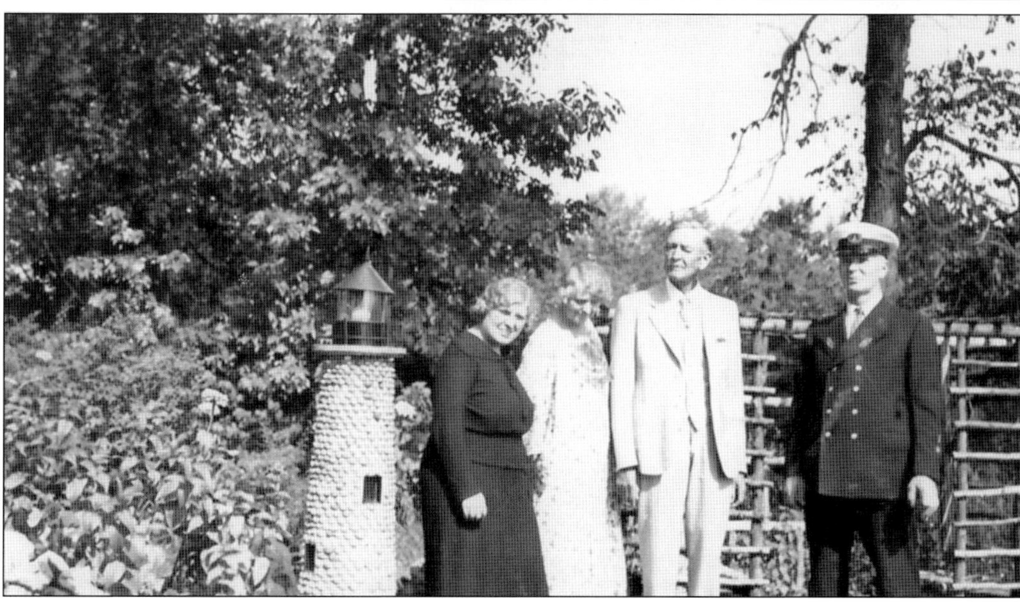

Keeper Reynold Johnson retired from duty at the North Point Lighthouse in December 1940 at the age of 60. He had been in the lighthouse service for 37 years at several Great Lakes lights. In an interview just prior to his return to civilian life, he pondered traveling and wondered what his days would be like away from the water. He stated that his rheumatism favored warm, dry destinations. (Courtesy of Dale Hanson.)

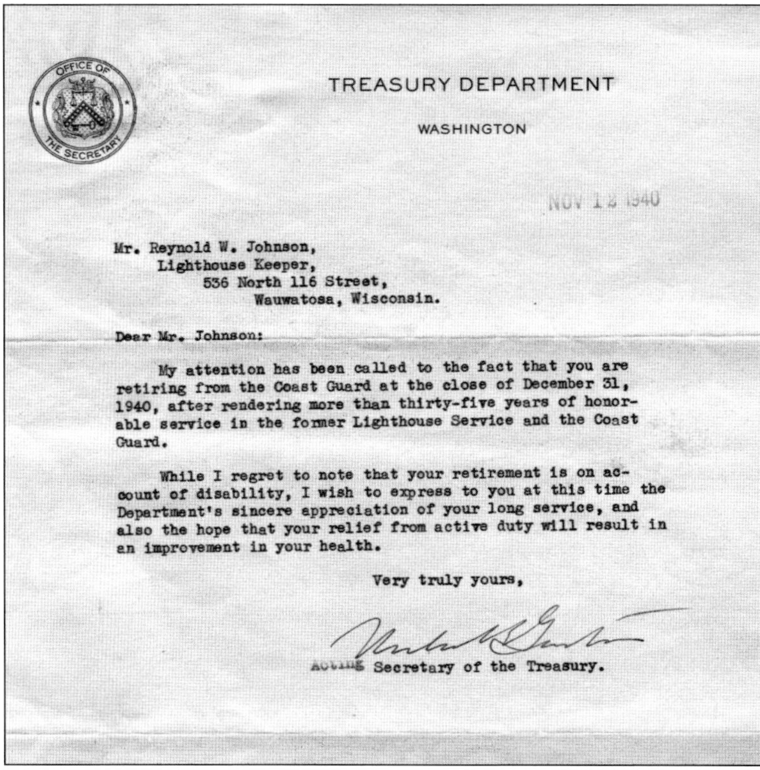

TREASURY DEPARTMENT

WASHINGTON

NOV 12 1940

Mr. Reynold W. Johnson,
Lighthouse Keeper,
536 North 116 Street,
Wauwatosa, Wisconsin.

Dear Mr. Johnson:

My attention has been called to the fact that you are retiring from the Coast Guard at the close of December 31, 1940, after rendering more than thirty-five years of honorable service in the former Lighthouse Service and the Coast Guard.

While I regret to note that your retirement is on account of disability, I wish to express to you at this time the Department's sincere appreciation of your long service, and also the hope that your relief from active duty will result in an improvement in your health.

Very truly yours,

Acting Secretary of the Treasury.

Keeper Reynold Johnson retired from active lighthouse duty on December 31, 1940. This letter, from the acting secretary of the treasury, states that he regrets that Johnson's end to his working years is due to disability. The government official proceeds to thank Johnson for his many years of service and wishes the light keeper improved health. (Courtesy of Dale Hanson.)

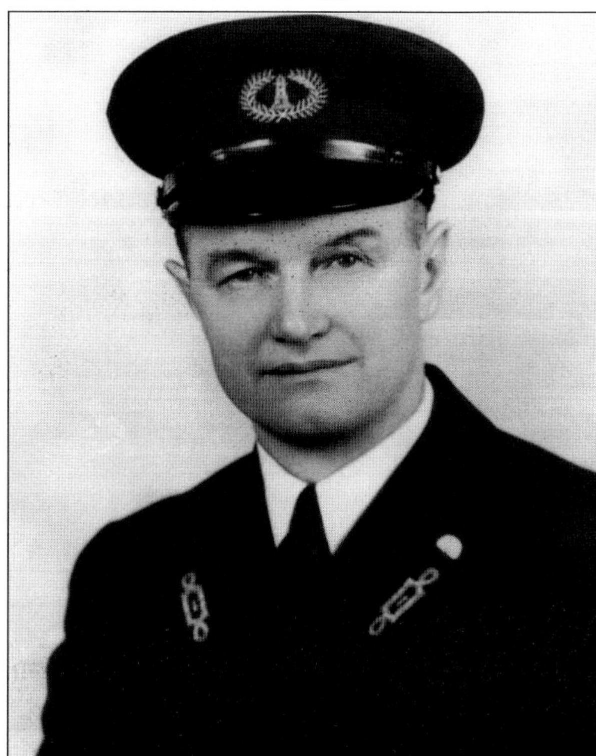

Charles Linsmeier was stationed at North Point from about 1925 to 1934. Some of that assignment was also spent at the Breakwater Lighthouse in the Milwaukee harbor, which shared personnel with North Point. Linsmeier's career in the Lighthouse Service spanned 34 years, with stints at the Cana Island Lighthouse in Door County, Rawley (Twin River) Point in Two Rivers, and the Sheboygan Breakwater and North Manitou Island Lighthouses. (Courtesy of Vivian Langer.)

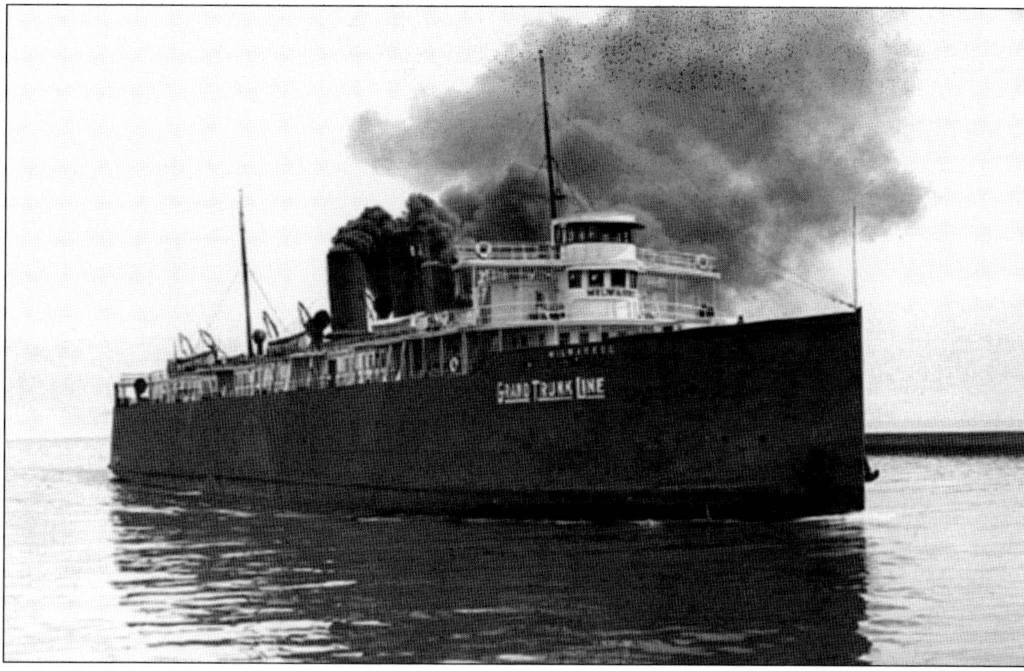

Assistant keeper Charles Linsmeier was in the lantern atop North Point on October 22, 1929, when the 338-foot car ferry *Milwaukee* left the city's harbor traveling east. Its destination was Grand Haven, Michigan. Through his binoculars, he could see the huge steel vessel briefly before losing it in a tremendous storm. More than 52 men perished when the vessel sank that day. The wreck lies about four miles northeast of North Point off of Whitefish Bay. (Courtesy of Kimm Stabelfeldt.)

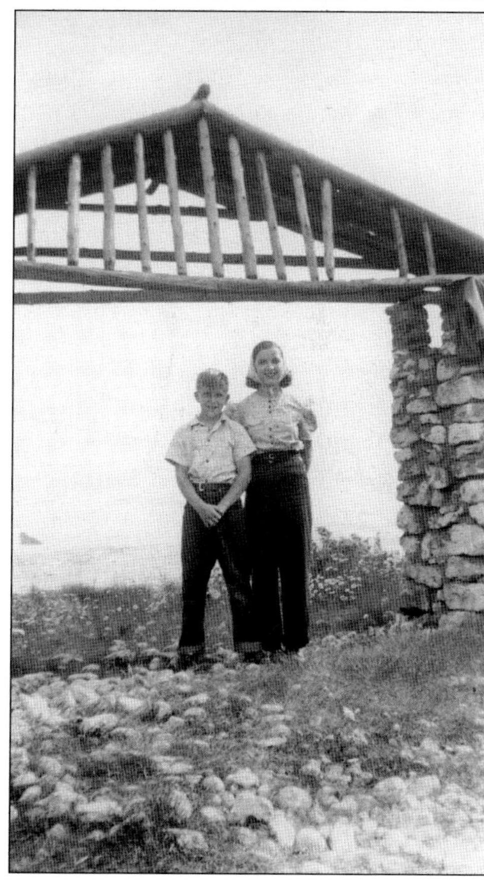

Charles Linsmeier and his wife, Esther, had two young children when stationed at the North Point and Milwaukee Breakwater Lighthouses. Siblings Chuck and Vivian Linsmeier are pictured here on a visit to one of Charles Linsmeier's previous assignments, Cana Island, Wisconsin. As an adult, Vivian recalled many special childhood lighthouse memories and stated that North Point was a great place to live during the Depression. She also offered another particularly poignant quote, saying that "North Point Lighthouse was a wonderful, even magical place to live." (Courtesy of Door County Maritime Museum.)

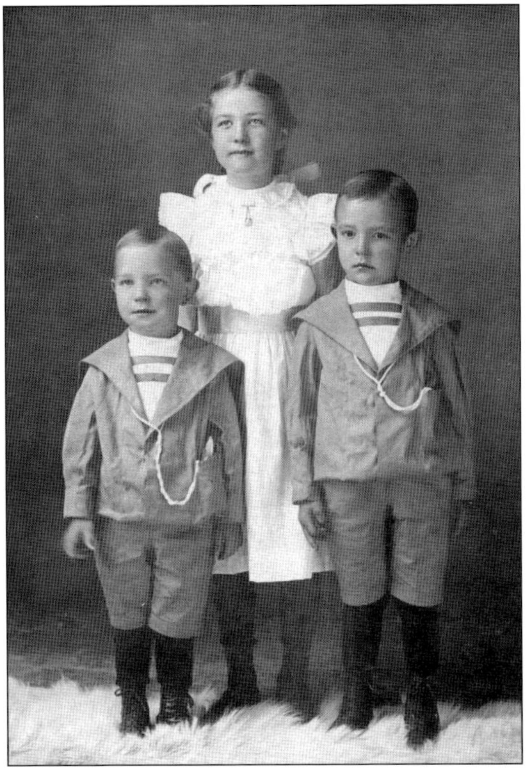

Future lighthouse keeper Herbert William Fadel (left) is pictured here with his older sister Elma and brother Allen around 1902. Born in 1897, Fadel took a civil service test and went into the Lighthouse Service in 1936. He was stationed at the Milwaukee Pierhead and Breakwater Lighthouses, and occasionally North Point, in the late 1930s, where he served under keeper Reynold Johnson. (Courtesy of Jane Fadel Murphy.)

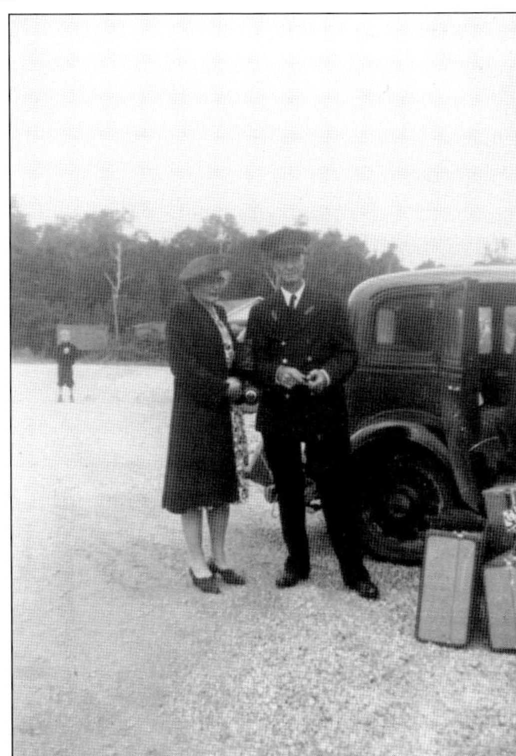

Herbert Fadel's lighthouse career took him and his family to lighthouses in cities other than Milwaukee. Here, he and his wife, Eva Simms Fadel, are shown in 1944 leaving Wisconsin's Washington Island. His longest tenure was 11 years at the Wind Point Lighthouse in Racine, where he was one of the last assistants before US Coast Guard personnel became responsible for lighthouses. (Courtesy of Jane Fadel Murphy.)

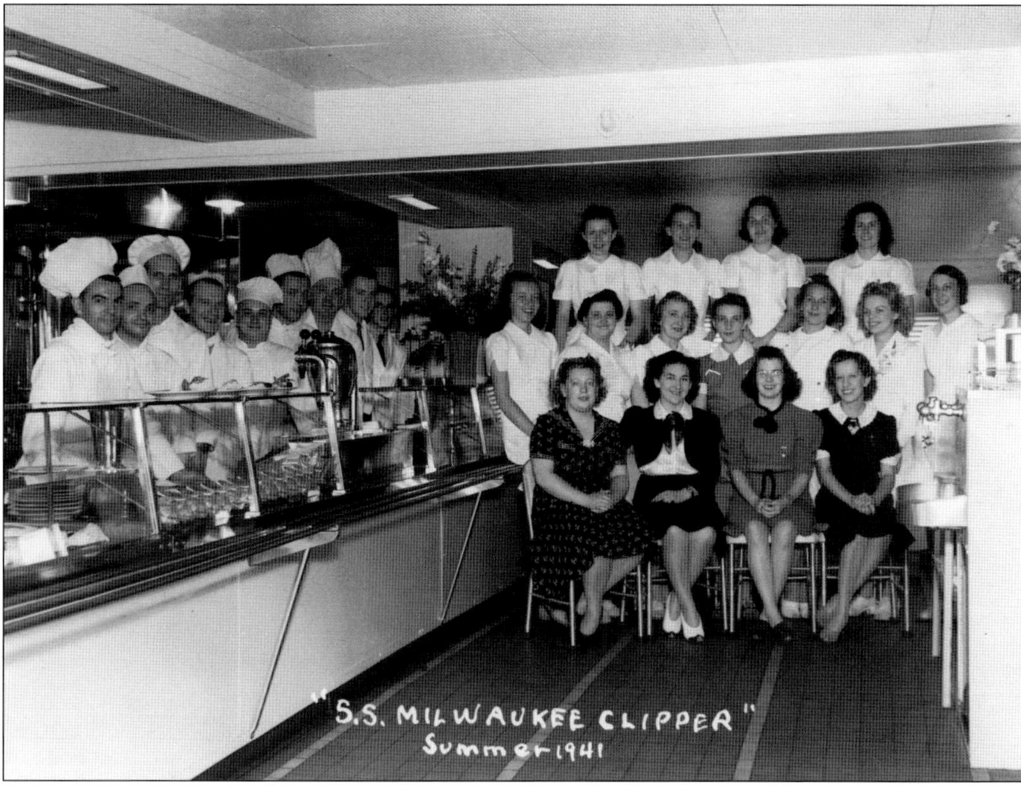

Light keeper Herbert Fadel's daughter Jane also played a role in Milwaukee maritime history. She was an employee on the *Milwaukee Clipper* cruise ship. Nicknamed the "Queen of the Great Lakes," the 361-foot vessel made her maiden voyage in 1941. It sailed primarily between Milwaukee and Muskegon, Michigan. Jane recalled getting seasick on rough crossings. She is shown here in the back row, second from the right. (Courtesy of Jane Fadel Murphy.)

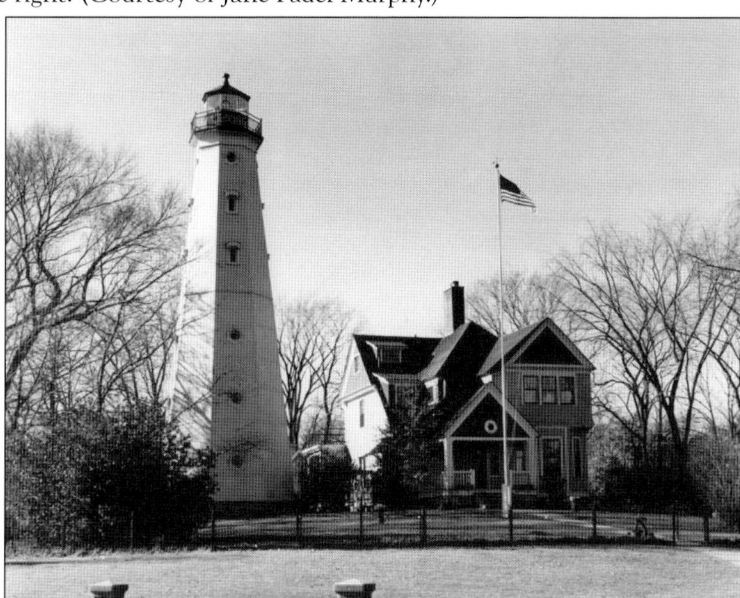
The North Point Light Station looked like this when Reynold Johnson retired in 1940. From all accounts, the facility was one of the best kept on the Great Lakes for many years. Johnson and other keepers at North Point took pride in their work and residence—it was an extension of themselves. This delightful photograph certainly reflects the care taken. (Courtesy of USCG.)

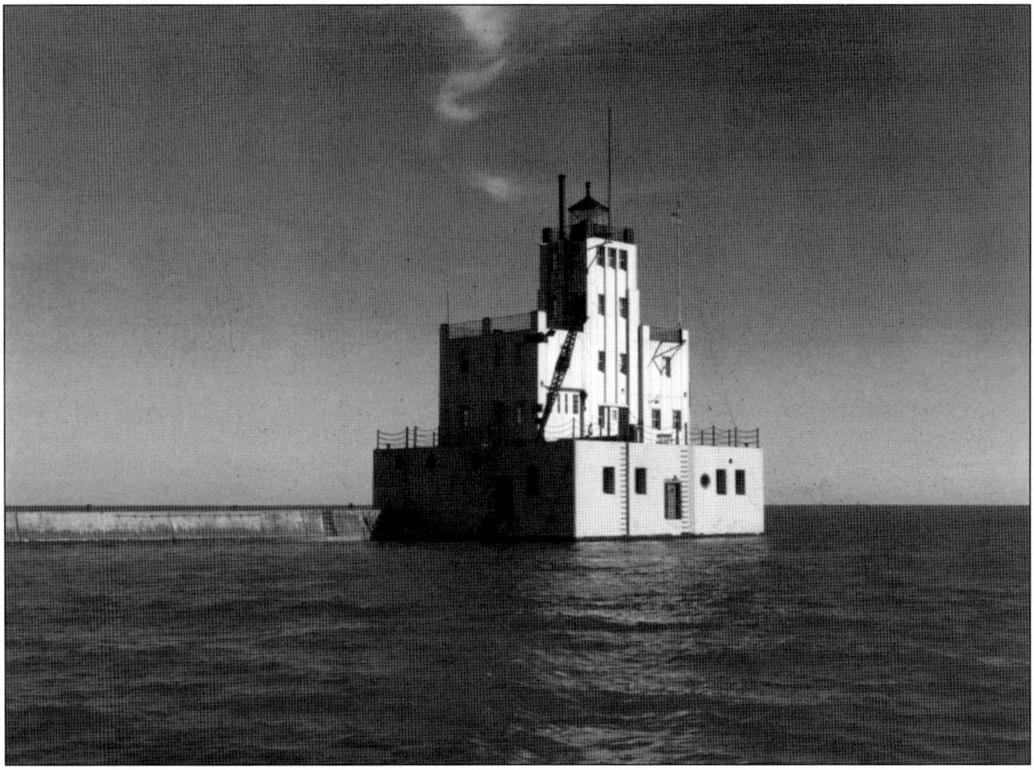

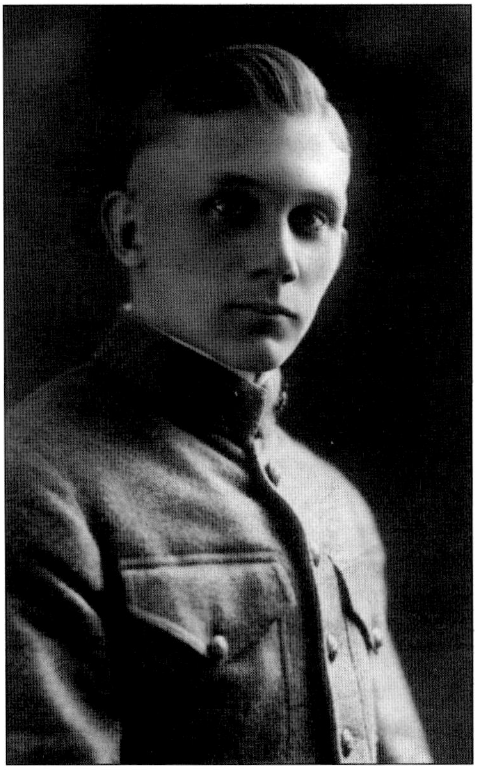

When the North Point and Milwaukee Breakwater Lighthouses were combined into one government entity, alternating crews rotated time at the two locations. While the length of duty varied over the years, it usually consisted of two teams of men that spent several days at North Point and then an equal amount of time at the breakwater. Inclement weather may have affected that schedule if harsh lake conditions prevented an exchange of personnel. The breakwater complex was automated in the 1960s. (Courtesy of USCG.)

A youthful Alexander Werner poses in his official uniform in this c. 1918 photograph. The number of his Coast Guard Station, 293, is shown on his collar. Like lighthouse keepers, surfmen were a hardy lot who braved ferocious Great Lakes storms and had to be prepared to assist ships in distress. Their duty was taken seriously, and many men paid the ultimate sacrifice. Their motto was, "You have to go out, but you don't have to come back." Werner would later serve at North Point in 1946 as a boatswain's mate. (Courtesy of Ed Werner.)

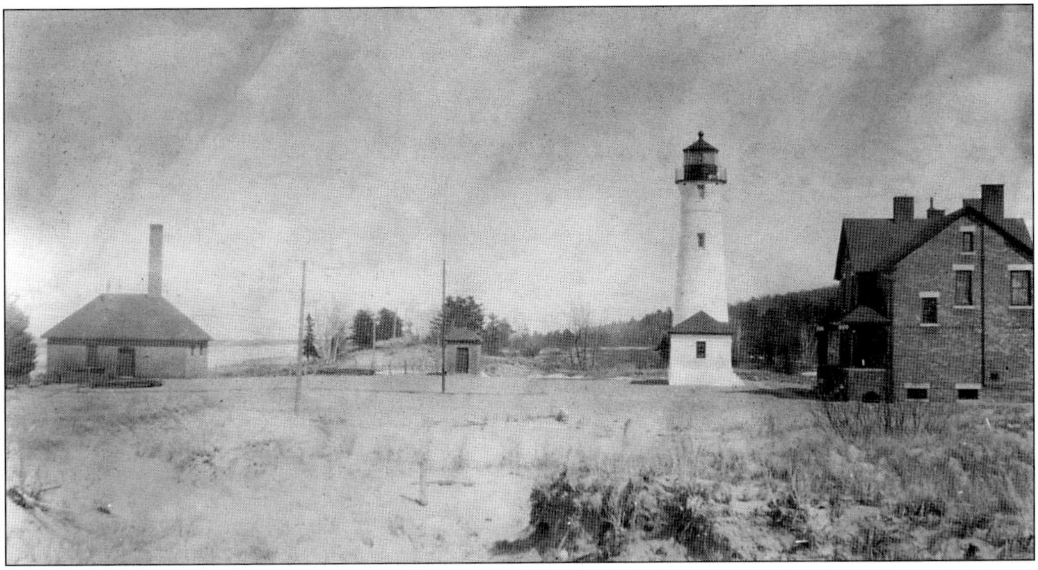

The southeastern Lake Superior coastline west of Whitefish Point, near the Crisp Point Lifeboat Station and the 1904 Crisp Point Lighthouse shown here, was called the graveyard of the Great Lakes. Many shipwrecks littered these shores. The big lake was respected by mariners, light keepers, and lifesaving crews in all seasons, particularly the stormy months. Alexander Werner was stationed at the lifeboat station in 1918. (Courtesy of Ed Werner.)

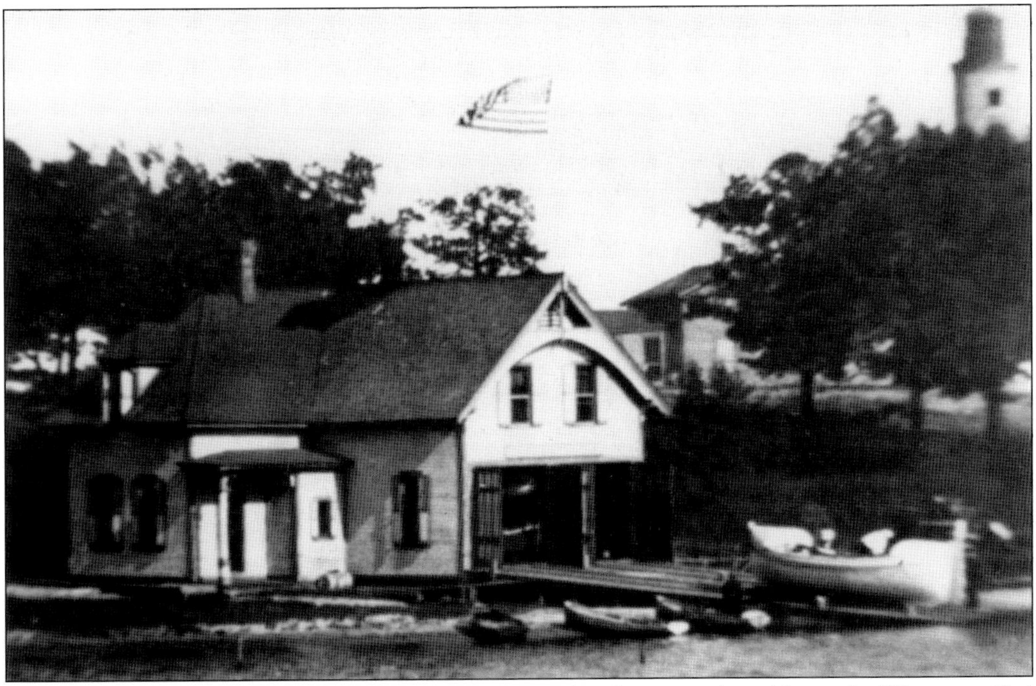

The Kenosha, Wisconsin, Lifeboat Station was another location that Alexander Werner called home for a portion of his Coast Guard years. He was a surfman in 1919 at Kenosha, pictured here. Situated on the Pike River, the Southport Kenosha Lighthouse was nearby and is seen in the upper right portion. Several Wisconsin cities had lifesaving stations in close proximity to lighthouses. (Courtesy of Ed Werner.)

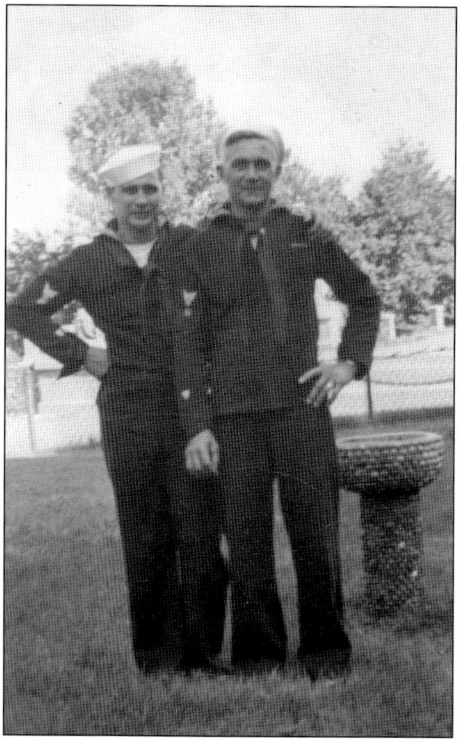

North Point Lighthouse saw its share of Coast Guard personnel come and go after the station was automated in 1943. Pictured around 1946 in the front yard at North Point are Boatswain's Mate First Class Alexander Werner (right) and colleague Boatswain's Mate Second Class Buyer. Behind the men are one of the stone lions and some of the ornamental and metal fencing surrounding the complex. An interesting ornate stone birdbath was also present in the yard. (Courtesy of Ed Werner.)

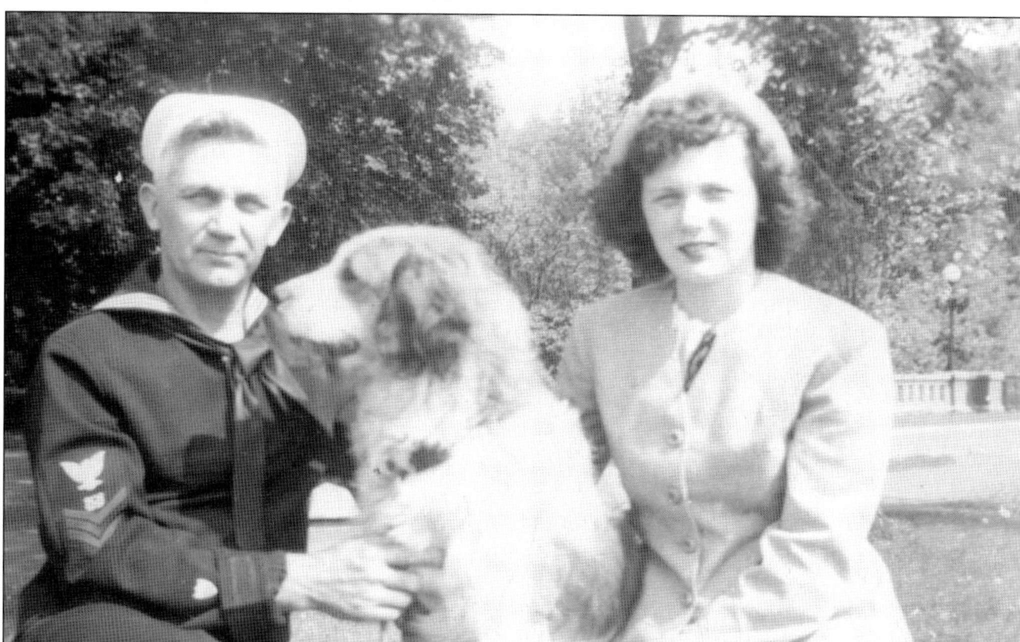

Alexander Werner was a Coast Guardsman at the North Point Lighthouse in 1946 for a relatively short time. Routine maintenance, such as painting, scrubbing, and window and screen repair, was still needed at North Point, although most personnel spent the majority of their duty hours at the Milwaukee Breakwater Lighthouse. Here, Werner shares a light moment with his daughter Jean and the family pooch Skipper. (Courtesy of Ed Werner.)

Lighthouse work at North Point came in many forms. While numerous jobs were routine, occasionally an unusual or special type of task needed to be performed. When the US flag became tangled in the nautical-style flagpole in 1946, Alexander Werner took the most appropriate and reasonable action—he shimmied up the shaft and untangled it. (Courtesy of Ed Werner.)

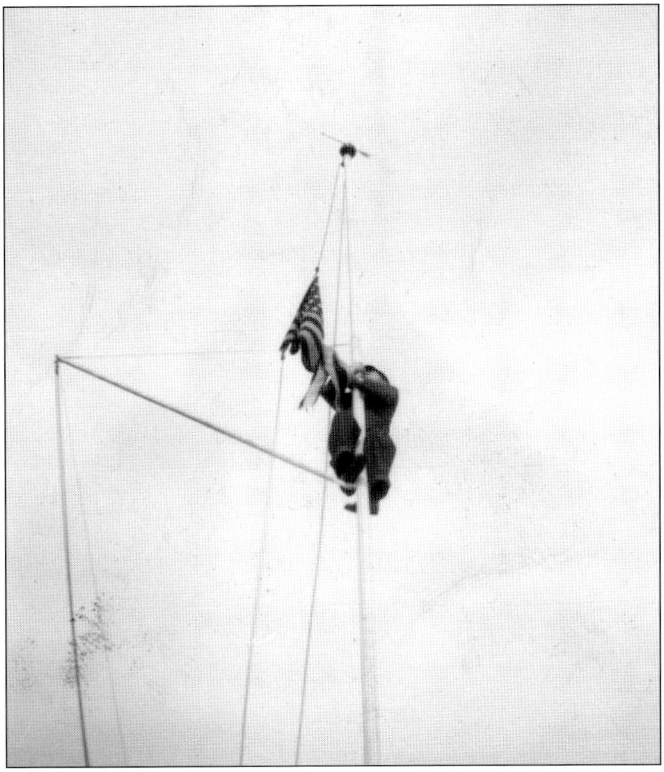

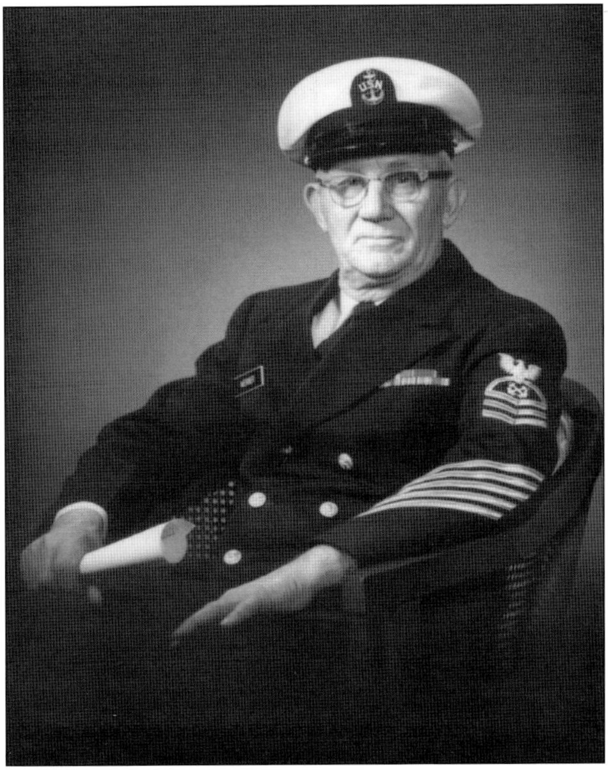

Alexander Werner's military career spanned several decades. In his 20s, he enlisted multiple times in the US Coast Guard. After serving in both World War I and World War II, Werner spent a short period of his service at the North Point Lighthouse. Later, he joined the US Naval Reserve. One of his sons and a grandson followed in his footsteps in the Coast Guard. He is pictured here in retirement in 1975. He was affectionately known as "The Chief." (Courtesy of Ed Werner.)

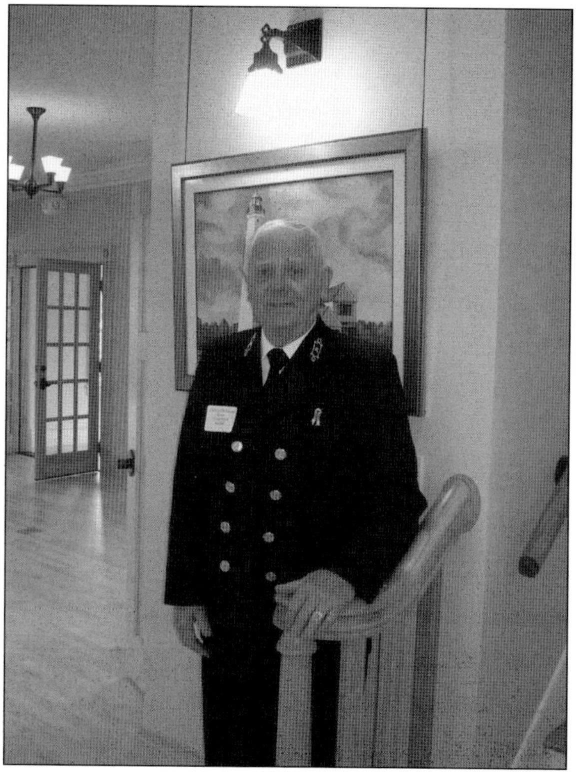

Retired US Coast Guard Lt. Comdr. Edward Werner revisits North Point Lighthouse in 2007 during festivities marking the lighthouse's completed restoration. Werner lived here in 1946 when his father Alexander was stationed at North Point. The young boy's small bedroom had a view of the lantern. Here, he is dressed in a replica lighthouse keeper's uniform that he also wears when giving educational programs for grade-schoolers in Kenosha, Wisconsin. (Courtesy of John Enright.)

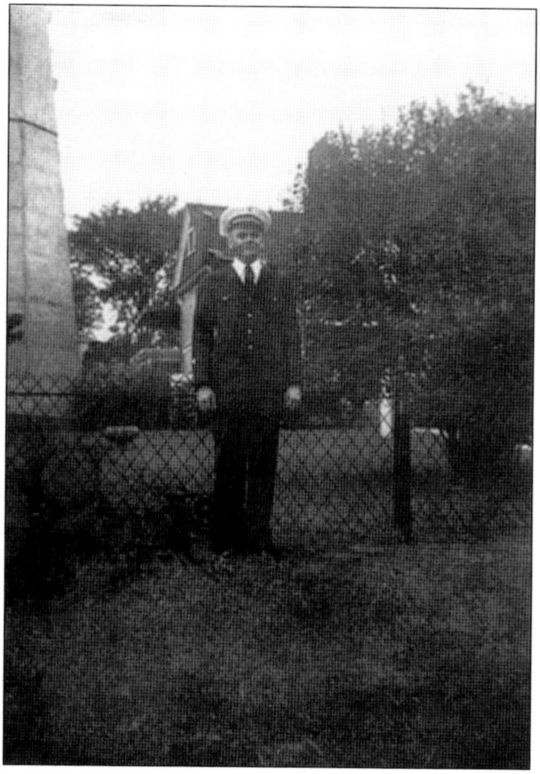

There are some people who served at North Point whose stories will remain unknown. The gentleman in this photograph might be one of them. The only information that accompanies the photograph is the name Adolph and the year 1940. Perhaps he was a Coast Guardsman or a relative of someone stationed in Milwaukee. Possibly, he was just a visitor. (Courtesy of NPLHF.)

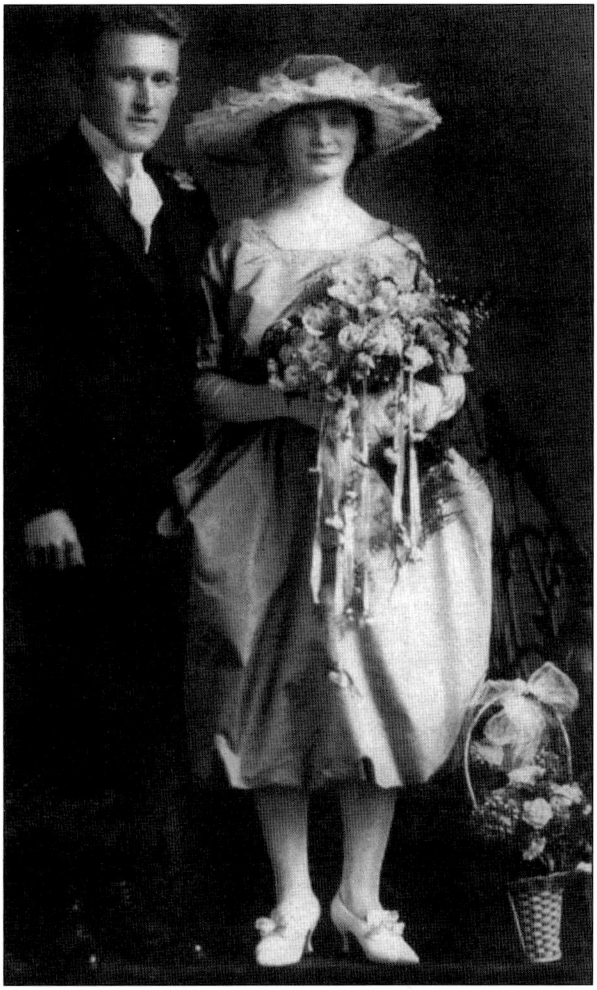

After the North Point Lighthouse became automated in 1943, the complex still served as living quarters for the personnel who manned the Milwaukee Breakwater Lighthouse. After the US Lighthouse Service was dissolved into the Coast Guard in 1939, the men who resided at North Point were Coast Guardsmen and not technically government lighthouse keepers. Pictured here is one of them, Michael M. Rotta, with his future wife, Theresa Damback. (Courtesy of Ellen Puerzer.)

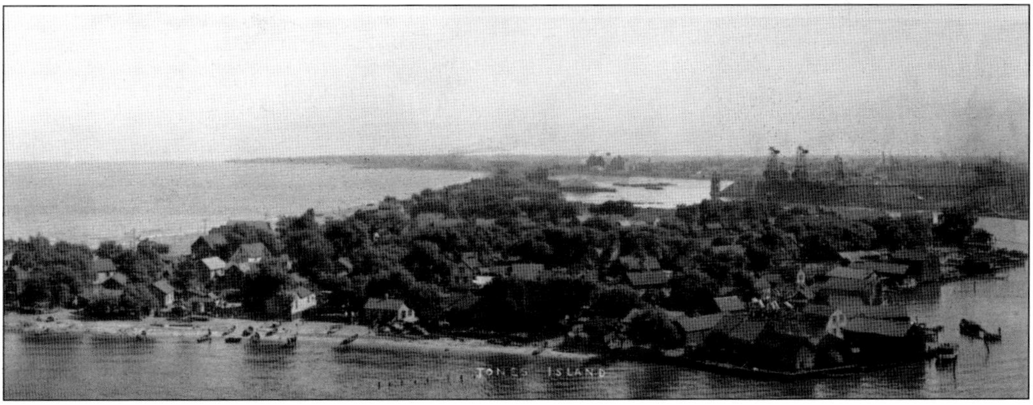

Michael Rotta was born on Milwaukee's Jones Island, an area immediately south of the city's harbor, in 1897. Originally a marshy area between the Milwaukee and Kinnickinnic Rivers, Jones Island was later home to an immigrant fishing village. The land was eventually channelized and filled in. Today, it is a heavily industrialized area that includes the Port of Milwaukee and one of Milwaukee's wastewater treatment plants. (Courtesy of MPM.)

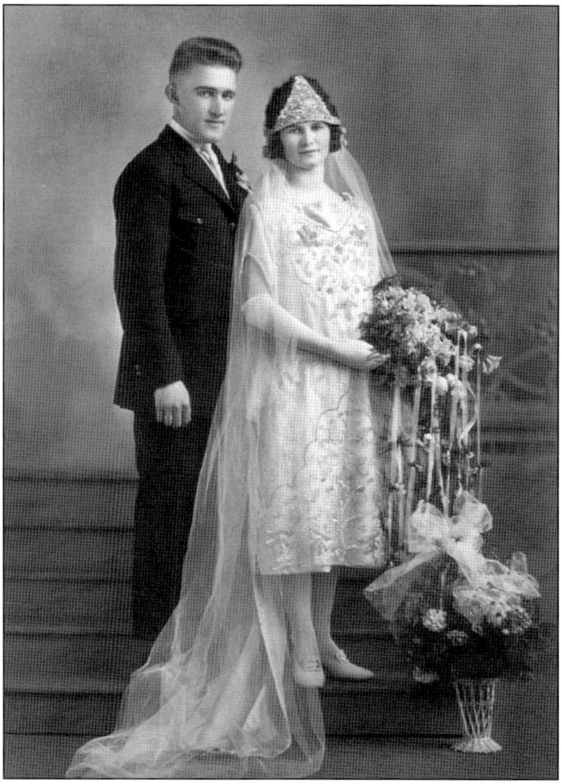

Michael Rotta and Theresa Damback are shown here on their wedding day. The Rottas had six children: Ruth, Michael Jr., Richard, David, Susan, and Michaelene. Nicknamed "Micky," Michael Rotta Sr. attended St. Stanislaus School in Milwaukee. Prior to his lighthouse service in Milwaukee, he also served on the lighthouse tender supply vessel *Sumac* and at the North Manitou Island Lighthouse on northern Lake Michigan. (Courtesy of Dorothy Peissig.)

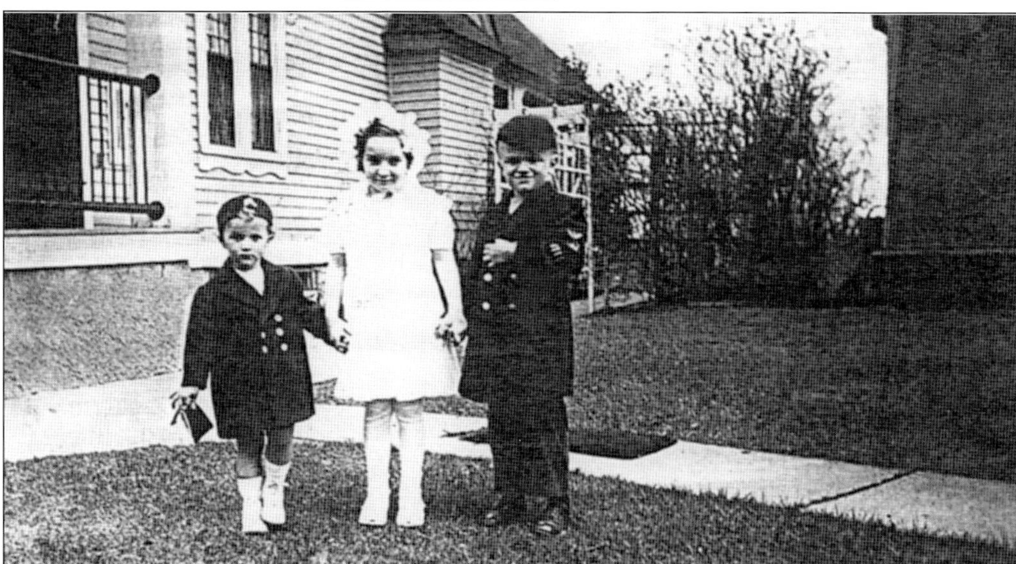

Two of the Rotta children, Susan (left) and David (right), flank their cousin Marcia Kozlowski in this 1943 photograph. Taken on the grounds at the North Point Lighthouse, they were celebrating Marcia's first communion, as evidenced by the young girl's beautiful dress. Note the base of the lighthouse tower in the upper right of the picture. Another Rotta son, Michael Jr., was tragically killed after being hit by a truck at age five. The young boy had said he wanted to grow up to be a lighthouse keeper like his father. (Courtesy of Dorothy Peissig.)

One of the Rotta's older daughters, Ruth, was also a member of the US Coast Guard like her father. Her rank was SPAR radioman, third class. In this 1943 photograph, Ruth stands with her proud father, both of them in uniform. Notice that Ruth's younger brother David, in the foreground of the photograph, also sports some Coast Guard emblems on his jacket. (Courtesy of Dorothy Peissig.)

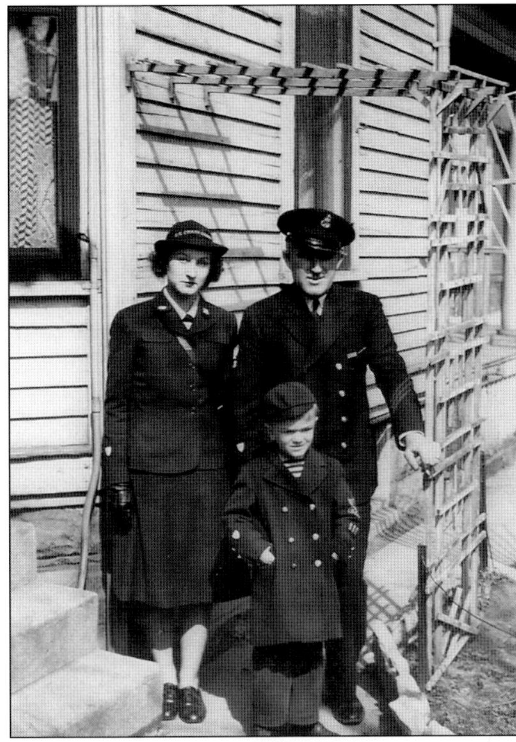

US Coast Guard Chief Boatswain Mate Michael Martin Rotta was only 54 years old when he died while on duty at the Milwaukee Breakwater Lighthouse. Chief Rotta was on a scaffold near the top of the lighthouse performing maintenance when it gave way, hurtling the keeper to the concrete 35 feet below. Rotta was a native Milwaukeean and called North Point and the breakwater lighthouse home for 24 years. (Courtesy of USCG.)

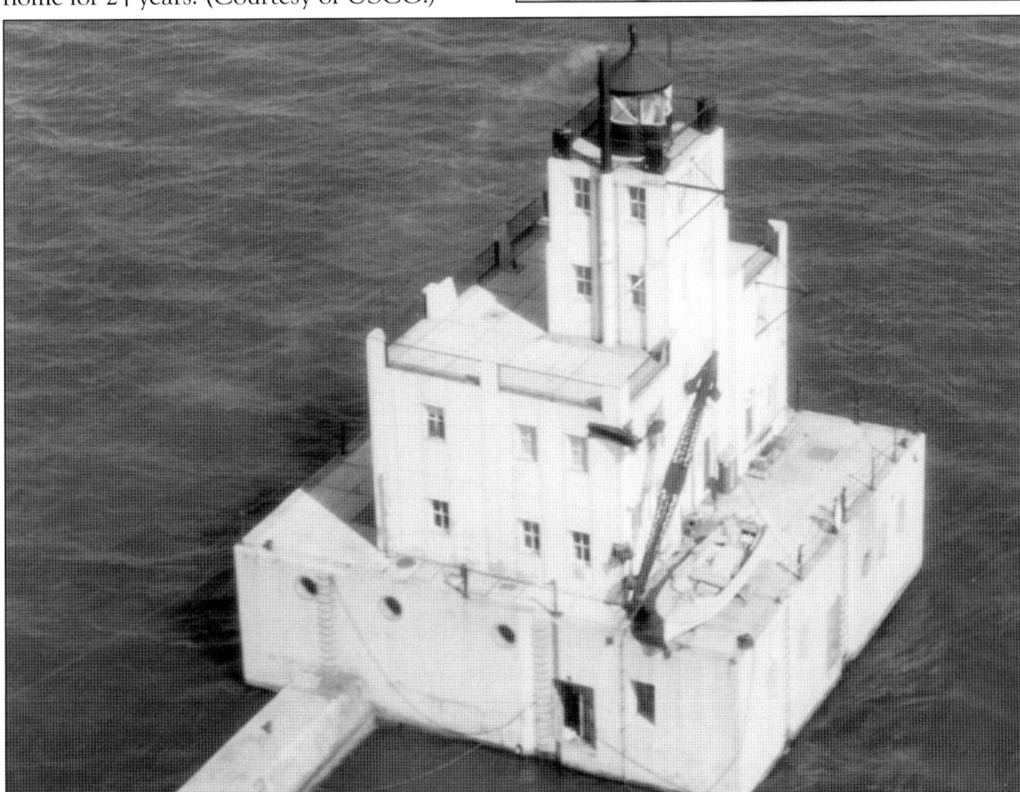

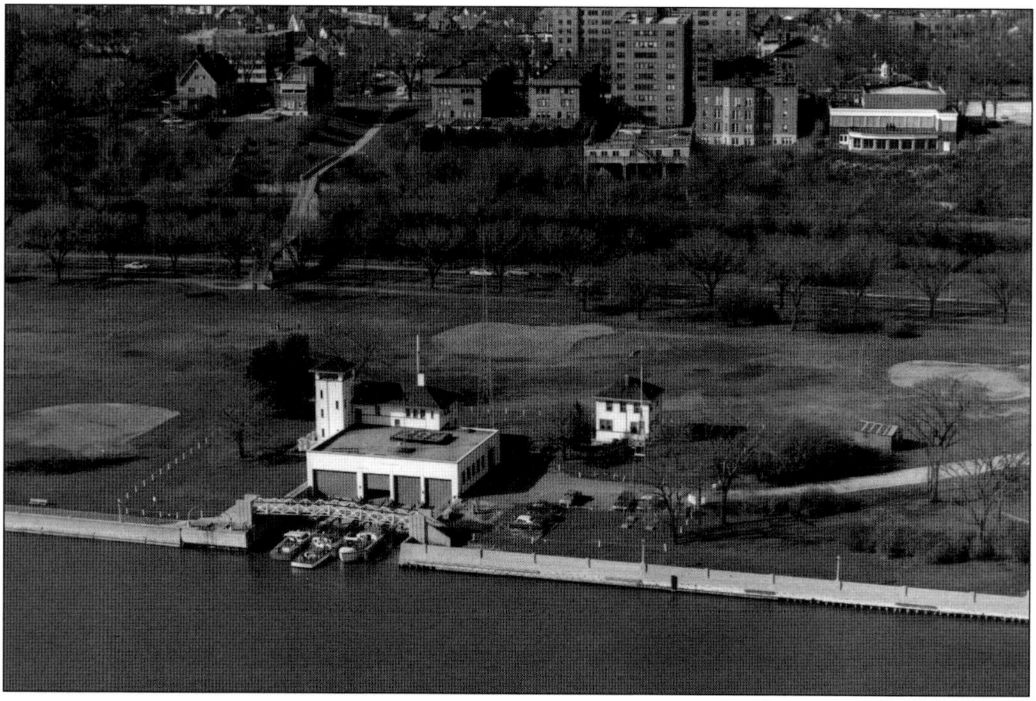

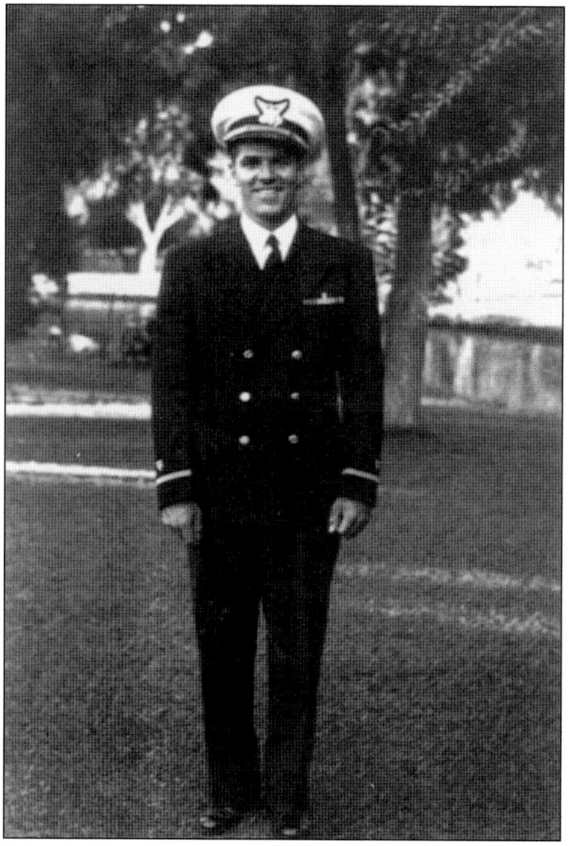

Chief Michael Rotta's partner, Richard Skolweck, was on a nearby ladder at the breakwater lighthouse and witnessed Chief Rotta's accident. Somehow, the ropes and tackle loosened on the scaffolding that Rotta was on. Skolweck telephoned ashore for help. A boat from the McKinley Marina Coast Guard Station (pictured here) was dispatched, and Rotta was brought to a waiting ambulance. Notice the various vessels ready for duty in the dock area. (Courtesy of USCG.)

Roger F. Erdmann was a Coast Guard officer stationed at North Point from 1959 to 1961. His family occupied the first floor of the keeper's dwelling. His nautical career spanned more than four decades and included time in the Pacific in World War II, a rescue of victims from the capsizing Italian ocean liner *Andrea Doria* off of Massachusetts in 1956, and the command of a Coast Guard weather ship out of Boston. (Courtesy of Mark Kuehn.)

Five

Renovation, Preservation, and the Future

North Point Lighthouse Friends

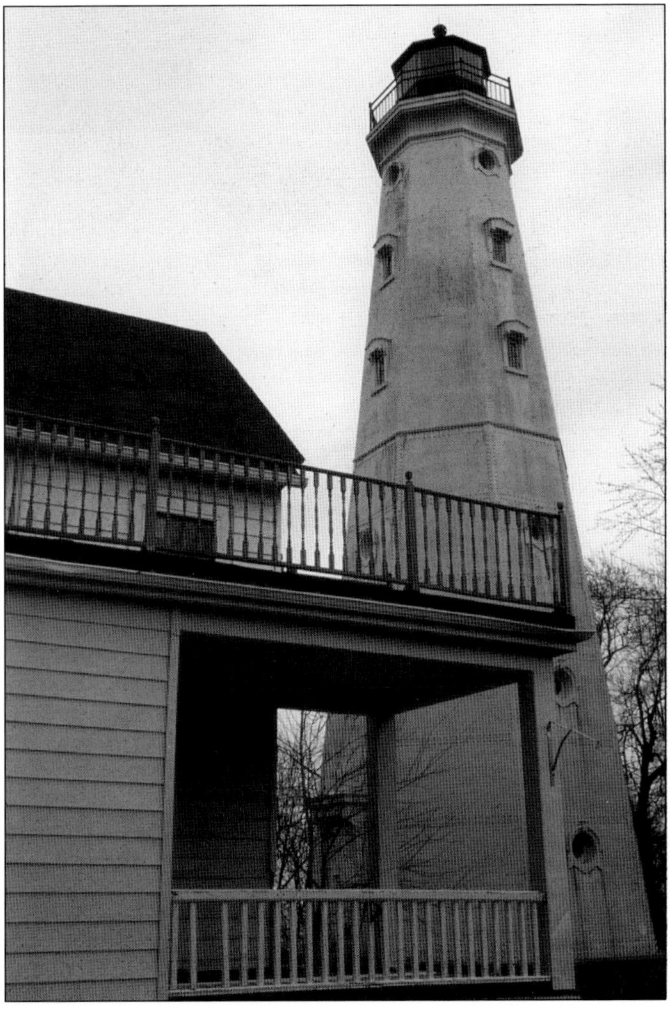

After the Coast Guard's presence ended at the North Point Lighthouse in 1994, it was boarded up and remained idle and vacant for a number of years. It was not long before the lighthouse showed signs of neglect. Fortunately, some community groups and concerned citizens came together in 1996 with the common goal of laying the groundwork for turning this decline around. It would require much effort, along with complex negotiations between many governmental bodies and private entities, to return the lighthouse to its former stateliness. (Authors' collection.)

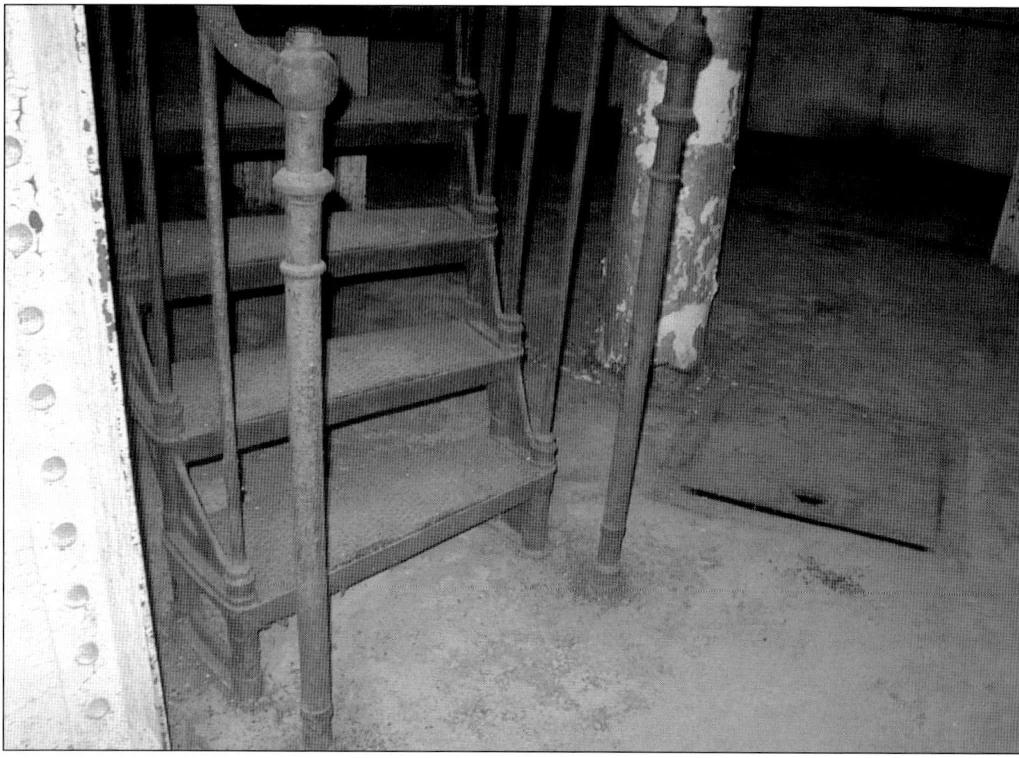

The North Point Light Station was placed on the National Register of Historic Lighthouses in 1980 and the National Register of Historic Places in 1984. Funding for the lighthouse's mammoth restoration came from grants and donations, while Milwaukee County and the federal government ironed out legal issues involved with the lighthouse property. Renovation design plans started in 2004, and restoration began in October 2005. The first hurdle was the lighthouse tower; the exterior had not been painted in many years, and the interior, with its circular stairways, was a mess. (Courtesy of Julie Bastin.)

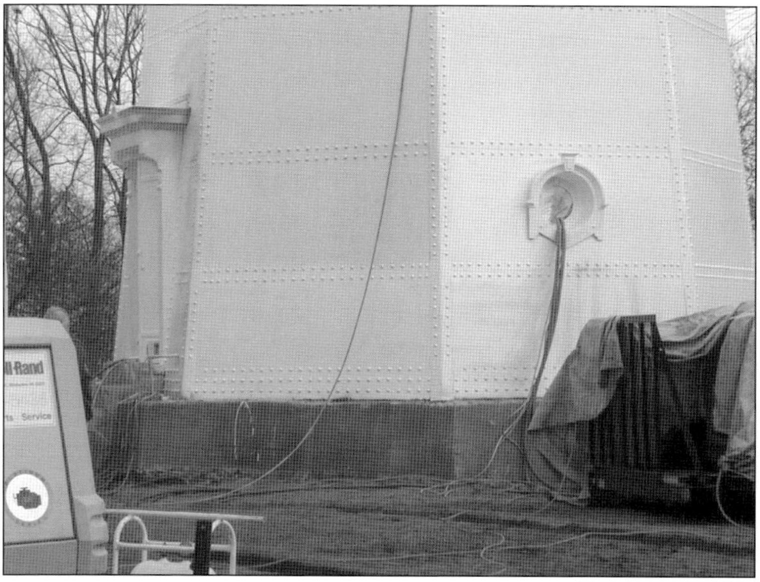

All of the wires, cords, and machinery that ran in and out of the North Point tower during its restoration gave the sad appearance of a lighthouse on life support. While the complex had deteriorated from neglect and a lack of care over the years, it was slowly resuscitated and revived, and its health and prognosis steadily improved. (Courtesy of Julie Bastin.)

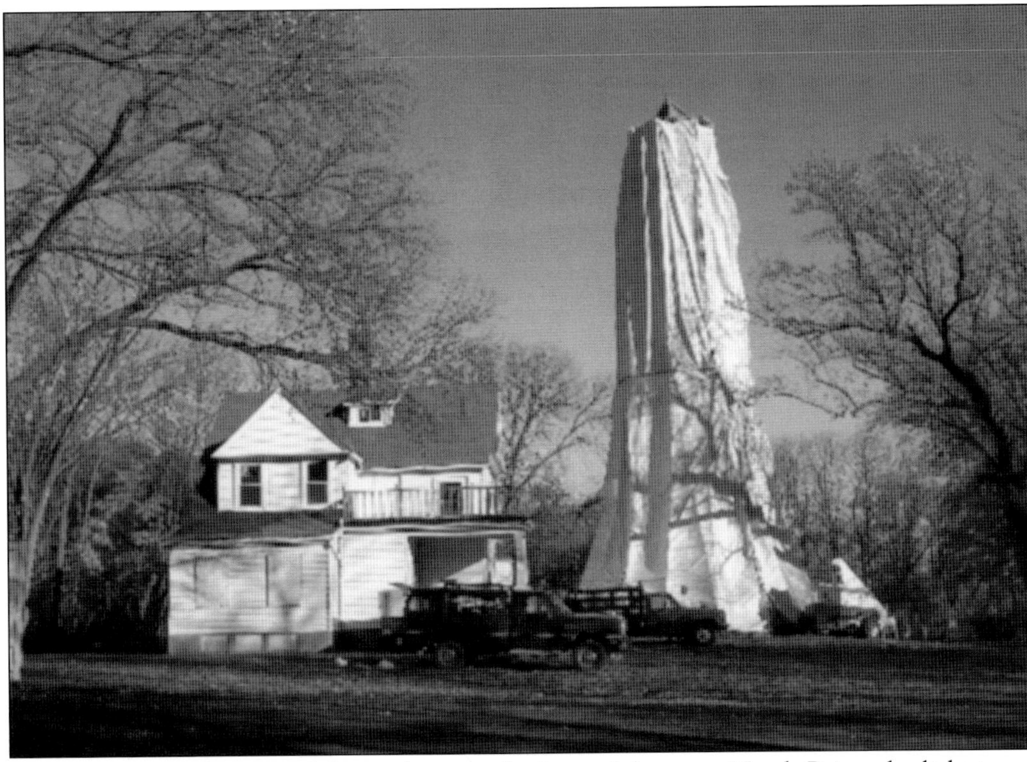

Prior to any significant work being done on the keeper's house at North Point, the light tower itself was completely rehabilitated. The light station had no renovation done on it for many years. Here, a shroud prevents paint and debris from contaminating the surrounding area. Sandblasting and the removal of lead-based paint took place before new coats of white paint were applied. (Courtesy of NPLHF.)

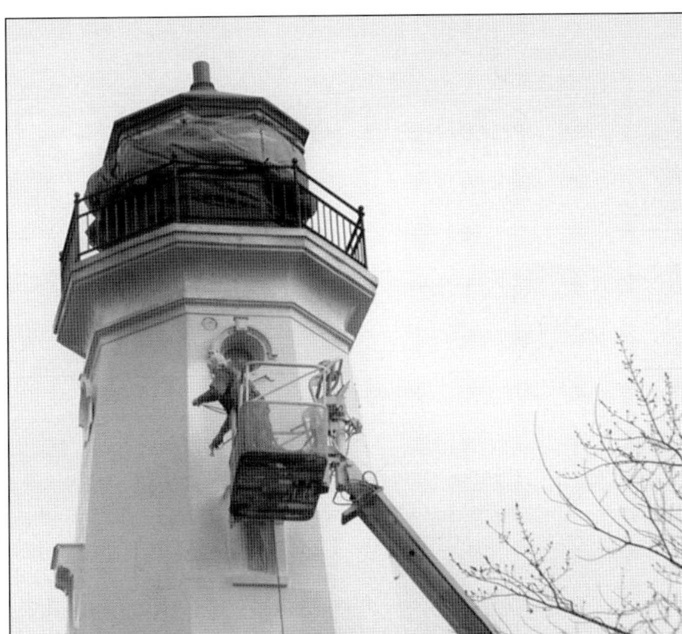

One of the biggest issues with the lighthouse tower was the lead-based paint that was used over the years. Approved lead abatement methods were employed, and many precautions were implemented to prevent the old paint from contaminating the soil or being released from the tower. Here, a technician applies new paint to the exterior of North Point's tower. The priming, sealing, and painting of the tower were completed in February 2006. (Courtesy of Julie Bastin.)

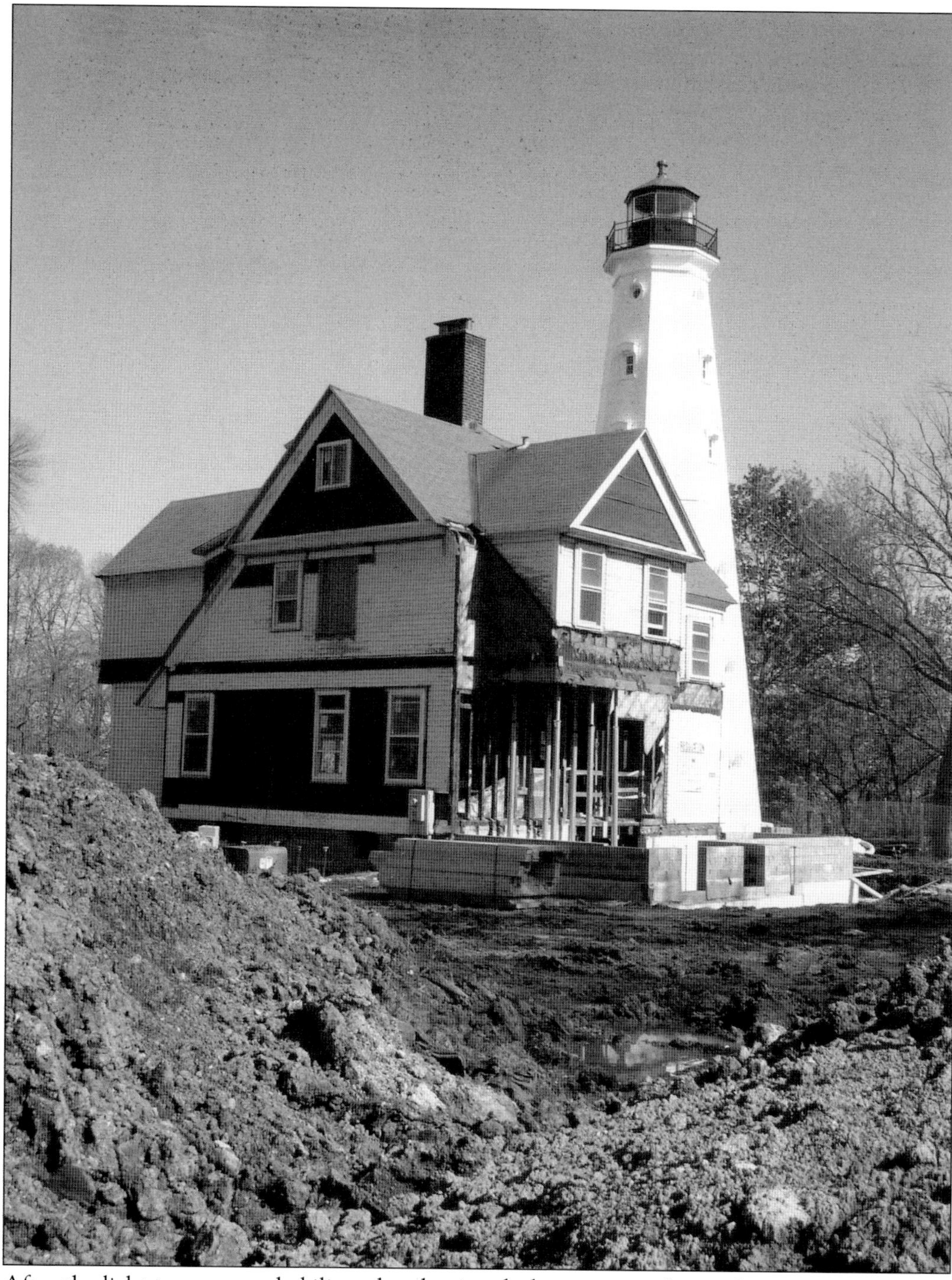

After the light tower was rehabilitated and painted, the next significant phase in North Point's journey back to greatness began in March 2007 with the renovation of the keeper's house. The building had been seriously neglected, and plans called for the structure to be considerably altered. Much of the interior was gutted, and the final exterior look of the building was different than when the station was manned. The old back porch area, pictured here, was removed and replaced with a new entrance. (Courtesy of NPLHF.)

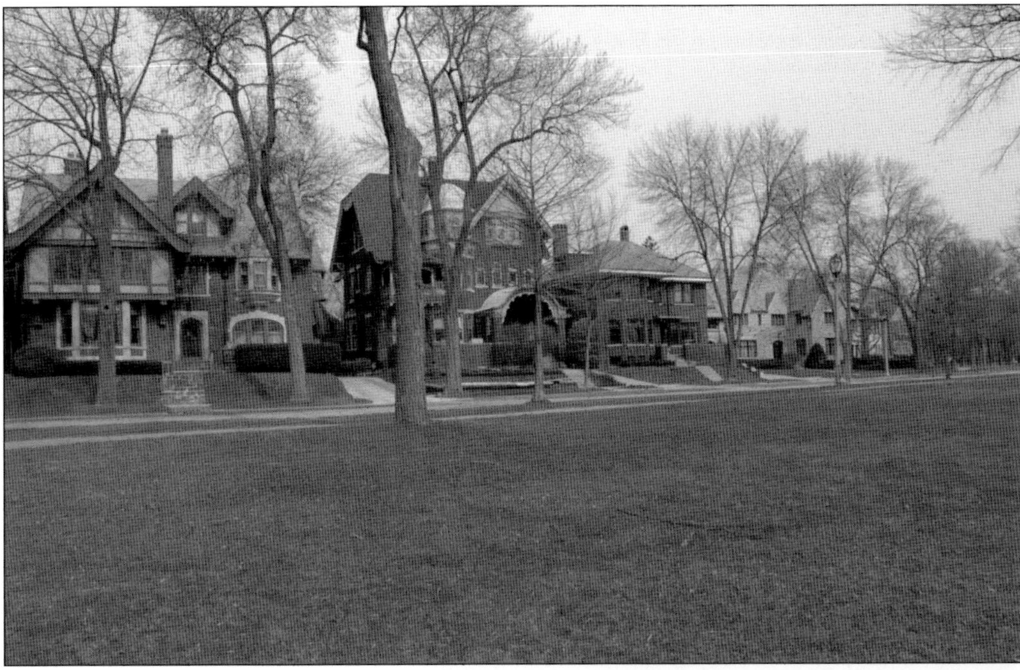

When the North Point Lighthouse Friends (NPLHF) formed in 2002 and restoration plans moved forward, one of the tasks facing the organization was taking into account what effect the increased activity might have on the surrounding homes and neighborhood, as well as on Lake Park itself. Some nearby residents had concerns about additional traffic and people at the new lighthouse attraction. (Authors' collection.)

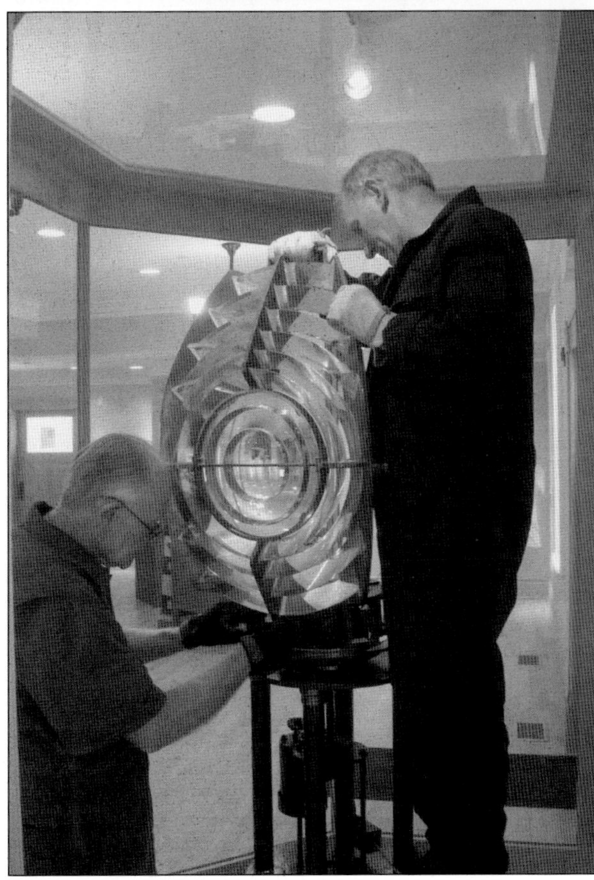

After North Point was mothballed in 1994, its Fresnel lens was placed in a conference room at the Milwaukee Coast Guard Station. In May 2009, the North Point Lighthouse Friends enlisted the services of lighthouse lens experts Jim Woodward and Frank Blaha. They oversaw the dismantling and reassembling of the lens and the drive mechanism, as well as its return to the restored facilities in the former keeper's quarters at the lighthouse. (Courtesy of John Enright.)

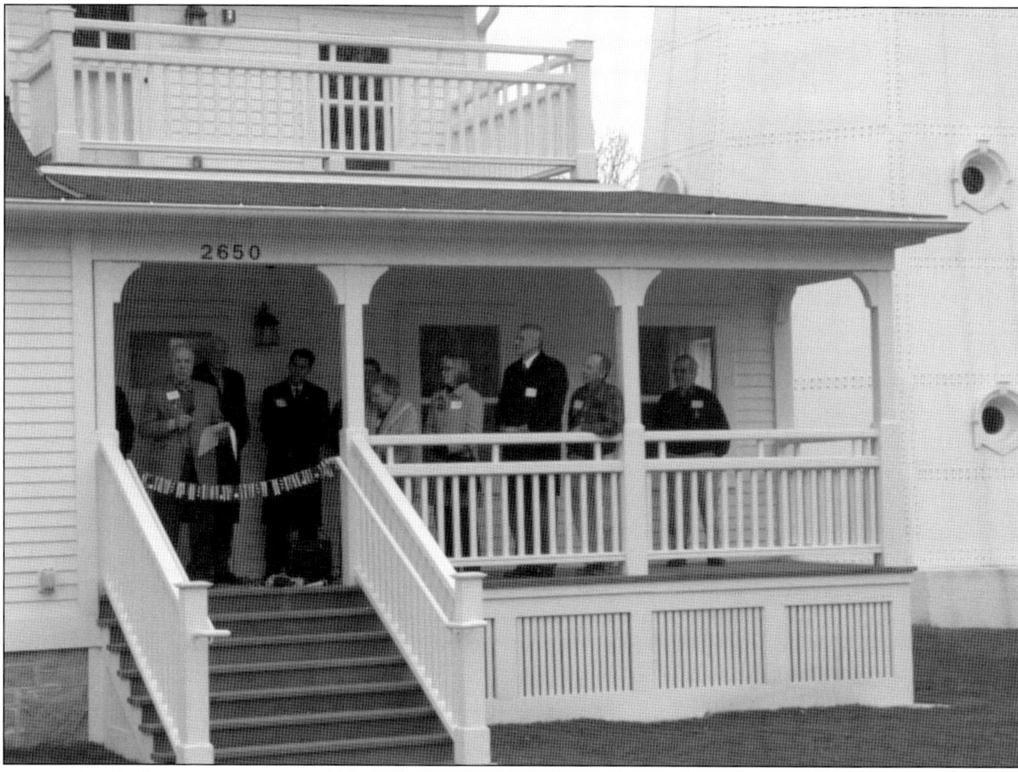

An official ribbon-cutting and rededication ceremony celebrated the restoration efforts at the North Point Lighthouse on November 16, 2007. With NPLHF Board president John Scripp presiding, public officials, including Milwaukee mayor Tom Barrett, Milwaukee County executive Scott Walker, state senator Alberta Darling, honored guests, and many of the Lighthouse Friends Board and volunteers that helped bring the project to fruition were all on hand. The renovated North Point tower stands in the background. (Courtesy of Julie Bastin.)

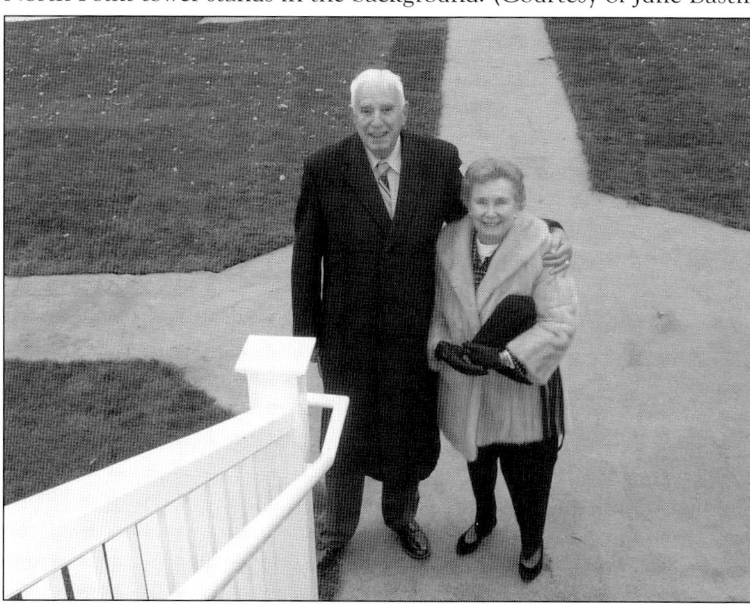

Col. Albert Kellogg "Buz" Stebbins III, along with his wife, Virginia, arrive as honored guests at the rededication ceremony at the North Point Lighthouse in November 2007. The two were very generous donors to the North Point Lighthouse Friends. They marveled at and were pleased with the renovation and restoration efforts. (Courtesy of John Enright.)

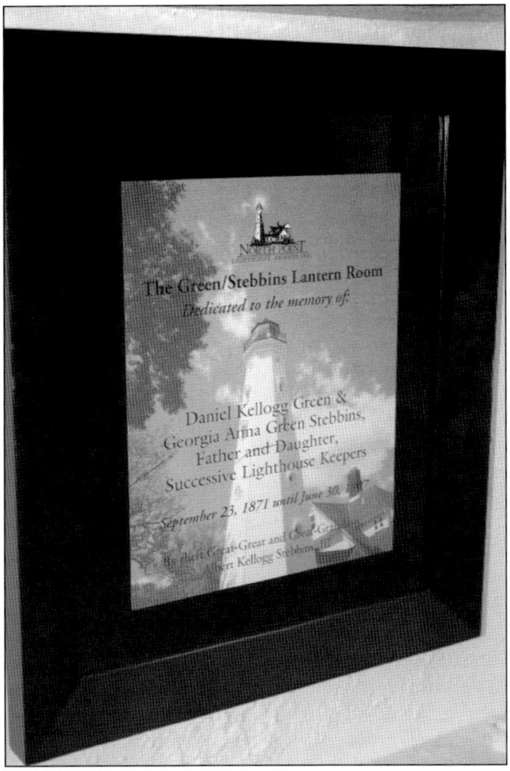

A plaque honoring the Stebbins and Green families for their more than 35 years of faithful service at North Point was affixed to the inside of the lighthouse tower in an appropriate place—the watch room, just below the lantern, a spot that D.K. Green and his daughter Georgia Stebbins passed hundreds of times over the years in their daily keeper trips to the light. (Authors' collection.)

Col. Buz Stebbins is the great-grandson of keeper Georgia Green Stebbins and the great-great-grandson of Georgia's father, keeper Daniel Green. Like his grandfather, Albert Stebbins Sr., Buz was a graduate of the US Military Academy at West Point. Here, Colonel Stebbins installs the padlock to the lantern at North Point for the very first time during ceremonies for the rededication of the lighthouse. (Courtesy of John Enright.)

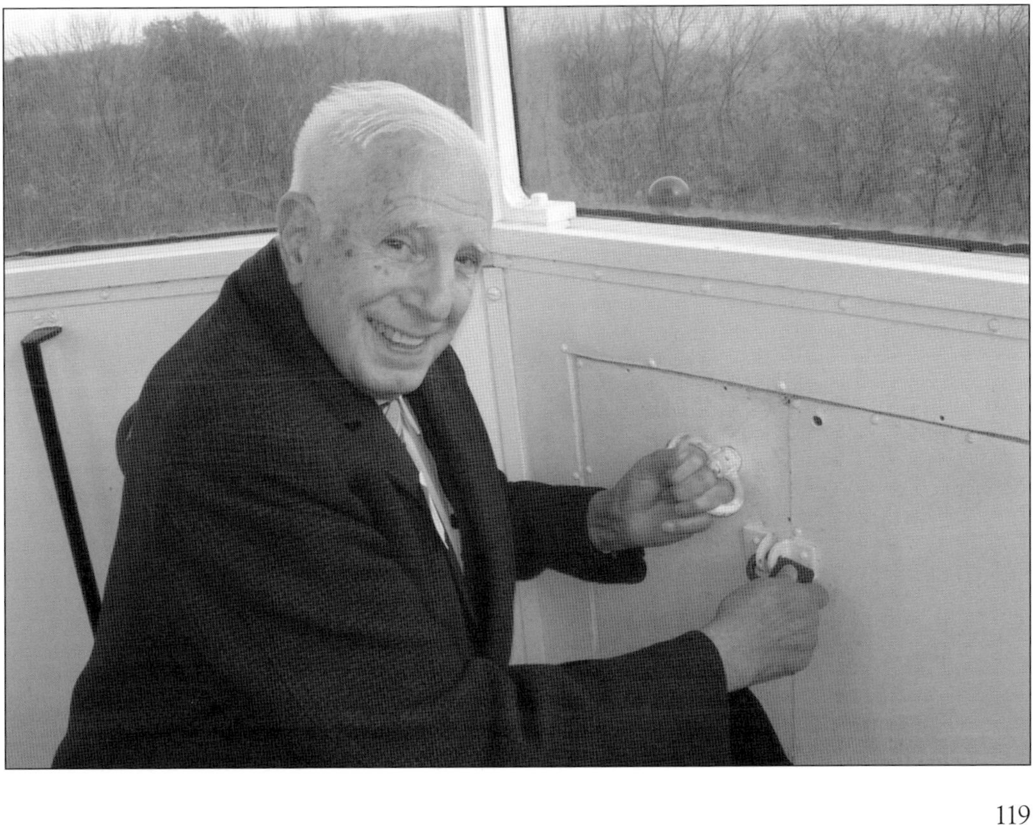

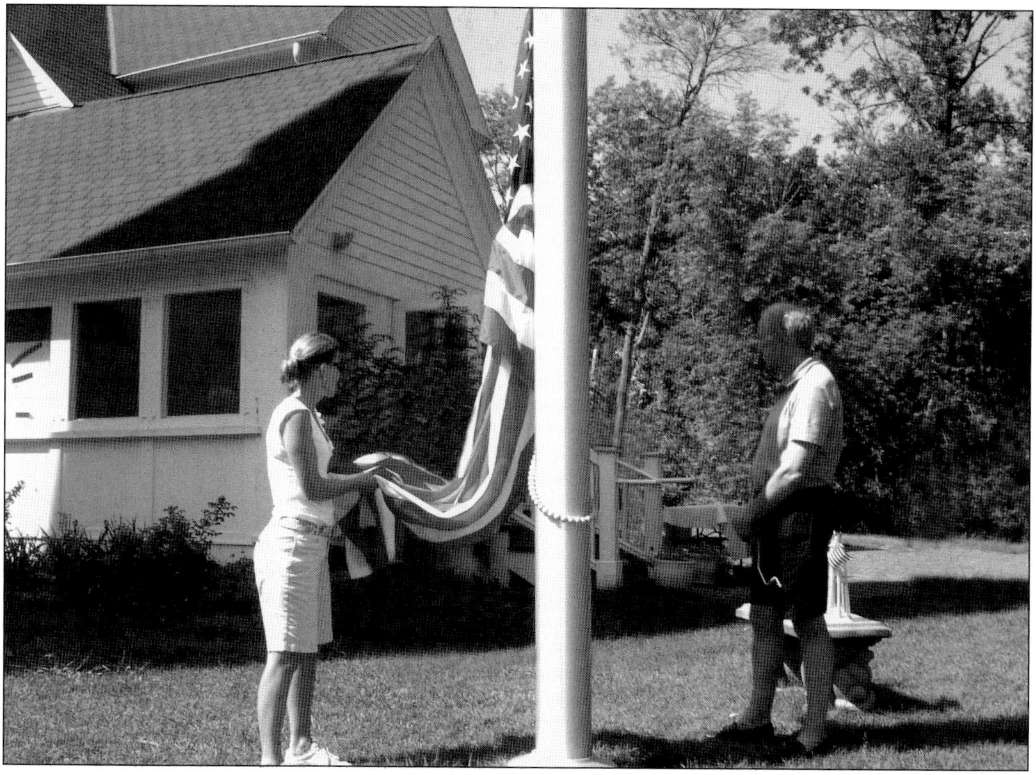

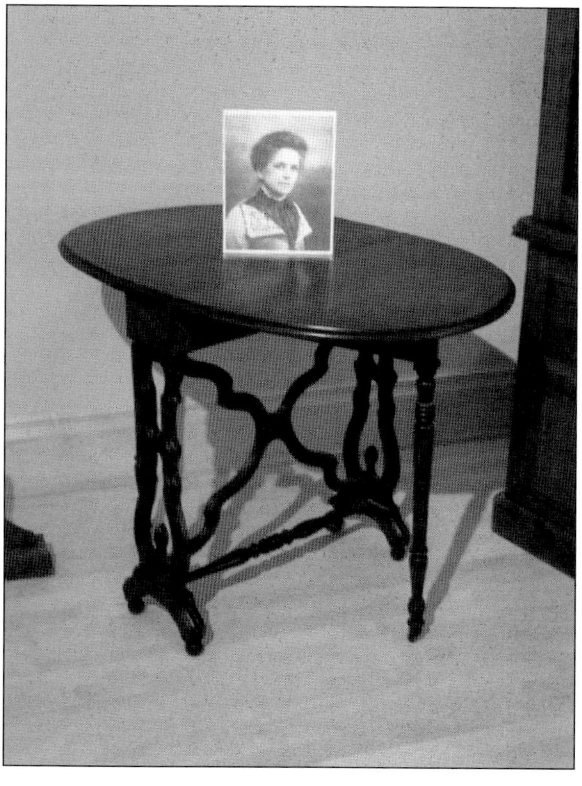

The NPLHF installed a flagpole in front of the lighthouse in the autumn of 2010. While the location of the station's flag varied somewhat over the years, when it was manned and active the North Point complex always flew Old Glory—since it was a government facility, displaying the flag was a requirement. (Courtesy of John Enright.)

The refurbished keeper's quarters at North Point contains several areas devoted to marine artifacts. There are also additional lighthouse-related items, including this Victorian drop leaf table used by keeper Georgia Stebbins. Handed down by family members through the years, this basic piece of furniture is a simple reminder of the connections to the keepers of old. (Courtesy of John Enright.)

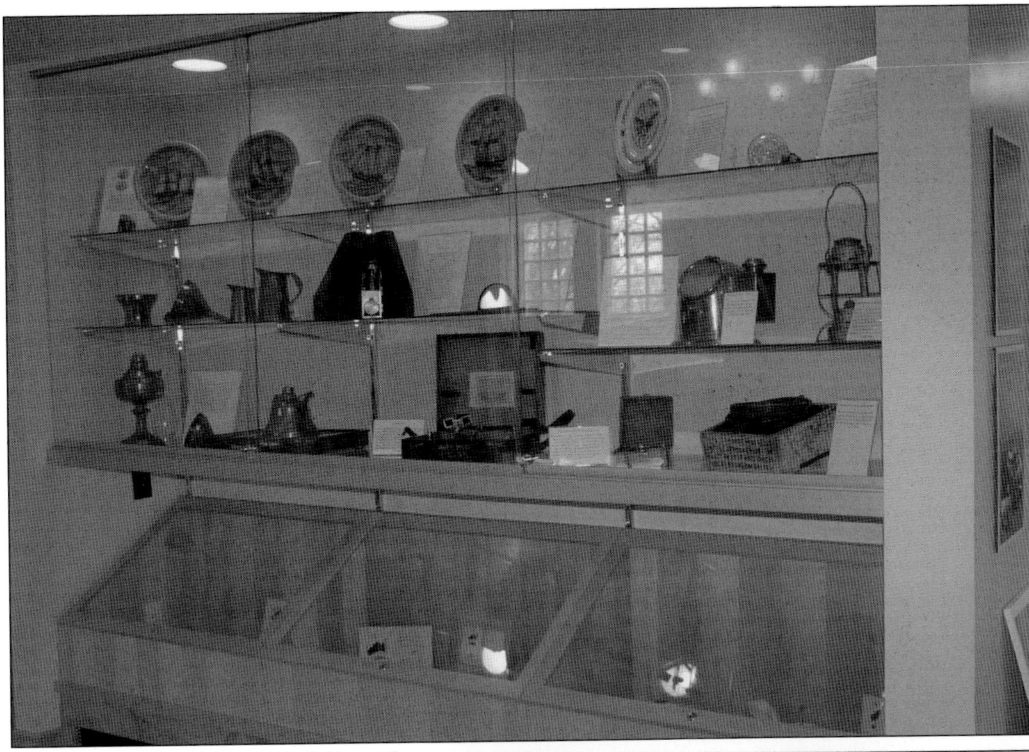

The end result of the remodeling of the keeper's house at North Point is a modern building with museum display areas showcasing nautical and lighthouse artifacts and history, as well as upstairs offices, a conference room, and a staging kitchen. The tower was once again connected to the home by a passageway, allowing visitors the opportunity to climb the lighthouse steps like the keepers did decades ago. (Authors' collection.)

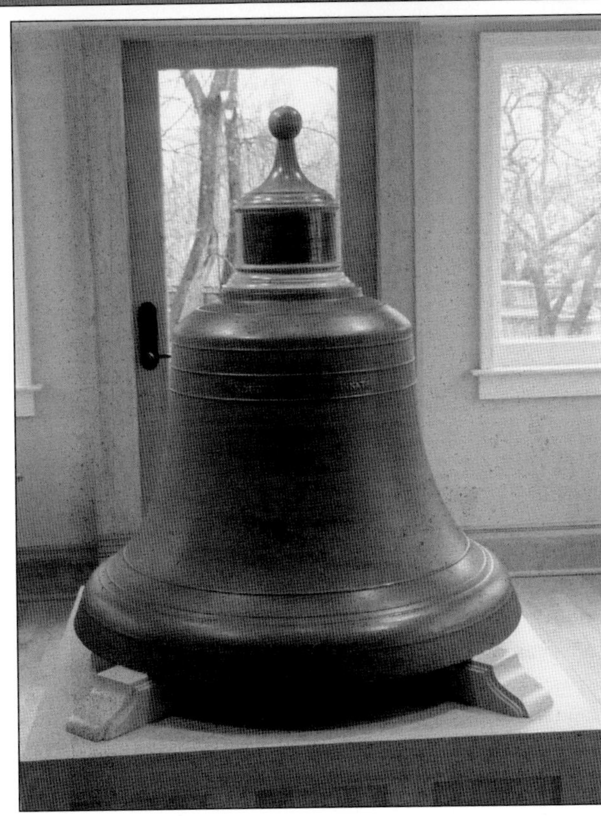

One very large maritime object at North Point is this massive fog bell. The inscription on it reads "Vanduzen & Tift Cincinnati U.S.L.H.E. 1893." The Buckeye Bell Foundry in Cincinnati cast bells from 1837 until about 1950. The partnership of Vanduzen & Tift operated it from 1866 until 1894. This bell rang for decades at the Milwaukee harbor north pier. It was removed in 1969. Today, it rests in North Point's display gallery. (Authors' collection.)

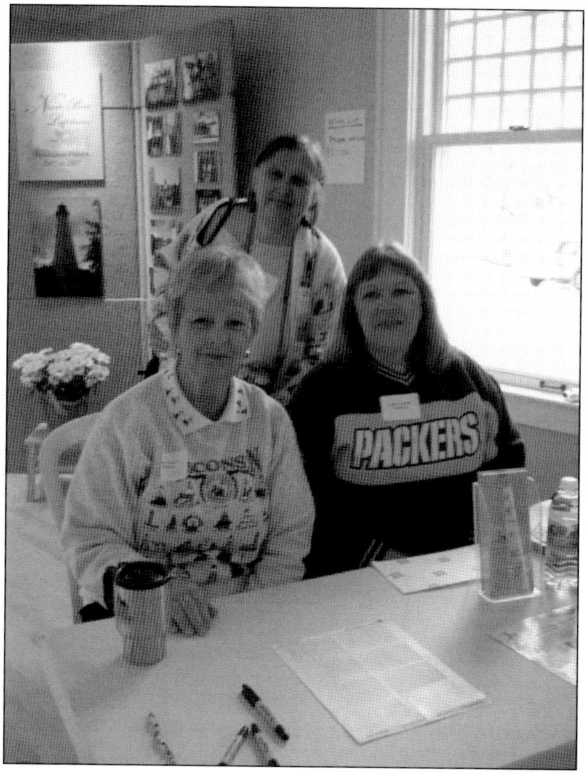

Lighthouse organizations rely heavily on volunteers. The North Point Lighthouse Friends are blessed with dedicated people who give freely of their time and talents to let the public know how special the lighthouse is. Without their collective efforts, lighthouse groups could not thrive. The ladies pictured here are, from left to right, Audrey Gloor, Mary Schrank, and Judith Dimmick. They welcome visitors, give guided tours of the light station, and staff the gift shop. (Courtesy of John Enright.)

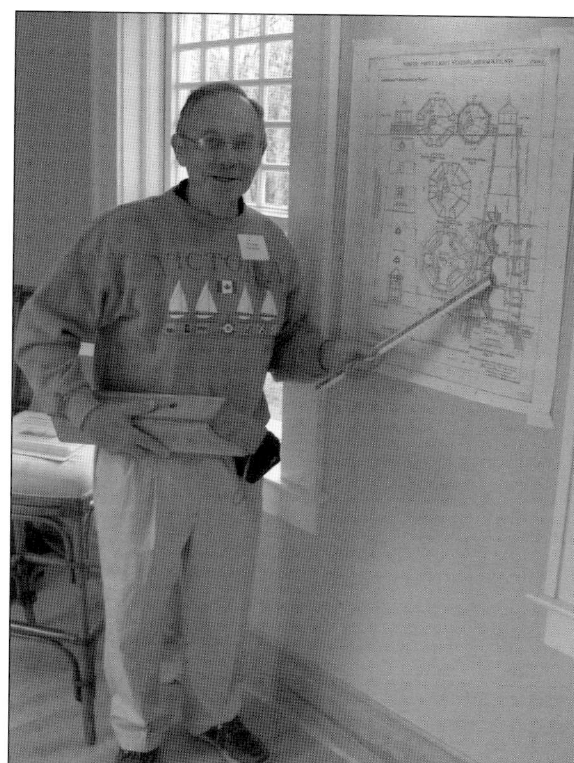

When people visit North Point, they are taken on an expert tour by one of the docents. Here, curator and NPLHF board member John Enright stands next to a schematic of North Point's tower sections ready to interpret its history. Efforts of the NPLHF Board, staff, and volunteer handiwork are seen inside the lighthouse, as well as around the grounds. Much like the work of the light keepers, the organization's labors are never completely done. (Courtesy of Paul Froehling.)

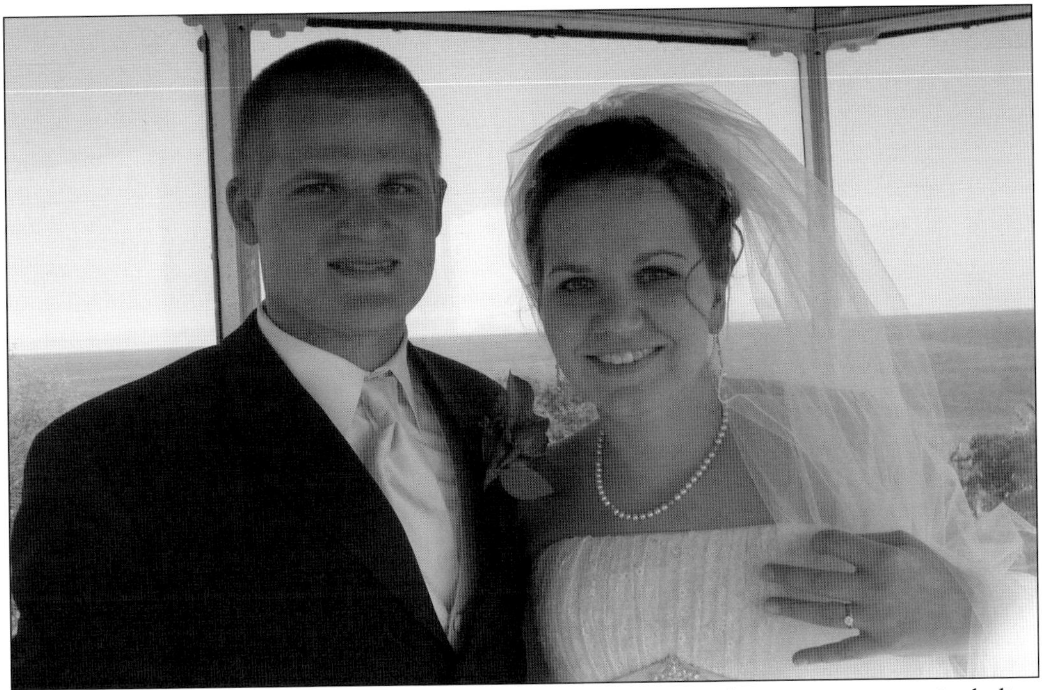

The restored North Point Light Station is a favorite destination for many activities, including weddings and special events. While some people actually exchange vows at the lighthouse, this newly married couple arrived on a Saturday afternoon to climb the tower. A NPLHF member took their picture in the lantern. This young pair had a grand view from this high vantage point on their special day. (Courtesy of John Enright.)

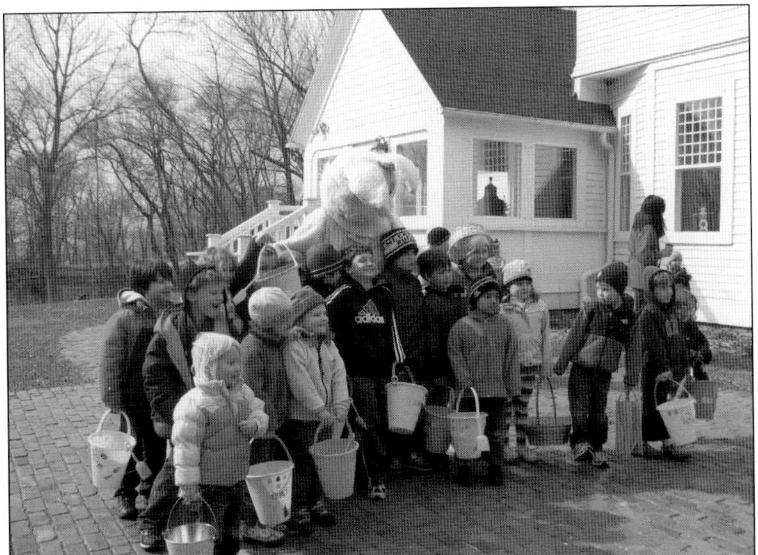

Young people enjoy many activities and entertainment at North Point's scenic lighthouse grounds and Lake Park, including educational programs and studies that feature maritime history. Summer camps, Halloween, and an Easter egg hunt—complete with the Easter Bunny—are popular with families. (Courtesy of May Klisch.)

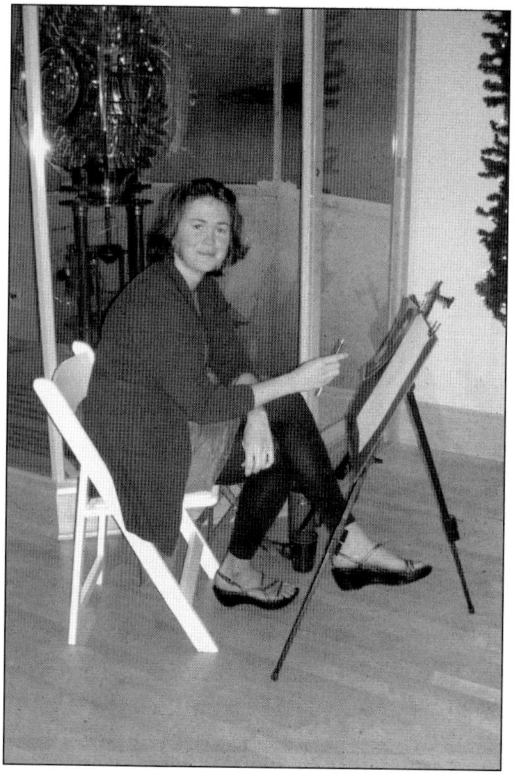

With North Point's fourth-order Fresnel lens in the background, artist Anne Kirwin sketches a portrait of the lighthouse's famed female keeper, Georgia Stebbins. The NPLHF offers many unique gatherings and enrichment opportunities at the lighthouse, including adult education programs and lectures, collaboration with local schools, summer camps, and other special events. (Courtesy of John Enright.)

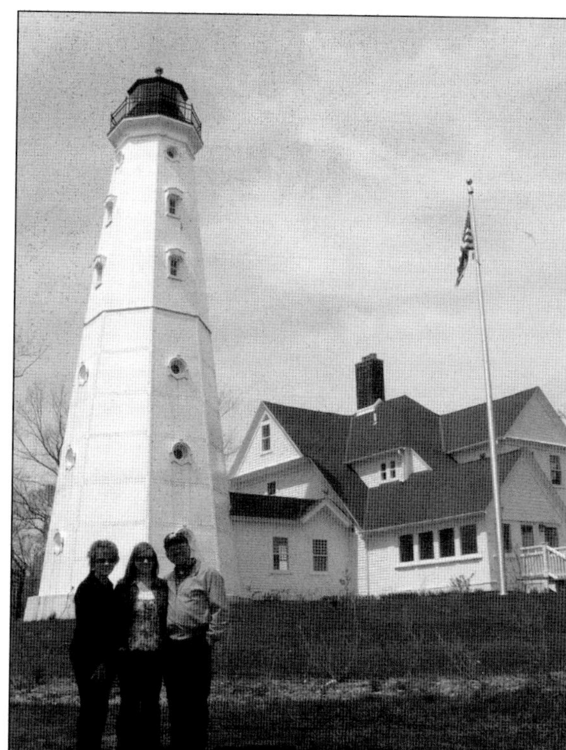

Families come to visit the lighthouse and stroll the paths in charming Lake Park during all seasons of the year. Many come to enjoy North Point's history, some come to stand on its sturdy base or climb the tower, others just want to relax and take in a bit of nature in an urban environment. Authors Barb Wardius (left) and Ken Wardius (right) flank their daughter Sarah on a pleasant Milwaukee spring day at North Point. (Authors' collection.)

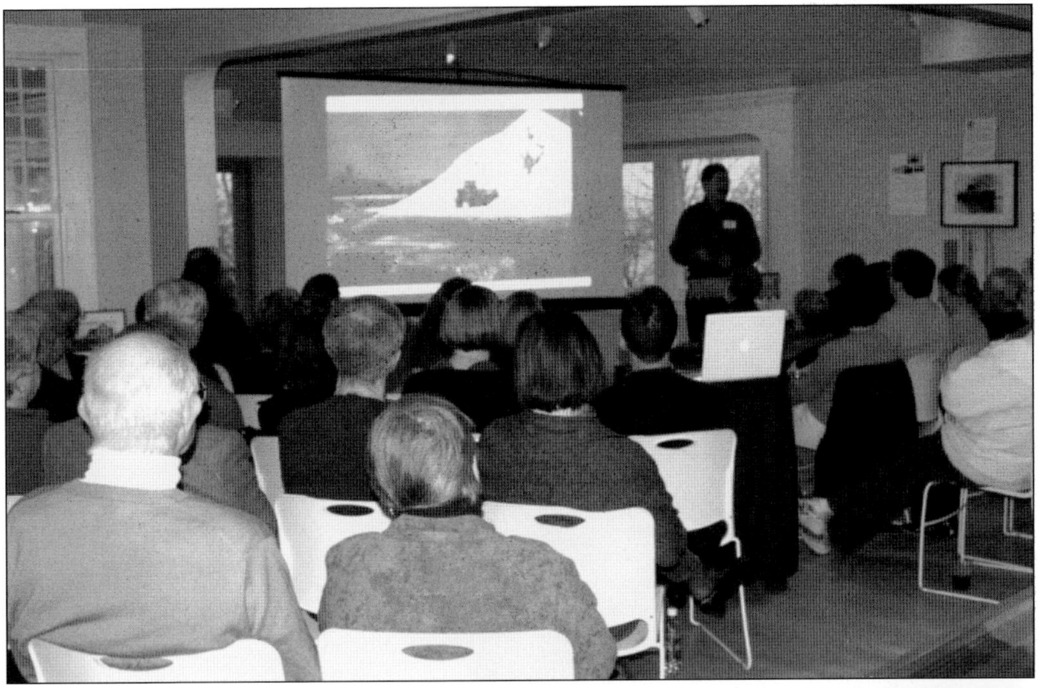

Today, the renovated keeper's residence at North Point serves diverse purposes. The North Point Lighthouse Friends host adult educational programming and unique experiences at the lighthouse. North Point can also be rented for fundraisers, private gatherings, and other events. Here, an audience listens intently to Milwaukee historian and author John Gurda as he presents a lecture on Milwaukee's Jones Island. (Authors' collection.)

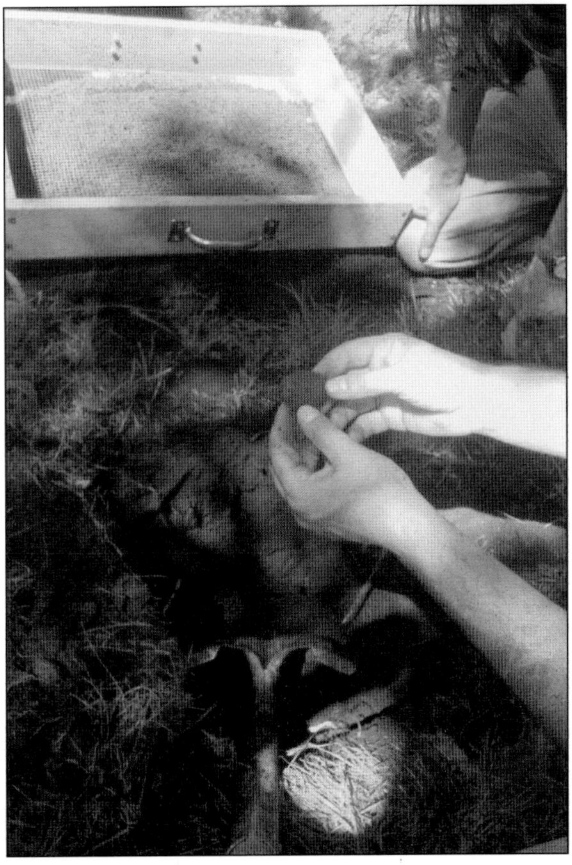

Historical research is still a work in progress at North Point. The precise location of North Point's original 1855 lighthouse is not certain. It is also debated whether the old lighthouse was demolished or simply just pushed down the severely eroding bluff. NPLHF members, along with expert assistants utilizing archaeology tools and principles, are shown here scouring a nearby bluff at North Point for clues through artifact collection. (Courtesy of John Enright.)

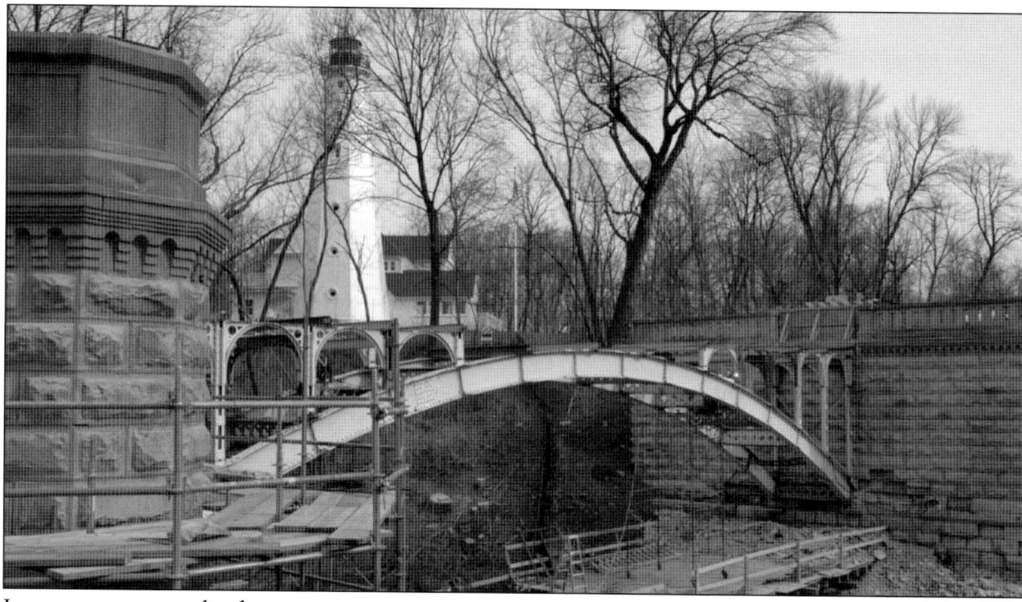

Improvements and other projects continue at North Point, as well as in other parts of Lake Park. The North Lion Bridge was renovated and rebuilt in 2010, and the South Lion Bridge was finished in 2011. There will always be something at the lighthouse that needs attention, just as when dedicated light keepers, who were conscientious of all of its needs, manned the North Point Lighthouse. (Authors' collection.)

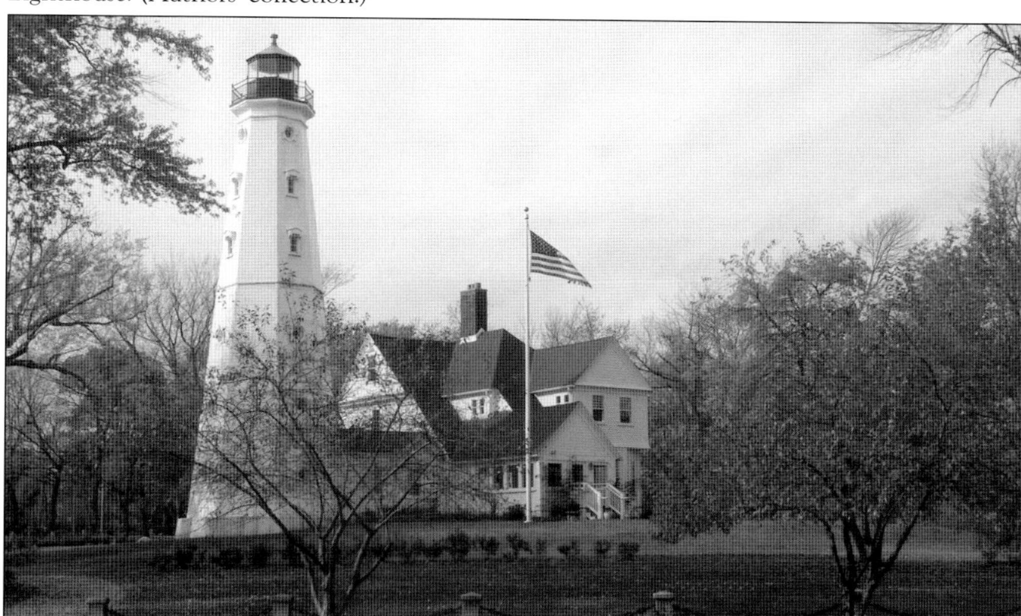

The mission and purpose of the nonprofit North Point Lighthouse Friends is to restore, rehabilitate, and preserve the lighthouse, inspire an appreciation of its history, and promote its use, consistent with Lake Park and the surrounding neighborhood, for the benefit of the public. The NPLHF motto is "preserving Milwaukee's light for future generations." Today, this maritime treasure is once again the grand jewel of Lake Park; this photograph is a testament to that statement. (Courtesy of John Enright.)

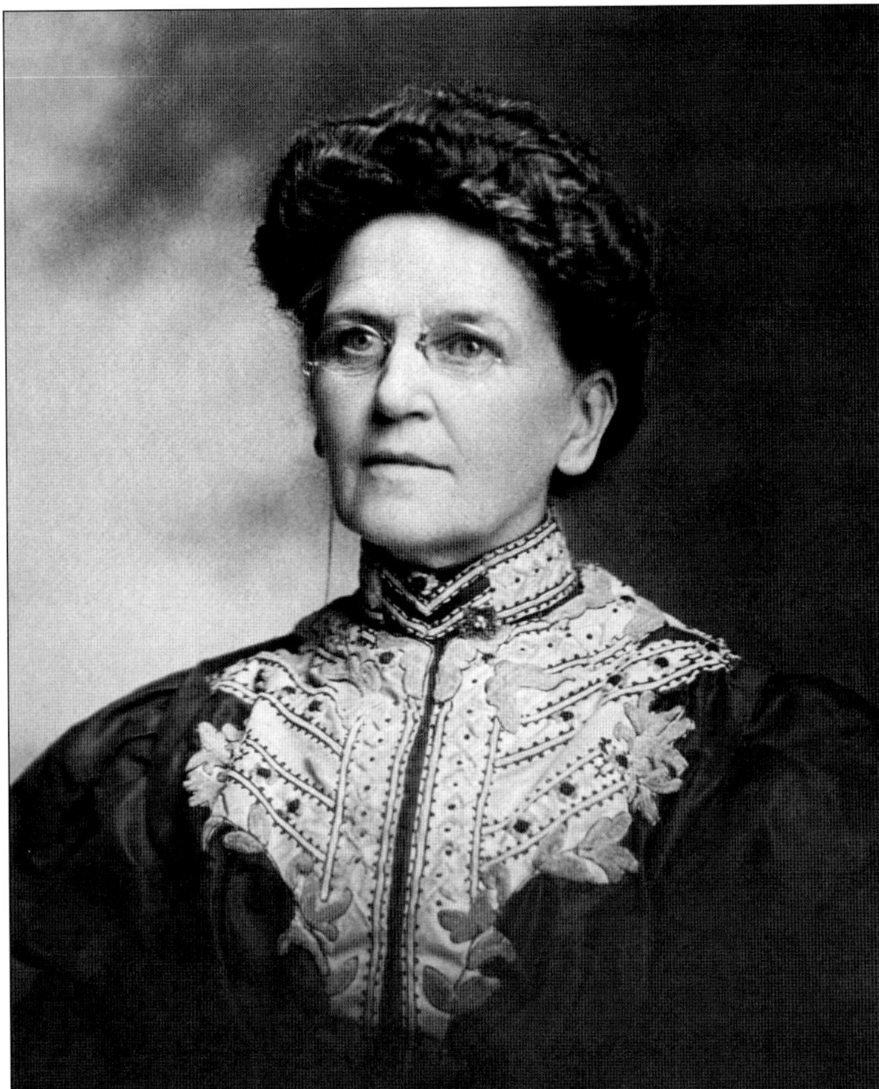

Georgia Anna Green Stebbins was dependable, hardworking, dedicated, and resourceful—a remarkable woman who served at the North Point Lighthouse for over three decades. She did not seek accolades for her years of hard work and devotion, but rather thought of herself as ordinary. Now, a century later, the same words pertain to the North Point Lighthouse Friends. With an eye toward the future and careful consideration and knowledge of the past, the NPLHF has insured that Georgia's legacy will continue. The lighthouse and keeper's quarters have been restored and rescued from a path of decay and ruin. The tower is open, and people can climb to the top, perhaps thinking of the past keepers who made the trek several times each day. Volunteer docents share stories of earlier times, while other volunteers supply hours of enthusiasm, energy, and donated time. Georgia would be pleased!

The lighthouse is open Saturdays and Sundays from 1:00 p.m. to 4:00 p.m. Contact the North Point Lighthouse Friends at 2650 North Wahl Avenue, Milwaukee, Wisconsin, 53211; the phone number is (414) 332-6754; the website is www.northpointlighthouse.org. (Courtesy of the Stebbins family.)